COLLINS COBUILD

COLLINS Birmingham University International Language Database

English Course

Jane & Dave Willis

Student's Book

2

Collins ELT
8 Grafton Street
London W1X 3LA

COBUILD is a trademark of William Collins Sons & Co. Ltd

© William Collins Sons & Co. Ltd 1988

10 9 8 7 6 5 4 3 2 1

First published 1988

Printed in Italy by New Interlitho Ltd

ISBN 0 00 370033 X

Design: Terry Smith
Cover design: Richard Morris
Photography: Chris Ridgers
Artwork: Jonathan Allen, Sarah Allison, Laura Boyd, Terry Burton, David English, Mike Mosedale, Kieren Phelps, Paul Shorrock, Clive Spong

This Student's Book is accompanied by a set of cassettes ISBN 0 00 370036 4, a Practice Book ISBN 0 00 370034 8, and a Teacher's Book ISBN 0 00 370035 6. A booklet containing transcripts of the unscripted recordings is included inside the back cover of the Student's Book.

COBUILD is the Collins Birmingham University International Language Database

Acknowledgements *(Figures in brackets refer to sections.)*

The syllabus of the Collins COBUILD English Course is based on the research findings of the COBUILD project at Birmingham University. Editor-in-Chief: Professor John Sinclair.

Liaison between COBUILD and Collins was co-ordinated by Antoinette Renouf. Computer support was provided by Tim Lane.

The authors would especially like to thank the COBUILD team for their detailed research and Michael Halliday and John Sinclair for guidance on the Grammar material. They are also grateful to students at the Cicero Language School, Tunbridge Wells for their advice in 209, and to teachers at the School for their co-operation. Finally, the authors would like to thank family and friends, especially their daughters, Jenny and Becky, for all their help and patience throughout the writing of this book.

Many people read and commented on the manuscript and it is impossible to list them all here. The publishers and authors are especially grateful to the following: Alistair Banton, Martin Mulloy, Georgina Pearce, Debra Powell, Hilary Rees-Parnall and Paula Walker.

The following participated in the unscripted recordings, and provided supporting texts and information to ensure the contextualisation of the recordings was accurate: Stephen Bowden, Jeremy Clear, David Foll, Caroline Frost, Bridget Green, Monica Janowski, Philip King, Danny Lim, Catherine McKinna, Jenny Maxwell, Ken O'Connell, Myf Sinclair and Jenny Vaughn.

Most of those in the published recordings also gave time to be photographed, as did the following: Brendan Barnes, Jane Burnell, Theresa Clementson, Claire Edwards, Marcia Jackson, Sian Mills, Paul Stokes and Maya Wilkie (all 128); Alan Dury (15); Deborah Blackburn and Dave Swabrick (182) and Jane Marr (14, 17).

The following allowed us to take photographs at their homes or premises: Argos Distributors Ltd (117); Stephen Bowden (14); The Trustees of the British Museum (157); Forfars Bakers Ltd, Brighton (42, 47); Caroline Frost (14); General Trading Company (1); John Mannion (1, 14); Playtime Playgroup in St Paul's C.E. School, Brighton (11, 42); St Martins Reference Library (14); The Window Box, Brighton (42); Y.M.C.A., London (2); Varndean School, Brighton (42); Selfridges (126).

The publishers are grateful to the following for permission to use original material in the Student's Book: Automobile Association for extracts from the A.A. Members' Handbook, 1986/87 (Great Britain) edition (7, 134, 198); Sunday Times for permission to redraw their original (18); and Reader's Digest (21, 45, 55, 73, 93, 164, 171, 188); Reader's Digest and T. McGuire (75); Spike Milligan for poems 'The Dog Lovers' and 'Holes in the Sky' (15); Dateline for part of application form (20); Northumberland County Council for extract from Northumberland Gazetteer (35); Country Farm holidays, Worcester for newspaper quotes (35); Just 17, EMAP Metro Publications for extracts (47, 78, 158, 162); Michael Rosen for poems 'Teachers' (58) and 'Juster and Waiter' (64); Guinness Publishing Ltd for three extracts from 1988 Guinness Book of Records (copyright 1987) (63); West Midlands Passenger Transport Executive (now obsolete) for Travelcard text (82); Reader's Digest and Alan Woodward (93); Carcanet Press Ltd for extract from William Carlos Williams, 'The Collected Poems 1909–1939', ed A. Walton Litz and Christopher MacGowan (1987) (95); Roald Dahl for 'The Hitch-hiker' from 'The wonderful world of Henry Sugar', Jonathan Cape 1977 and Penguin 1982 (97, 114, 121, 136, 147, 152, 161, 167, 174, 179, 189, 193); Reader's Digest and A. H. Andrews (103); Guardian Royal Exchange for part of a claims form (108); British Rail for timetable (110); Time Out London Student Guide for extract (110); B.M.W. (121); Reader's Digest and H. Morris (144); Thomson Local Directories, Farnborough GU14 7NU for extract (176); Milk Marketing Board 'Dairy Diary' for extract (178).

The publishers are grateful to the following for the use of photographs: Irish Tourist Board (1, 38); Cheshire County Council (1); Gazette series, Middlesex County Press (7); Catherine McKinna (9, 64); Dateline (20); Britain on View (BTA/ETB) (28, 35, 114, 116, 139, 144, 186, 198); English Life Publications Ltd (28); Sunday Times (39); Bahamas Tourist Board (38); Lyons Maid (42); All-Sport Photographic Ltd (42); Ford Motor Company Ltd (42); Spectrum (49, 51, 62, 69); British Heart Foundation (63); DHSS (63); John Mannion (64); Hoverspeed Ltd (68); Air France (68); Hot-Air Balloon Company Ltd, London SW6 2AG (68); Sealink Ferries (68); Kobal Collection (75); Birmingham Post and Mail Ltd (80); Toshiba (U.K.) Ltd (91); Topham Picture Library (97); Guinness Publishing Ltd (101); Knutz (116); Collins Road Atlas Great Britain (based on Ordnance Survey maps with the permission of the Controller of Her Majesty's Stationery Office, Crown copyright reserved) (134, 198); Ian Brown (134); Police Review (143); Museum of London (191); Mary Evans Picture Library (198); Glasgow University Library (201).

Every effort has been made to contact the owners of copyright material. In some cases this has not been possible. The publishers apologise for any omissions, and will be glad to rectify these when the title is reprinted if details are sent.

Contents

Unit 1
So I'm going to move on

1 Who's who?

a Introduce yourself to the people near you.
Find out their names and where they come from.

b Read the quotations. Say which person you think they are about.

How old are your children?

I've got two ... I've got a three year old, a girl, called Lucy Claire and a nearly one and a half year old, who's called Neil.

I work in Hillingdon, which is in West London.

She was born in Dublin ...

John Mannion

He comes from Warrington ...

At the moment I'm looking for jobs, maybe moving out of London.

Dublin, the capital of the Republic of Ireland.

Catherine McKinna

Before I had the children I was an insurance broker.

My son's called Joe.

How old is he?

He's about 15 months – just about learning to walk ...

I used to work at a desk and have files of clients ... businesses in front of me and I would deal with their insurance needs.

Warrington, an industrial town in the north of England.

c Work out where these places are.

Warrington Dublin Hillingdon Birmingham

in the north of England
in West London
in central England
in Ireland

not far from Scotland
quite near Wales
in Cheshire
near Manchester

d Introduce the person next to you to one or two other people in the class. Say where they come from, where they work or study and a little about their family.

1e e Listen to the quotations. Find out who says what.

5

2 Background

2a **a**   Listen to Catherine asking John about himself.

What kind of work does he do?
Why does he want to move on?
How far will John's family have to travel if he gets the job he is now applying for?

b   Later, we asked John to write about Catherine.

CATHERINE by John

Catherine describes herself as a wife and mother. She has two children, one, Lucy Claire who is three and Neil who is eighteen months. Before having children she worked in insurance. She was born and lived for the first seven years of her life in Dublin. She still has an Irish accent, in reaction to the 'very English' community in which she lived. Her parents moved back to Ireland and so she returns there often.

How much did you know already?
Where do you think she lives now? How do you know?

c   Now read what Catherine wrote about John. What additional information does she give us?

JOHN by Catherine

He is a teacher of English at a Catholic school in Hillingdon, London. He comes from Warrington which used to be in the county of Lancashire but is now in Cheshire. He is married with a 15 month old son called Joe who, he says, is just starting to get interesting and mischievous. John is trying to get a new job and is busy sending application forms and CVs all over the country.

d   Find out things like this about one or two other people in your class. See if you or they have anything in common with each other.

▶ Write a paragraph about one person, but do not write their name.

Give your paragraph to your teacher to read out loud. Who is each paragraph about?

▶ How many people in your class have things in common with you? Tell each other. ◀

3 Language study

a   **Questions**

2a   Write down the questions that Catherine asks John. Do they refer to past, present or future time?

Write down questions that you used when talking to people in section 2d above. What words do your questions begin with?

b   **so, well, …**

2a   Why does Catherine use the word **so**?
What words does John use to begin his answers? Why?

4 Wordpower

about

How many meanings does **about** have? Look at the cartoons. Who is saying what? Then look up **about** in the Lexicon. What other meanings are there?

Help us to bring about political change.

What I like about him is his sense of humour.

Can you ring back later? We're about to have dinner! Oh, about 9, 9-30 O.K?

A letter from school? Oh, what's it about?

Where would you hide it?

Discuss with your neighbour the best place in the room on the right to hide something small (like money or keys) if you were playing a game. Decide exactly where you would put it. For example:

In the vase on the bottom shelf of the bookcase on the left of the fire.

Here are some words to help you.

on	between	at the bottom/top
behind	by	next to
below	in	over
beside	in front of	under

See how quickly you can guess which places other people have decided on. Ask them questions. They can only answer 'yes' or 'no'.

▷ Can you write any sentences of twelve words or more to describe where to hide the object? ◁

⬛ **5** We asked two people where they would choose. Listen and find out if they decided on the same places as you.

6 *Language study* ·······························

Verbs with prepositions

Can you explain what these examples mean?

1 *a b c d f g h – which letter has been* left out?
2 *Work out where these places are.*

3 *Find out their names and where they come from.*
4 *Could you* pass *the books* round *please?*
5 *Look up the word **about** in the Lexicon.*
6 *There are twelve books and ten students. How many books are* left over?

7 A town you know

*Hillingdon is a suburb of London with a population of about 230,000.
It is two miles from Uxbridge and fourteen miles from the centre of London. Early closing is on Wednesdays. There is no market Day.
The main hotel in Hillingdon is the Master Brewer on Western Avenue, (A40) telephone Uxbridge (0895) 61199.
It is a large hotel with 64 rooms, each with bathroom.
It has parking for about 200 cars. J.W.
(from facts taken from the AA members' Handbook. 1986/87)*

a Hillingdon, where John works, is a typical West London suburb. Could this be a picture of a town in your country? Why not? What things in this photo strike you as being typically English?

What can you find out about the town of Warrington (which is where John originally comes from) from this *AA Members' Handbook* entry? Read the description of Hillingdon above, then see if you can guess what the signs and symbols for Warrington mean.

WARRINGTON 135,568 Cheshire (STD 0925) Map33sj68 EcThu MdWed/Fri/Sat Bolton 21, Chester 21, Liverpool 18, London 190, Manchester 20.
***Fir Grove Knutsford Old Rd Tel 67471 rm38 (18 bath 20 shower)
100P B&B (e) (f)[price range from £35–45]
**Patten Arms Parker St (GW) Tel 36602 rm43 (29 bath 14 shower) 25P B&B (e)

▷ Write a full description for Warrington using the handbook entry.

b Find out about a town your partner knows well. Ask questions and then write a short description. Give it to your partner to check.

▷ Write a description of a town you know well. Make one factual mistake. See if your partner can guess what the mistake is.

8 Grammar revision ··

am, is, are, was, were

Look at these uses of the verb **to be**.

1 Who or what
It's a very pleasant school.
I was an insurance broker.

2 Describing
He's about fifteen months.
She's quite small.

3 Where
It's near Birmingham, isn't it?
That was in Warrington.

4 With **-ing**
He's getting to the more interesting stage isn't he?
At the moment I'm looking for jobs.

5 With **-ed, -en**
He's married.
Where were you born and brought up?

Which category do these examples belong to?

a *John is trying to get a new job.*
b *It's a new town I think.*
c *Now it's in Cheshire.*
d *Hillingdon is a suburb of London.*
e *It's two miles from Uxbridge.*
f *His son is called Joe.*
g *Joe is just starting to get mischievous.*
h *Catherine left Dublin when she was seven.*

9 Childhood

guess
hated
worse
long
?
Words to guess

Catherine's family

9a **a** John and Catherine talked to each other about where they were born and brought up, and where they lived as children.

Before you listen, say whether you think these sentences are true or false.

a *John's parents have lived in the same house for more than twenty years.*
b *John enjoyed going to school.*
c *There were no girls at John's secondary school.*
d *John likes going back to Warrington.*
e *Catherine started school in Ireland.*
f *Although she is Irish she has an English accent.*
g *They had a lot of Irish friends as children in England.*
h *Catherine still lives near her mother and father.*
i *She used to live in a small Irish community in London.*

After listening, correct the sentences which are false.

community	over	**L** Words
left/leave	remain	to look up
brought up		

b How does each of them feel about the community in which they lived as children?
Being away and going back – what does each of them say about this?

8 Where do their parents live now?

10 Language study ··············

a Which phrases don't always refer to past time?

in those days   some time ago
then   at that time
every year

b Study the transcript of **9a**.

1 Can you find five phrases which show how John felt about his schools and Warrington itself? e.g. *I didn't like it.* Did he give any reasons?

2 When each person starts speaking, what are the first two or three words that they say? e.g. *I was born ...   What was ...   Erm sometimes, ...   Ah! I beg your pardon.*
How do they relate to what has gone before?

3 What do you think they were going to say? Can you finish their unfinished sentences?

What was ...? Did you like where you lived?
Was it ...?
But living there was ...
I haven't been back since, really. (since when?)

4 Which one of these words/phrases did Catherine say? Which two others would also be possible here?

Actually   In fact   But   Funnily enough

CM: Oh, I go back there every year ... _____ I'm going on my holidays there tomorrow!

11 Your partner's childhood

Find out as much as you can about your partner's childhood. Write notes so that you can tell the class about the most important things.

▶ Tell the class about your partner. ◀

12 | Languages you've learnt

a What languages can you speak? How many foreign languages have you learnt, or tried to learn?

12b **b** Catherine talked to someone called Stephen about the languages they knew. Listen and make a list of the languages they knew, and say how good they were at each.

12c **c** Many people say that the British are very lazy about learning foreign languages, because they think that when they go abroad they will usually be able to find someone who speaks English.
To find out if this was true, we asked a variety of British people from different walks of life about their language learning experiences.
Some of their comments and stories are written here. Read them. Do you think the British *are* lazy about learning languages?

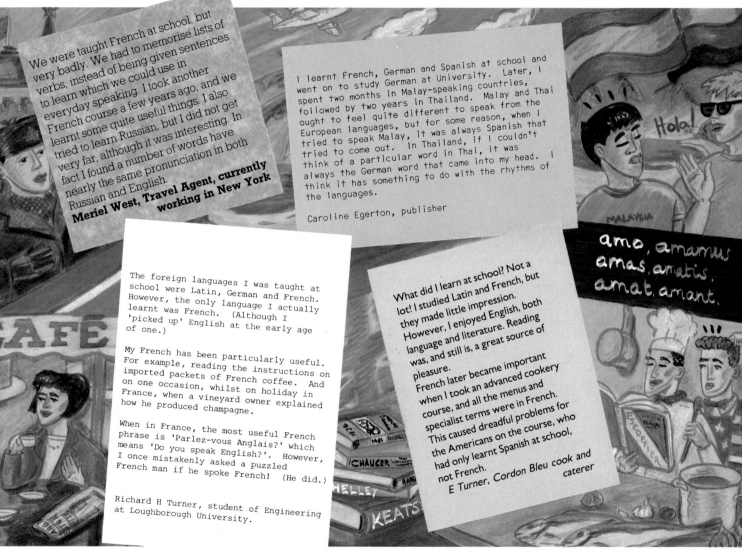

We were taught French at school, but very badly. We had to memorise lists of verbs, instead of being given sentences to learn which we could use in everyday speaking. I took another French course a few years ago, and we learnt some quite useful things. I also tried to learn Russian, but I did not get very far, although it was interesting. In fact I found a number of words have nearly the same pronunciation in both Russian and English.
Meriel West, Travel Agent, currently working in New York

I learnt French, German and Spanish at school and went on to study German at University. Later, I spent two months in Malay-speaking countries, followed by two years in Thailand. Malay and Thai ought to feel quite different to speak from the European languages, but for some reason, when I tried to speak Malay, it was always Spanish that tried to come out. In Thailand, if I couldn't think of a particular word in Thai, it was always the German word that came into my head. I think it has something to do with the rhythms of the languages.

Caroline Egerton, publisher

The foreign languages I was taught at school were Latin, German and French. However, the only language I actually learnt was French. (Although I 'picked up' English at the early age of one.)

My French has been particularly useful. For example, reading the instructions on imported packets of French coffee. And on one occasion, whilst on holiday in France, when a vineyard owner explained how he produced champagne.

When in France, the most useful French phrase is 'Parlez-vous Anglais?' which means 'Do you speak English?'. However, I once mistakenly asked a puzzled French man if he spoke French! (He did.)

Richard H Turner, student of Engineering at Loughborough University.

What did I learn at school? Not a lot! I studied Latin and French, but they made little impression. However, I enjoyed English, both language and literature. Reading was, and still is, a great source of pleasure.
French later became important when I took an advanced cookery course, and all the menus and specialist terms were in French. This caused dreadful problems for the Americans on the course, who had only learnt Spanish at school, not French.
E Turner, Cordon Bleu cook and caterer

d Which of these people do you think is most serious about learning languages?
Which of them do you think has the best sense of humour?

e What do you think is the best way of learning a foreign language?

By reading a lot	Reading a dictionary
Doing grammar exercises	Translating
Trying to speak it, even though you make mistakes	Watching English or American films on TV

f What experience do you have of learning English? Write a short paragraph.

g Language survey

Design a survey form. Practise the questions you might ask. Ask other people in your class.

Tell each other which person you think speaks the most languages.
Who has learnt the most languages in the class as a whole?

a Questions and answers

Make questions that you can match with some of the answers below.

| Do | you . . . ? |
| Did | |

What . . .	do	you . . . ?
Where . . .	did	
How many . . .		

English, French and some
Japanese.
Quite near, yes.
I live about three miles from here.
Not much, just a few words.
Well. I did, yes, but . . .
Oh, er, about four.
No, outside London.
Well, I used to speak five . .
I work for GEC.
Not really, no.
No, I don't . . .
No, I didn't, really . . .

Do you speak English?

b Classroom phrases

Who might say each of these – teacher, student, or either?

Sorry, I didn't understand.
Sorry? Can you say that again?
What's the meaning of . . . ?
Can you guess what it means?
Try and work out what it means.
Excuse me. What does 'community' mean?
I don't know the word for xxxx.
Okay. Your next task is to find . . .
Shall we start?
We've finished.
Well, that's about it.
I don't know what to say next.
Tell them about . . .
Ask them about . . .
On your own . . .
Help each other.
Excuse me. Can you help me?
Get into groups, and . . .

c How good are you at languages?

I know a tiny bit of Italian.
I can speak a little Spanish, but not much.
I can get by in French.
I picked up some Greek from travels.
I was taught Latin, French and German at school.
I've forgotten my German.
I can read English all right, but I can't speak much.
I'm quite good at . . .
I can understand quite a lot of . . .
But I find it difficult to say what I want to say.
Catherine has a slight Irish accent.

d ????

What's the missing word?

He is married _____ a 15 month old son called Joe.
What words do your questions begin _____ ?
. . . is a suburb of London _____ a population of . . .
It is a large hotel _____ 64 rooms, each _____ bathroom and shower.
It has something to do _____ the rhythms of the language.
Do you have anything in common _____ any other students?
. . . wait a moment and I'll be _____ you.

In which sentences does the missing word mean 'and has'?

e Not

Not much, just a few
words.
Not a lot!
Spanish, not French.
Not really, no.
Not many.
Not bad.

I'm not very good
at languages.
Finished? Not yet!
It's not time yet.
Not me!
Why not?
Of course not.

f Common uses of wh- words

1 To describe
I work in Hillingdon, *which is in West London.*
. . . Americans, who had only learnt Spanish.

2 After words like **say, find out, ask**
Say *where they come from.*
We asked John to write *what he could remember.*

Find 3 sentences like those in 1, and 3 like those in 2.

a *Find out their names and where they come from.*
b *Now read what Catherine wrote about John.*
c *He comes from Warrington, which used to be in Lancashire but is now in Cheshire.*
d *He has a son called Joe who, he says, is just starting to get interesting.*
e *You are often asked to send a curriculum vitae when you are applying for a job.*
f *Write down questions that you used when talking to people in section 2d above.*
g *And what about these?*
h *Decide exactly where you would put it.*
i *Hillingdon, where John works, is a typical West London suburb.*

How many sentences are left over? What are the **wh-** words in them and how are they used?

Important words to remember (34 so far)					
alright	deal L	introduce	particularly	remain L	task
apart L	foreign L	Ireland	partner	Russian	text
bring L	guess	Japanese	pleasant	Spanish	tiny
capital	hate	learning	population	struggle L	worse
community L	hotel	literature	reaction	study	
county	industrial	particular	ready	tape	

Unit 2

Have you any idea what they're like?

John

14   What can you tell from a photo?

a   How much can you tell about a person from their looks? Look very carefully at the photos.

Stephen

Caroline

Try to guess which of these people:

- definitely has a sense of humour
- has had to get remarkably fit and healthy since having children
- absolutely hates sport
- is fairly interested in sport but hates football
- enjoys some sports (mostly squash, tennis and swimming) but is not terribly good at them
- makes friends fairly easily
- likes most sociable activities which involve meeting and talking with people
- smokes a lot, and so feels they cannot be considered terribly healthy
- likes food and cooking but mainly eating
- is still at university, after studying one academic subject after another
- is interested in the Arts, especially cinema, and reads a lot
- used to be a medical student but got bored and took up anthropology
- leads a hectic social life and smokes
- seems to like animals
- has been to America and likes football
- loves to travel and hopes to go abroad again soon

Catherine

Monica

14b   **b**   You will hear four of these people introducing themselves. Which people? What kind of work do they all do?

c   Which two of the descriptions on the left apply best to you? Which two would you guess best applied to your teacher? And your partner?

15 Describe a person

| John | Alan | Catherine | Caroline | Monica | Stephen | Jane |

> Take turns at describing one of the people here today. You must not say their name. Can your partner guess who it is?

15a a We asked Monica and Caroline to play this game. Listen and work out which of these people Monica is describing. Does Caroline guess correctly? Then listen to Caroline describing one of these people for Monica to guess.

b Now can you play the same game with a partner? First describe one of the people in the photograph above.
Then look around the class and describe one of your classmates to your partner. Be careful not to look at the person and give the game away!
Finally, play the game again, without mentioning any colours.

c If you had to describe yourself to a stranger so that they would recognise you easily in a crowded place like a hotel, station or airport, what would you write?

> 21 Park Road
> Harefield HW3 4IL
> 12 December '87
>
> Dear Mr Shaw,
> Thank you for offering to come and pick me up on the 22nd. I hope we won't miss each other.
> I'm fairly tall, and not exactly thin... I have long fair hair, and will probably be wearing a dark red jacket.
> I should be at the meeting point by 6.30 p.m. but I may be slightly later.
> Looking forward to meeting you all,
>
> Marie-France

Write the same kind of thing about another person in the class, so that someone else would recognise them easily. Do not write their name.

16 *Phrase-building* ....

Make some phrases and say them quickly.

| quite
fairly
rather | tall / short / slim / well-built / plump |

| reasonably
slightly | thin / slim |

medium height
not what you would call thin
not exactly thin

with long hair
with longish hair
with long dark hair
with long dark straight hair
with fairly long straight hair and brownish eyes
with long hair, darkish and straight, and brown eyes
she has longish hair, dark and straight, brown eyes and glasses

I'll be wearing a suit / dress
I'll be wearing a light suit / dress
I'll be wearing a light blue suit / dress
I'll be wearing a light blue suit/ /dress with a flower in my buttonhole

17 Biography

We asked Monica to write a brief biography of herself. She was, in fact, about to set off on a trip to South East Asia, to do some research in Sarawak. Find out how many countries she has lived in.

> I was born in the United States and lived in the Mid West of America until 1962 and I have only been back once since then, when I was fourteen. I've mostly lived in England since leaving America, although I spent two years in Rome while I was still living with my family. I studied History at Sussex University and since then I have been teaching English in Poland and in Malaysia. In 1983 I started postgraduate work in Social Anthropology and I am now doing a PhD at LSE.

Tell your partner the same kinds of things about yourself. Try to find out if you have anything in common.

Now write a short biography for yourself. Don't put your name.

Read other people's biographies. Which person's experience is the most similar to yours?

Sports and injuries

a Find out what kind of sports the people in your group and their families take part in. How many are (or could be) dangerous sports? Prepare to tell the class.

▶ *Sports Survey* Tell the class. Listen and work out which seem to be the two most popular sports among you all. ◀

b Look at the picture opposite of a professional footballer. It shows all the injuries he has had in his ten-year career. What injuries has he had, and how many?

`18b` Listen to the group counting up his injuries. Did they get the same ones as you did? Did they get the same number?

c Can you beat the footballer? Get into groups. What injuries have you had between you? (They need not only be sports injuries. Any injuries at all.) Find out what happened in each case.

Have you as a group had more injuries than this footballer?

▶ Plan a summary of your group's injuries to tell the class. ◀

Find out which is the most common injury that people in your class have had.
Can your class beat the footballer?

What do you say in your language if something hurts you? In English we say **Ow!** or **Ouch!**

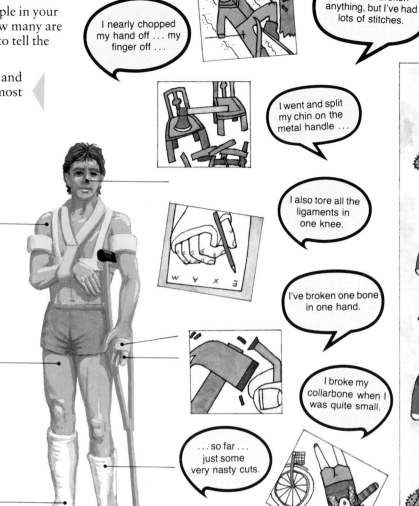

`18d` **d** Find out:

1 Which person did which of these things, and how they did it.
2 What were the reactions of the others? What did they say or do?
3 Which drawing is not mentioned at all?

Language study

a Verbs in past tense form
Check that you know the present forms of these verbs.

> lived spent studied started broke
> fell had to spend gave went split
> had to sit and write tore got had

b and, but, so
Read the summary of what happened to Catherine, and say where **and, but, so** could fit.

When she was quite small, Catherine fell off her bike _____ hurt herself badly _____ nobody realised how serious it was. She went to bed _____ it was very painful _____ she didn't sleep the whole night. The next morning, they took her to the doctor's _____ he said she had broken her collarbone _____ she had to have it bandaged up.

c Below are 30 common verbs, starting with the most common. What are their past tense forms?

be	say	take	use	like
have	mean	want	give	feel
think	see	put	call	become
do	go	look	tell	help
know	make	find	need	bring
get	come	leave	seem	lose

Put the past tense forms in categories according to their pronunciation. e.g. **gave** and **made** have the same sound.
How many do you have left over?

20 Who would you get on with?

> Imagine that you were applying to a Computer Dating Agency. Write a short piece about yourself to enclose with your letter to the Agency.

3. Your Interests

Indicate the interests and activities you enjoy by placing a tick ✔ beside the.
please indicate with a cross ✗. Otherwise leave the box blank

THE MUSIC YOU ENJOY		
Classical		
Opera		
Pop		
Jazz		98.
Folk		99.
		100.
		101.
		102.
		103.

AN EVENING OUT
Theatre
Concerts
Opera/Ballet
Cinema
Dancing
Parties

We asked everyone in the group to do this task. Read what two of them wrote about themselves.

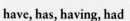

I am 29 years old and work for a publishing company. I enjoy travel and lived for five years in Papua New Guinea, where I was a teacher. Although I intend to stay in Britain for a few years, I hope to see more of the world in the next ten – definitely South America and Africa.

I enjoy living on my own although I love to be with friends and lead a hectic social life. My main preoccupations are reading, music, travel and friends. I like food and cooking – but mainly eating.

cr

My name is Catherine McKenna and I am 32 years old. I was born in December 1953 in Dublin, Republic of Ireland. I am one of five children and am an identical twin. I am 5ft 2½ ins tall and have red hair, blue eyes, fair skin and freckles and an reasonably slim.

My hobbies include reading, sewing, cinema, theatre going and most sociable activities which involve meeting and talking with people. I also enjoy some sports (eg, squash and tennis although I am not very good at them) and swimming and other pastimes like playing boules or croquet and sitting in the shade on a sunny day.

I have had a varied career but lastly I was an insurance broker working for an International Insurance Broking House based in Hampton Wick and, of course, the City.

c.M.

a Think of a friend of yours who would get on well with one of these people. Explain to your partner why you think so.

20b **b** Listen to John and Catherine talking about what they would write.
What did Catherine say? Did she actually write what she said she would?

Make a list of what they have in common.

▶ Tell the class. Do you all agree? ◀

c Write about yourself. Start by talking through with your partner what you want to write.

▶ Write in a similar style to the texts above. Read each other's and comment. ◀

21 Funny Story

21 San Francisco disc jockey Don Sherwood tells of an argument in a friend's house after a weekend of sports television. The wife complained, 'You love football more than you love me.'

The husband replied, 'Yeah, but I still love you more than basketball.'

22 *Grammar revision*

have, has, having, had

Look at the sentences 1–10. Find:

a at least two sentences where **have** goes with **to**. What do they mean?

b two where someone **has** something in their character.

c two sentences describing someone.

d two where **have** goes with part of the verb like this:
I have lived in London for almost as long as I can remember.

e two sentences where **have** means 'own' or 'possess'.

1 *We had to look in the atlas to find out where it was.* (2)

2 *I would need to meet someone who also had a sense of humour.* (20)

3 *Do you have any pets?*

4 *Do you have a favourite colour?* (128)

5 *I've never broken anything but I've had lots of stitches.* (18)

6 *I do pride myself on having a good sense of direction.* (140)

7 *She has dark hair.* (15)

8 *I have a travelcard, so I don't have to pay.* (80)

9 *I have eaten the plums that were in the icebox.* (95)

10 *Have you finished?*

In which five sentences could you use **got** after **have**?

23 Are you a lucky person?

How many ways are there of winning money in your country?

Find out if other people in your class have ever won any money, and how. Who is the luckiest person in your class?

23 Catherine won some money two years running. How? How did she feel? What did she do when she heard she had won?

24 *Wordpower*

bit

Find someone in the pictures who might be saying or thinking the following:

(a) It's a bit much, 25 minutes late again!

(b) Ow, hey! Your dog bit me!

(c) Have you had to wait a bit?

(d) I got a bit of shopping done.

(e) Like a bit of cake?

(f) Just a small bit, thanks.

(g) Sorry he's making a bit of a mess.

(h) Ah, he knows a bit of Chinese.

(i) Your son is a bit smaller than my son.

Now look up **bit** in the Lexicon.
What other **bits** can you see in the pictures?
What other phrases with **bit** could you make up?

25 Animals

a   Animal categories

How many different ways can you think of to categorise these creatures?

25a Which categories did Caroline and Stephen think of? Who do you think is an animal lover?
Stephen says 'Rats get a really bad deal.' Why?

What animals do these things in English?
   purr   growl   bark   squeak

What noises do animals make in your language?

What kind of noises are these?
'The car engine purred quietly ...'
'What's your name?' the policeman barked loudly.

26 Poems by Spike Milligan

26a   **a   THE DOG LOVERS**

So they bought you
And kept you in a
Very good home
Central heating
TV
A deep freeze
A very good home
No one to take you
For that lovely long run –
But otherwise
'A very good home'
They fed you Pal and Chum
But not that lovely long run,
Until, mad with energy and boredom
You escaped – and ran and ran and ran
Under a car.
Today they will cry for you –
Tomorrow they will buy another dog.

Do you agree or disagree with these statements?

1 This is a poem about people who are nice to animals and who gave a dog a very good home.
2 The poet says that dogs need more than just food.
3 The dog's owners just never took him out for a good long walk.
4 The people in the poem didn't realise what they were doing was wrong.

26b   **b   Holes in the sky**
Now listen to another poem. Learn it.

a fairly, very, quite, a bit etc.

Find the words like **fairly, very, quite, a bit** etc. that go with the adjectives in the phrases.

[27a] Listen to how they are said. Which words are stressed? There are some phrases where they make the adjective stronger in meaning, and others where the adjective remains fairly neutral. Can you hear the difference? The sentences marked (x2) you will hear twice. How is the meaning different each time?

e.g. *I'm fairly interested in sport.* neutral
Not very tall. neutral
They're ever so small. strong
It's a very pleasant school. strong

She's got a very strange accent.
... squash and tennis, though I'm not very good at them.
English and American, which are fairly similar.
I make friends fairly easily.
It's quite a close community. (x2)
She's quite small. (x2)
They are ever so small.
It was so painful.
It's extremely cold outside.
It can be terribly cold in winter.
... who was not terribly interested in sport.
I absolutely hate sport!
I was really very very unwell.
She looks a bit tired.
You're a bit late!
A bit shorter than you.
A lot shorter, in fact.
Much shorter.
Generally quite healthy. (x2)
It's rather expensive. (x2)
Extremely expensive!
That's quite enough!

b Using measurements

I'm 5 foot 2½ inches tall.
That's about 1 metre 58.
How tall are you? What height are you?
It's 50 metres long and 25 metres wide.
How long is the swimming pool near you?
How wide is it?
It's about 5 miles (8 kilometres) away.
Around 20 minutes away, by car.
How far is your house from here?
It's over 30 degrees Centigrade.
How hot is it where you live now?
How cold is it in winter?

c back

Use the Lexicon to find out what these uses of **back** mean.

a *I've only been back to America once.*
b *... way back when I was a paperboy ...*
c *... he was in the back of the police car.*
d *My back garden ...*
e *... I backed the car out of the garage.*

Now think of situations when you might hear or say these.

f *Can I have my book back please?*
g *Oh, that music brings back memories!*
h *Can you ring me back later? We're in the middle of dinner.*
i *To come back to what we were saying before, ...*
j *All right then. Go out now, but be back by 11. Okay?*
k *Let's go back to your first point ... the first thing you said.*
l *Never look back!*
m *Stand back.*

d Odd word out?

There is one word/phrase that is the odd one out in each set. Which is it?

a medical, fit, well, unwell, healthy, ill, sick, energy, pain, intelligent, hurt
b university, degree, academic, intelligent, subject, argument
c How awful! Dear me! Oh dear! What a dreadful thing! Great! How terrible! How sad!
d very very, fairly, really, extremely, terribly, absolutely, ever so, dreadfully, awfully

e Absolutely okay or generally all right?

Match these questions with the answers below. They all have at least, two possible answers.

1 *What do you think, then?*
2 *What's he like as a teacher?*
3 *Do you agree?*

a *Yes, on the whole. There are just one or two things ...*
b *Really very good. First class.*
c *On the whole, it should work well. But perhaps ...*
d *Very pleasant, on the whole.*
e *I think you're absolutely right.*

f Whole or part?

Match 1–7 with the phrases below.
1 *Which piece would you like?*
2 *Will you be at home in the morning?*
3 *There are five more bits to fit in.*
4 *When will you be away?*
5 *Did her father know?*
6 *Which bit of the town is nicest?*
7 *Just in India?*

a *I'll be in the whole day.*
b *Then you've done the whole lot.*
c *The whole family had heard about it.*
d *The whole place is lovely.*
e *Can't I have the whole thing?*
f *The whole of July.*
g *No, in the world as a whole.*

Important words to remember (98 so far)

absolutely	bored	dog	health	metal	sad	United States
academic	boring	easily L	healthy	mostly	shade	whole
afterwards	category	energy L	hole	nasty	sick	win
agency	character	escape	hurt	noise	skin	writer
animal	characteristic	extremely	ill	otherwise	smoke	
apparent	computer	fairly	international	pain	spread L	
argument	condition L	fall L	knee	painful	sweet	
background L	consider L	fell	mad	reasonably	tall	
bird	creature	fit	mainly	respond	terribly	
bit L	disease	funny	medical	response	thin	

A good place for a holiday

28 A nice active week's holiday

a Whereabouts in England is Northumberland?

Which of these words might be used to describe the Northumberland National Park?

beautiful	noisy	historical
crowded	quiet	ancient
peaceful	busy	wild

How do you think tourists spend their time in this area?
What do you think they go to see?
What sort of holiday do you like?
Do you think you would enjoy a holiday in Northumberland?

b Which of the following can you see on this page?

mountainous regions	seaside/lakes
areas of forest or woodland	rocky coastline
grassy hills	sandy beaches
desert	small harbours
farmland	large ports
green valleys	ancient buildings

Could any of these pictures be somewhere in your country? Which ones? What kind of scenery is typical of your country? How does it compare with Northumberland?

c Jenny Maxwell spent a week in Northumberland on holiday with her two children.
Make a list of six things you think they did.

17

29 Jenny's holiday

a   Jenny talked to a friend, Jeremy, about her holiday.

Before they began their conversation they had the instructions opposite. (They did not see each other's cards.)

29a   Listen to the tape, and then read the transcript and say how many of the questions you think Jeremy was able to answer.

Listen and read again and count how many questions Jeremy asked. Did he ask four, or more than four?

29b   b   Now listen to Jeremy's answers and see if you were right.
How many questions did he answer correctly?

c   Look at the six things you guessed in section 28c. Were you right?

Jenny

Talk to Jeremy about your last holiday. When you think you have told him all the important things, say "And that was how we spent our holiday."

Jeremy

Jenny is going to talk to you about her last holiday. You may ask her a maximum of four questions. At the end of the conversation you must answer as many of the following questions as you can.

a   How many people did she go on holiday with?
b   How did they travel?
c   How long was the holiday?
d   Where did they stay?
e   What was the weather like?
f   How did they spend the time?
g   Have they ever been on a similar holiday before?
h   Will they go back to the same place again?

When Jenny says, "And that was how we spent our holiday." that is the end of the conversation.

---

30 Being indirect

a   Avoiding the question

In Britain, people don't like being asked how much money they earn, or how old they are. So if you are asked directly, you try to say something else, or give an answer that is vague, or a joke.

Well, how much do you get a month?	*Not enough!* *Less than you, I expect.* *Oh, about what a school teacher normally gets.* *Well, it depends . . .*

Think of things you could say if for some reason you didn't want to answer these questions.

1   *How old are you?*
2   *What time did you get home last night?*
3   *Who were you with last night?*
4   *How much money did you actually spend?*
5   *Why didn't you come to the party?*

31 A holiday you've had

Working on your own, make a few notes about a holiday or day out you had recently. Your teacher will divide you into A and B groups and give you further instructions.

b   Asking indirectly

Now think of the different ways of finding something out without asking directly.

Instead of asking: *How old are you?* you could:

1   indirectly find out what year the other person left school etc. and work it out from that.
2   ask questions like *Do you remember when the Beatles first became popular?*
3   give the same information about yourself, e.g. *Well, I'm 43 and . . .*

Think of what might you say in order to find out:

1   how much rent someone pays
2   if they have had a nasty argument lately
3   how much they spent on their last holiday

32 *Language study*

a   do, did

Jenny says: *We did a lot of walking along the coast.*

What did you do on your last holiday?

a bit of climbing   some swimming
a lot of boating   a lot of sightseeing

What do the phrases with **do** mean here?

a   *Who does most of the meals in your house?*
b   *I'll do the list.*
c   *Who does most of the talking in your home?*

b   That was why/how etc.

Jenny and her children had never been to Northumberland. Jenny says:
      That was why we wanted to go.
They did a lot of different things.
      That was how we spent our holiday.

Now look at these.

I liked science subjects but I think that was because the teachers were very much better. (58)
You have to get on a train and come all the way back again. That's why it's always better to catch a taxi.

a Read the two postcards. Speculate about who the senders are and their reasons for sending the postcards. What do you think will happen as a result of these postcards?

Dear Dave, Jane, Jenny + Becky 3/5
My sister lives very close to this picture. The Blue Mountains are spectacular. We're having a family time here till we leave on Friday 11/5. This is to inform you that we've changed our flight. We're flying direct from Sydney on QF1 e.t.a 21.10, just in case you're thinking of coming to the airport.

See you soon

Mandy

AIR MAIL

DAVE + JANE WILLIS
c/o The British Council
Rubber House
Collyer Quay
Singapore 1
SINGAPORE

Dear Becky,
Sorry you couldn't come to the airport. Miss you lots. Say hi to your parents from me. Thanks for the weekend. Please write Anne-clare has my address Amanda

BECKY WILLIS
21 FOLLESTONE RD.
MEDWAY PARK.
S'PORE 0513
SINGAPORE

PAR AVION
AERPHOST
O E 78

O'Connell Bridge, Dublin, Ireland. Photo: P. O'Toole, John Hinde Studies.

b What do you think about the first postcard?

33b Listen to John and Monica. Did they say the same as you?

c What about the second postcard?

33c Listen to John and Monica again.

Why do they use these words and phrases?

Perhaps	Do you suppose
It sounds as though	I don't know
Maybe	Probably
I suppose so	

d Imagine you are on holiday abroad. You write a postcard to a friend. Your real purpose is to persuade them to meet you at the airport or station. But of course you want to do this without actually asking them directly.
Write the postcard.

34 *Wordpower* ....

time and money

1 **time** = minutes, hours, days, week, months etc.
Mummy and Daddy went back to Ireland some time ago. (9)

It'll rain all the time. (38)
How did they spend the time? (21)

2 to have a _____ time.

It sounds like you had a good time. (29)
We had a dreadful time.

3 **time** = an occasion when something happens

The second time was when we went to eat at a hamburger restaurant.
I've already boarded this flight five times and every time I ended up in Cuba.
This time our friend left a warning note. (150)

4 **time** = two o'clock, 8.30, 17.20 hours etc.
What time is it? Do you have the time?

5 **times**
The taxi cost five times as much as the bus.

Which category do these examples belong to?

(a) Took a very long time getting there. (21)
(b) People we met on it said they'd been many times before. (29)
(c) Look at the time. We're going to be late.
(d) But next time I knew I could do it. (58)
(e) We had a very busy time at work last week.
(f) My job is a hundred times more difficult than playing the piano. (174)

Spend goes with money as well as time. What other words are like **spend**?

(g) That's very expensive. We can't afford it.
(h) You'd waste a lot of time and you'd feel exhausted when you got there. (69)
(i) Business is bad. We're losing quite a bit.
(j) How much did you actually spend?
(k) If you go by taxi you'll save ten minutes or so.
(l) We are saving for our holidays.

35 Discover the North Pennines

a The North Pennines, as the name suggests, are at the Northern tip of the Pennine Hills, the backbone of England. A spectacularly beautiful and undiscovered area, some of the wildest open landscape left in England.

WHERE TO STAY

Hotels, inns, guesthouses and farmhouses provide a wide choice of accommodation.

What the critics say ...

A farmhouse holiday is ideal for a family – good food, a friendly atmosphere and a lovely setting. – Carol Chester, **Daily Express**

Excellent value for good food, peace and quiet and beautiful scenery. – Paul Hughes, Daily Mirror

Read through the passage below and find phrases that could act as captions for the pictures.

provide
guesthouses
farmhouses
ideal
atmosphere
excellent value

?
Words to guess

discover
choice
finding

L
Words to look up

Northumberland is a paradise for everyone who enjoys the open air. There are magnificent walks over hills, moors and dales, including a rugged stretch of the Pennine Way, and in summer you can bathe from miles of smooth sandy beaches. The streams and rivers of Northumberland provide some of the finest trout and salmon fishing in Britain, and there is excellent sport along the coast for sea anglers. With the sea or the moors for a background, you can play golf on superb courses, and there are good facilities for other sports and pastimes, including pony-trekking, sailing, gliding, tennis and bowls. Horse-racing, Association and Rugby football can be enjoyed in nearby Newcastle.

If you are thinking of a motoring holiday, there's no better place than Northumberland, where parking problems are few, and you can drive for miles without seeing another car. In fact there are several roads where you are more likely to surprise a pheasant or a hare than to pass another vehicle. Wherever you decide to stop you can always be sure of finding comfortable accommodation, a good meal, and a real warm-hearted Northumbrian welcome – Northumbrians have a reputation for being the most hospitable folk in Britain. There's plenty of entertainment too, especially in the larger towns. National ballet and opera companies visit the region regularly, and there are first-class theatres in Newcastle ...

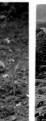

open air
streams
region
pastimes
fishing
comfortable
accommodation
plenty
regularly

?
Words to guess

b Think of a tourist place that you know very well. How many of these phrases might be used to describe it? Choose any five phrases and complete them.

There's no better place than ... excellent sport/ shopping/entertainment ... magnificent ... superb ... can be enjoyed ... You can always be sure of finding ... There's plenty of ... There are good facilities for ... There is/are first-class ... The people have a reputation for ... Ideal for ... a wide choice of ... excellent value for ...

36 *Phrase-building*

Make some sentences from the first table and after each one add a suitable comment from the second.

We did	some a fair bit of quite a lot of a lot of plenty of too much far too much	sunbathing. fishing. shopping. walking. climbing. sightseeing. driving.

That's	how why	you	got so tired. have no money left. saw so much. enjoyed yourselves. got so many things. spent the time.

Grammar revision

been

Sometimes **been** means 'gone to' or 'visited'. How many sentences are there here where **been** means 'gone to' or 'visited'?

Have you been there before?
I don't know London. I've never been.

a *How long have you been away from there?* (9)
b *I haven't been back since.* (10)
c *I've only been back once since.* (17)
d *Since then I have been teaching English.* (17)
e *We'd been collecting firewood for a bonfire.* (18)
f *Have you ever been to a zoo?*
g *Have you ever been bitten by a dog or a snake?*
h *So the weather must have been sunny and nice.* (29)
i *I've never been to Charles de Gaulle airport.* (69)
j *His stories have been translated into many languages.* (97)

38 Future holidays

38a **a** Stephen is telling Catherine about his next holiday. Who do you think says these things?

a *That sounds really lovely.*
b *Why can he get you tickets?*
c *How lovely!*
d *I'll just laze in the sun.*

Listen and see if you were right.

38b **b** What are Catherine's plans? Find the phrases with these words in the transcript.

next holiday	with my parents
with me	for the children
in a week's time	mainly
most of the time	looking forward

c Work with a partner. Ask five questions to find out what your partner will do for their next holiday. Take notes and then write a short piece about your partner's holiday.

39 Board and lodgings

Write a question to act as a heading for five of these paragraphs, e.g. What is B&B? Is breakfast included?

BED BREAKFAST & EVENING MEAL

Can tourists find anything like B & B in your country?
How much does it cost for a comfortable bed for the night?
Is that more or less than B & B in Britain?
What food is there that is typical of your country and that tourists like?

Write something similar about holiday accommodation in a country that you know well.

'B & B'. A HOME AWAY FROM HOME
Bed and Breakfast, or B & B as it is often known, is a form of holiday accommodation for which Britain is world-famous.

It gives you the opportunity to stay in a private house that has one or two spare bedrooms, or a small guest house.

And it also gives you the chance to make friends and see some of the most attractive and less well-known parts of the country ranging from John O'Groats to Land's End.

In most cases it will be run by the owner who lives on the premises and you will be treated as a royal guest.

The welcome will be warm and friendly but your privacy will be respected and you can have all your meals in a separate dining room.

In addition to a comfortable bed, your host will prepare you an English breakfast fit for a King.

Prices range from £7 to £16 per night.

Contact your local BTA for information on budget accommodation.

40 Language study

Look at the transcripts for sections 38a and 38b. How many ways of referring to the future can you find? e.g. *I'm going to have a holiday.*

a What do these sentences have in common?

1 *You will be reading about two people.*
2 *What do you think they are going to say?*
3 *I intend to stay in Britain for a few years.*
4 *Tomorrow they will buy another dog.*
5 *My next holiday is tomorrow hopefully.*
6 *If I'm lucky my roommate will be able to get us tickets.*
7 *My husband is joining us in a week's time.*
8 *We're flying direct from Sydney on QF1.*
9 *I'll go home when I've finished this.*
10 *We'll come round and say 'Goodbye' before we leave.*

b Punctuation

Match these, then see if you can find one example of each of these punctuation marks on this page.

a comma	' '
a full stop	;
an apostrophe s	.
a question mark	( )
an exclamation mark	–
quotation marks/inverted commas	,
a semi-colon	:
a colon	/
a hyphen	?
a dash	's
brackets	!
dot dot dot	-
a stroke/slash	…

c Which meanings of these words are used here?

1 *I found Chinese very difficult to learn. I expect you will, too.*
2 *I've got no idea which person on the board of directors to ask.*
3 *There's such a wide choice of banks – go to the one which will give you the top rates of interest if you want to save money.*
4 *I was working in the garden when I discovered this funny black object.*
5 *It was hidden in a small space right under a tree root, and was very difficult to reach.*
6 *The person next door said it would be a good idea to contact the museum who might be interested in the strange object.*
7 *Although I tried several times to phone them, I couldn't reach the man I needed to speak to.*

d northern, southern, eastern, western, European

What words commonly follow these?

Western Europe will be cold with snow in some northern parts. Southern areas of Eastern Europe will be warmer but heavy falls of snow may effect European airports.

e likely, unlikely

Say whether you think these things are:

(almost/practically) definite/certain
likely/probable   possible
(almost/practically) impossible   unlikely

1 *Catherine enjoyed her holiday in Ireland.*
2 *Jenny and her family will be going back to Northumberland.*
3 *Stephen had a good holiday in Bermuda.*
4 *If you go to Ireland you will be able to do a lot of sunbathing.*
5 *If you go to Bermuda it will rain all the time.*
6 *If you stay in a B & B you will be well looked after.*
7 *The Willises went to meet Munling and her family.*
8 *You will be going on holiday sometime in the next year.*
9 *You will be going abroad.*
10 *You will enjoy your holiday.*

f What's the missing word?

1 I've lived in London ____ years.
2 Where are you going ____ your next holiday?
3 You can drive ____ miles without seeing …
4 … breakfast, fit ____ a king.
5 It's ideal ____ a family.
6 … a good place ____ walking.
7 B & B accommodation ____ which Britain is world-famous.
8 What does it cost ____ a bed?
9 What's ____ homework?

Important words to remember (164 so far)					
accommodation	central	dry	king	queen	southern
active	choice L	eastern	likely	quiet	spend
activity	choose L	European	lovely	quietly	stream
afford	Christian	expect L	lucky	range	swimming
ancient	Christmas	fish	managed	reach L	unlikely
atmosphere	coast	fishing	maximum	region	value
beautiful	comfort	friendly	northern	regular	waste
beauty	comfortable	guest	opportunity	relaxed	western
beach	crowd	ideal	peace	royal	wet
board L	dangerous	island	plenty	sand	wide
boat	discover L	join	provide L	separate	wild

Unit 4
They're probably worth the money

Well paid or badly paid?

How many different jobs and professions can you find on this page? Which would be the best paid in your country? Which would be the worst paid? Which *should* be the best paid, do you think?

Mr. Matthew Stewart,
The Manager,
National United Bank,
57 High Street,
Risborough,
RB1 5AP.

Which of these statements do you agree with, if any?

a 'Anybody who handles money tends to get paid a lot.'
b 'Dentists are well paid; they're probably worth the money though.'
c 'Teachers are definitely underpaid.'
d 'Anybody who's paid more than me is probably overpaid.'
e 'In general, women receive the same pay for the same work as men.'
f '...women have a slight advantage; they tend to get tipped more generously than men.'
g 'Anybody who is expected to work eight and a half hours a day should be receiving more than just £1.20 an hour.'
h 'The Union would probably insist on a wage of at least £108 per week.'

L profession/al
  worth
  least

23

43   Best paid and worst paid

a   Look at the list of jobs below.
In groups, discuss which are the three best paid jobs and the two worst paid in your country. Write a list.
Do you think that any of the jobs on the list are overpaid or underpaid in your country?
Have you any idea which are the best and worst paid in Britain?

    a nurse in a hospital
    a miner at the coalface
    a shop assistant
    a car assembly worker in a factory
    a bank manager
    a dentist
    a schoolteacher
    a plumber
    a top professional footballer
    a nuclear scientist

▷   Tell the class what you have decided. ◁

Listen to the other groups and see if they think the same as you.
How many groups had the same person at the top of their lists?

43b   **b**   What did Caroline and Stephen think? Draw a table like this one, and fill it in after you have listened.

Best paid	....
Worst paid	....
Overpaid	....
Underpaid	....

Compare their opinions with:

what you think about your country.
what you decided about Britain.

44   *Language study* ············

44a   **a**   Listen to Caroline and Stephen talking about the schoolteacher and the nurse. How many times do they use the words **say, think** and **know**? What phrases do they use with them?

b   How many ways could you categorise these phrases?

> *paid reasonably well*
> *get a lot of money*
> *Too much!*
> *paid a lot*
> *the lowest*
> *are underpaid*
> *were the worst paid*
> *gets even less*
> *get well paid*
> *the same pay*
> *get less pay*
> *earn more than just £1.20 an hour*
> *at least £108 a week in wages*
> *the salary is just not enough*
> *can earn as much as $200 a day*
> *a low income*
> *a highly paid job*
> *gets a good salary*

45   Two jokes

a   **At the dentist's**

Do you like going to the dentist? Why not? How much does it cost (roughly) to have a tooth out in your country?

Compare prices with other students.

What could be the last four words of this joke? Decide what you think they are then tell the class.

> A woman went to a dentist in Baghdad to have a tooth out and was told it would cost the equivalent of £30.
> 'But that's ridiculous! she said. 'My husband has to work two hours for that.'
> 'Madam,' the dentist replied, 'If you like, I _____ _____ _____ _____.'

b   **If you call the plumber . . .**

The five parts of this joke have been mixed up. Can you work out the joke?

FINALLY HE CALLED A PLUMBER WHO FIXED EVERYTHING IN ABOUT HALF AN HOUR AND GAVE HIM A BILL FOR £75.
MY BANK MANAGER HAD A LOT OF TROUBLE WITH HIS HOT WATER SYSTEM.
"I'M NOT SURPRISED," SAID THE PLUMBER, "NEITHER DID I WHEN I WAS A BANK MANAGER."
"BUT THAT WORKS OUT AT £150. AN HOUR.
"I'M A BANK MANAGER AND I DON'T MAKE THAT KIND OF MONEY."

45c   **c**   Listen to the jokes.

46   When I was a paperboy

What kind of work can schoolchildren or young students do in your country to make some money? Tell each other.

Caroline and Stephen talk about their jobs as baby-sitter, paperboy and factory-worker. Stephen also mentions a friend who's a waitress.

Put their jobs in order from worst paid to best paid.

46   Listen and see if you were right.

47 Equal opportunities

a Letter to the Editor

Read this letter which was written by a teenager who had just left school and started work. Was it a young woman or a young man who wrote it?

I thought you might like to hear about my job in a bakery. I start work at 6 am, at the latest, and often work past 3 pm. That's at least 8½ hours work each day (I'm allowed a half hour break). Often the work is unpleasant – standing up all day, working near hot ovens (especially in summer), carrying heavy weights about – flour, baking trays, etc.

From my basic 40 hour week I get £1.20 an hour, which I think is awful. OK, so this is my first job, straight from school, but I do think my wages are bad. In an average four-week month I get to take home only about £160.

I saw in *Just Seventeen* that 5½ million working women earn less than the 'decency threshold' wage of £108 a week. Well, I'm one of them and would like to hear other readers' opinions.

HB, Worcester

L | heavy

| least
| union

If this person gets £1.20 an hour, and works an eight and a half hour day, how does that work out at £160 a month?

What are your opinions? What do you think this person should do?

> Together plan what you would put in a letter to send to the Editor responding to HB's letter. Write about three sentences, giving your opinions, and one or two pieces of advice, but don't write the whole letter.

Read your opinions and advice out to the class. Did you all suggest the same kind of things?

b Fair pay?

```
Read the letter about the job in the
bakery.  In general, do you think women
receive the same pay for the same work as
men?  What do you think about this
particular job in this letter?
```

47b Listen to what Caroline and Stephen thought.
Would you agree with them?
Who said these phrases?

On the other hand.
I don't think that should make that much difference.

48 Wordpower

clear, clearly

Which phrases could go with which person or which picture?

(a) The line of its footprints was clear.
(b) I hope that's clear.....
(c) The sea was so clear you could see everything on the bottom.
(d) Large areas of forest were being cleared.
(e) It was not clear whether the meeting had begun or not.
(f) Women are clearly underpaid in some jobs they do.
(g) Sorry but I'm not clear about what we have to do....
(h) Could you possibly write more clearly?
(i) The table needs clearing.

Look up the word **clear** in the Lexicon.

49 Keyhole picture

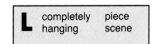

a Discuss what kind of job this person might do.

49a What jobs do John and Catherine think he might do?
Make a list of the things they think they can see.

e.g. *something hanging down from his chin*

b Looking at the picture above, what might the man be doing at this moment? What do you think John and Catherine will say? They mention five things he could be doing.

49b What five things do they think he could be doing?
Do you think John is 'completely wrong'?
Tell the class what you think now.

L	completely	piece
hanging	scene

50 *Preposition spot* ·············

in

In can refer to *time* and *place*. Find the phrases with **in**, and say which they refer to. When they refer to time, what do they mean?

a *... less injuries than he had in about ten years* (18)
b *There are holes in the sky where the rain comes in.*
c *My husband is joining us in a week's time.* (38)
d *... the highest hill in Northumberland ...* (29)
e *... and we went out in a boat one day ...* (29)
f *... especially in summer ...* (47)
g *... a plumber who fixed everything in about half an hour ...* (45)
h *I was born in 1956 in Warrington ...* (9)
i *... a competition in which the first prize was one week ...*
j *... if someone dropped in unexpectedly and stayed for a meal ...* (86)

What about these phrases? What word does the **in** go with?

k *... who wasn't terribly interested in sport ...* (20)
l *Even taking part in sport?* (20)
m *... what do they have in common?* (20)
n *In fact there are several roads where ...* (35)
o *In addition to a comfortable bed ...* (39)
p *I think in general they don't* (get equal pay). (47)
q *... some difficulty in finding a successful position.* (52)
r *... just in case you're thinking of coming to the airport.* (33)
s *He was in such a hurry that ...* (136)

51 Now what?

Discuss in groups what you now think the man does and where you think he is. What are all the things that he has with him? Tell the class.

51 John and Catherine discuss this picture, then finally they look at the whole photograph. What else can they see? What particular things complete the picture?

52 About your work

a We asked Stephen and Catherine to do this task.

> If you have a job, write a short account of the work you do. Are you happy with this job/type of work? Or you could write about someone else.
>
> If you do not have a job, write about what you would like to do, or have done in the past, and say very briefly what it involves. (max. 10 lines).

Read what Stephen wrote and find out how many different types of work his present job involves.

Really I am a student, but during the summer I work to make some money. This summer I am working for my father's publishing company, doing odd jobs. Some days I am the receptionist, on other days I make the tea. In between times I use the word-processor to send letters to authors and other publishers. Once I had to show a visitor from Korea around the office, another time I was commissioned to draw maps and illustrations for a new book. But most of the time I am filing invoices and stuffing envelopes. It's OK for the summer, but I wouldn't want to do it every day of my life.

L odd draw

my father's publishing company

b Catherine talked to John about the whole process of applying for jobs and about the job he had applied for in a school in Telford.

1 Find out exactly what post he wants in Telford, and if he thinks he'll be successful in getting it. Make brief notes.
2 What can a word-processor do that a typewriter cannot? How does this help John?

After their conversation, Catherine wrote about John.

> John is trying to get a new job – and is busy sending application forms and CVs all over the country. He wants a promotion to Head of Department, but as he is still relatively young and lacks seniority, he anticipates some difficulty in finding a successful position.

? briefly
the whole process of
lacks
it's just a question of
relatively
irrelevant sections

I discovered the joys of word-processing the other day.

c In pairs, interview two other people in your class. Find out something about the work they do, or a job they have done or may do.

▷ Together, write a few lines about one of them. Then give it to them to read and check.

▷ Write a few lines on the same subject about yourself or a friend. ◁

d Read Catherine's text on John again to find the phrases that go with the words in the box.

| trying | successful | relatively |
| application | difficulty | |

Language study

a Can you find nine or ten phrases that refer to time in Stephen's piece on page 26? Write them down.
   e.g. *during the summer*
b What's another way of saying **once**?

Grammar revision

Verbs and adjectives with 'to'

The class should be in two groups – one group of A students, and one group of B students. Look carefully at these phrases with **to** in them. A students look at set *A* below, while B students look at set *B* on page 29.

a How many *verbs* can you find that are often followed by **to**? Write a list of them.

b How many *adjectives* are there (e.g. *happy to*)? Write them down too.

c In which examples does **to** mean 'in order to', ('for the purpose of')?

Compare lists. Do you have any similar examples?

Which **to**'s are left over? What do these phrases mean?

Set A. Examples with 'to'

1 *... a very pleasant school and I'd be sorry to leave it ...* (2)
2 *... very difficult to tell anybody anything about me.* (20)
3 *She used to work at a desk.* (1)
4 *Although I intend to stay in Britain for a few years ...* (20)
5 *I hope to see more of the world ...* (20)
6 *That was why we wanted to go.* (29)
7 *You weren't going to tell me that ...* (29)
8 *Wherever you decide to stop you can ...* (35)
9 *... it is possible to visit the ...*
10 *I use the word-processor to send letters ...* (51)
11 *Once I had to show a visitor round ...* (52)
12 *John is trying to get a new job ...* (52)
13 *He wants a promotion to Head of Department ...* (52)

14 *A woman went to a dentist in Baghdad to have a tooth out ...* (45)
15 *My husband has to work two hours for that.* (45)
16 *... stood around with nothing to do.* (55)

55 Success or failure??

Read these stories, and try to work out how best to
complete them. Write your ideas down.
Read them out to each other.

A On his first day selling ice-cream in the cinema,
an assistant sold more during the interval than
anyone had ever done before. When this
success was repeated day after day, the
manager decided to keep an eye on him. He
found that ten minutes before the interval the
enterprising assistant _____.

C Upon returning to his office, my husband
stopped at his secretary's desk to see if there
were any messages for him. There were none,
but he couldn't help noticing a note to his
secretary from a recently hired young clerk-
typist. It read: 'Dear Ida, I'm in the lounge.
_____ coffee break. Sally.'

B In the sweet shop, one sales assistant always had
customers lined up waiting while other
assistants stood around with nothing to do. The
owner of the shop asked the popular one for her
secret. 'It's easy,' she said. 'The other assistants
scoop up _____ of sweets and then _____. I
always scoop up _____ and then _____.'

🎧 55 Listen to the complete stories and see what the
missing words actually were.

Discuss in groups.

1 Does anyone in your family eat a lot of sweets? Are
they good or bad for you? Why?
2 What does ice-cream make you think of? Has it
any associations or memories for you? Has ice-
cream ever melted and made a mess over your
clothes?
3 Do you know anyone who tends to be rather lazy,
like Sally in the story here? In what ways are they
lazy?

▶ Write a brief account of what your group
thought about one of these topics. ◀

Write it clearly, then pass it round for other groups to
read. Then tell each other briefly about any other
interesting ideas you had.

▶ Tell one of the stories again, but from
the point of view of one of the other
characters in it. ◀

e.g. *I'm the manager of the local cinema
here. Last winter, we employed a new
assistant. Part of his job was to sell ice-
cream during the interval. This young
man sold so much more ice-cream than ...*

56 Phrase-building

... stood around with nothing to do.

Think of some places you have been
to recently. Make some sentences
about them using these ideas.

e.g. I sat in the dentist's waiting room
with nothing to read.
I went to my friend's house and we had
so much to talk about.

Where could you add words like
**interesting, exciting, special, cheap,
really nice** etc?

There was We had ... with	nothing something a lot lots quite a lot quite a few lots of things so much	to	eat/drink/read/look at/do.

There wasn't ... without We didn't get/find	much anything anywhere anything	to	see/buy/eat/visit/go.

28

a   any, anybody, anyway, etc

Look at these sentences with **any**. How many of them are negative or interrogative sentences?

He stopped at his secretary's desk to see if there were any messages for him. There were none.
Anybody who handles money gets paid a lot.
Anybody who's paid more than me is overpaid!
An assistant sold more ice-cream during the interval than anyone had ever done before.
That piece of string doesn't appear to go anywhere, does it? It's just hanging . . .
That's what I would say, anyway.
A: When shall we come? B: Any time you like.
A: Where shall we sit? B: Anywhere. It doesn't matter where.
Is there anything you need to ask? Anything that's not clear?

anybody, everybody, somebody, nobody

b   Odd ones out

Find two odd ones out in each group.

1 businessman, General Manager, profession, secretary, Head of Department, the Management, scientist, decision
2 rates of pay, fair pay, equivalent, earnings, Unions, wages
3 In general, On the whole, In my opinion, Usually, On the other hand, Normally, Generally, It tends to be . . .
4 failure, highly paid, professional, successful, business-like, awful, worth the money
5 low paid, unsuccessful, bad working conditions, trouble with, Headquarters, at least, the worst, badly paid, pretty awful

c   Game: Spot the pairs!

Can you find twelve pairs of similar words? Is each word in the pair used with the same meaning?

We've got it completely wrong.
We've made the wrong decision.
A difficult decision to take.
Hey, wait a minute! Take it easy!
Is it easy to draw maps?
The bus drew away before I could get on.
It's nice to go away, especially in summer.
Can you keep it secret? Especially the bit about me.
What was the secret of her success?
I hope your application is successful.
John has gone to a lot of trouble applying for jobs.
The trouble is, the whole process is a long one.
It takes time to complete such a process.

d   often, tends to

Which of these sentences are true as far as you are concerned?

Often my work is unpleasant.
I often work past 6 p.m.
Anyone who handles money tends to get paid a lot.
Rats tend to live in unattractive conditions.
I think women tend to get better tips than men.
Do you know anyone who tends to be lazy?
I tend to worry about . . . I lie awake at night thinking.
I tend to wake up early in the morning. Do you?
I often wake up late.

e   Set B. Examples with 'to' (see page 27)

1 *. . . that half an inch is very important to me.* (20)
2 *. . . will be able to get us tickets to go down to Jamaica . . .* (38)
3 *. . . you have to expect rain . . .* (38)
4 *I'm looking forward to it.* (38)
5 *Very lucky to get to the top of it . . .* (29)
6 *. . . had never managed to get to the top . . .* (29)
7 *In addition to a comfortable bed . . .* (39)
8 *. . . we will be happy to help select the holiday.*
9 *Anybody who handles money tends to get paid a lot . . .* (42)
10 *. . . it's hard to know isn't it?* (43)
11 *I think anybody who is expected to work eight and a half hours a day . . .* (47)
12 *Seems to be a street scene* (49)
13 *. . . it looks like a window behind him to me.* (49)
14 *. . . that piece of string doesn't appear to go anywhere . . .* (49)
15 *. . . could it belong to the door of the car?* (49)
16 *. . . during the summer I work to make some money.* (52)

Important words to remember (238 so far)						
amount	completely L	equivalent	joy	partner	senior	worst
anybody	decided	experienced	lack	piece	somebody	worth
anywhere	decision	factory	least L	plastic	somewhere	
apply	dentist	fair	low	profession	string	
assistant	department	failure	manage	professional L	success	
awful	difficulty	fixed	management	scene L	successful	
basic L	dollar	generally	message	science	surprise L	
brief	draw L	handles	minister	scientific	surprised L	
chin	earn	hang L	nobody	scientist	trouble L	
clear L	earnings	heavy L	nurse	secret L	union L	
clearly L	easy	income	opinion	secretary	wage	
company	engineer	joke	pair	sell	wake	

sport/PE (physical education)

languages

technology

economics

home economics

music

business studies

58 **Schooldays**

history

maths

art

biology

geography

chemistry

physics

science

a Favourite subjects

In groups, tell each other a little bit about your favourite subject at school. Also which subjects you like or liked the least and why.

▶ Summarise the findings of your group survey so that you can report to the class. ◀

Find out:

1 the most popular subjects
2 the least popular
3 the most common reasons why people dislike certain subjects
4 whether the men and women in the class like the same subjects

58a Compare your findings with Catherine's group. Write notes about Caroline, Stephen and John.

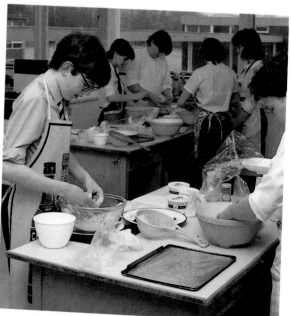

b Talk about teachers

What kind of things do schoolteachers complain about in your experience? Are they always right?

58b Do you agree with what Rodge (Roger) says in this poem? He is talking about what it's like being a pupil at Primary School.

TEACHERS

Rodge said,

'Teachers – they want it all ways –
You're jumping up and down on a chair
or something
and they grab hold of you and say,
"Would you do that sort of thing in your own home?"

'So you say, "No"
And they say,
"Well, don't do it here then."

'But if you say, "Yes, I do it at home."
They say,
"Well, we don't want that sort of thing
going on here
thank you very much."

'Teachers – they get you all ways,'
Rodge said.

Michael Rosen

We asked Stephen to write what he thought about this poem.

I remember thinking that way about teachers. After class, or on the way home, I would work out what I should have said to the teacher, to shut him up completely. But when it happened, I never had any reply at all. I had to just sit back and take it. But next time, I knew I could do it!

58a **a** Find the transcript for 58a.

1 Look at the sentences in the transcript with **like**. Which two '**like**'s have a different meaning from the others?

2 Find four examples of the word **got**. Does it have the same meaning in each case?

3 Find seven examples of **that**. How many different meanings does it have here? What about the word **those**?

4 Find about six more phrases that tell us how much or little they liked their subjects. Write two more in each column of a table like this.

like	quite like	not liking it at all
my favourite was English		*the least favourite was Maths*

Then add any other phrases you know expressing 'like' or 'dislike' in the suitable columns.

What information surprised Catherine? How do you know?
Which of these expressions also express surprise?

Oh, my goodness!   *Did you really?*
Ouch!   *My God!*
How sad!

b   Find phrases with these words in the poem in section 58b.

or   so   and   well   but   of   … then

60 Asking indirectly and dropping hints

Oh dear! The smoke is making my eyes run!

Very sorry. I've nearly finished it.

Group A students together think of ways you could ask people indirectly to do the following things to help you.

Group B students together think of ways to answer A, politely, avoiding the issue, and not doing what the other person will be asking.

a A wants to borrow some money from B.
b A wants someone to help them do some homework.
c A's car has gone wrong – it needs to be repaired.
d A wants B to stop smoking in the office for good.

A and B students in pairs practise some of the situations above.

Then change over, and do the ones below.

e A wants B to put his/her cigarette out now.
f A has no-one to go to the cinema with.
g A lent B some money and now wants it back.
h A wants to borrow B's bike/car.

or

Look at this example:

JM: … Is it a tie? Or, is it a piece of rope or something?

61   Listen again up to the phrase 'a plastic bag'. How many examples of **or** can you hear? Where does it come in the sentence? What words follow it?

62 Balloon man

Memory challenge

Look at the picture for one minute. Close your books. How many things can you remember? Make a list. Say where they were and what colour.

e.g. *a piece of grey string, round the man's neck*

63 The human body

a Other meanings

Find three meanings for the word **head** and two for the word **foot**. If you are talking about the human body in your own language how do you say **head, hand, heart, foot, leg, arm**?

What other meanings do these words have in your language?

63a Look at the pictures and then listen to John and Monica talking about them. How many of the uses of these words do they find? Which ones do they miss?

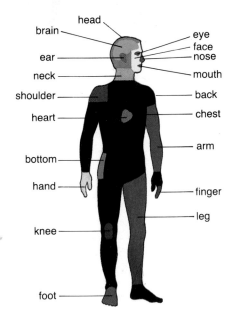

Parts of the human body

b Useful phrases

When do you think you might use the phrases below? For all except one, there is a possible situation given on the right but they are mixed up. Which one is missing?

1 *Could you hand me that one please?*
2 *Oh dear, I can't face it!*
3 *Keep an eye on this for me please.*
4 *The body was pale blue.*
5 *Where are you heading for?*
6 *Could you give me a hand?*
7 *Right in the heart of Africa.*
8 *On the other hand, …*
9 *In my heart I knew she was wrong.*
10 *It's two feet wide and roughly six feet long.*
11 *I got it second hand.*
12 *You must ask headquarters.*

a When you want someone to look after something.
b When you want someone to help you.
c When saying how big something is.
d When you really don't want to do something.
e When you want someone to pass something.
f When you want to know where somebody is going.
g Saying where a place is.
h When you want to give the opposite point of view.
i When talking about a car.
j If you need the permission of head office.
k When you buy something which isn't new.

c Believe it or not!

Allen Doster, from New York, self-employed, donated 1,840 pints of blood between 1966 and 1986.

Brain of Britain Quiz
The youngest person to become 'Brain of Britain' on BBC radio was Anthony Carr, aged 16 …

Give blood – save a life!
The National Blood Donors' Association

YOU CAN SUBSTITUTE HEART VALVES WITH PLASTIC ONES AND HIP JOINTS WITH METAL ONES.

THE OPERATIONS, HOWEVER, REQUIRE ONE THING FOR WHICH THERE IS NO SUBSTITUTE

BLOOD

AND THERE'S ONLY ONE PLACE WE CAN GET IT FROM

THE NATIONAL BLOOD TRANSFUSION SERVICE
"We're asking you to help us."

Heart stoppage
The longest recorded heart stoppage is a minimum of 3 hr 40 min in the case of Miss Jean Jawbone, 20, who was revived by a team of 26 in the Health Sciences Centre, Winnipeg, Canada on 8 Jan 1977.

The British Heart Foundation

Look after your heart!

d Riddles

Do these riddles first, then write some more for your friends to answer. (The pictures above may help you.)

What has a face but no eyes?
What has feet, a back, sides and arms but no hands?
What has a mouth and runs, but can't eat, speak or walk?

The human brain as compared to a sheep's brain.

Childhood

John   Catherine

a   Dreams and ambitions

>
> What were your childhood dreams and
> ambitions? What did you want to be when
> you grew up? What were your parents'
> attitudes? Write down one or two things
> that you can remember.

Read the card. Write notes about yourself.

64a Listen to John and Catherine. Take notes.

> Tell one another about your childhood
> dreams and ambitions.

How many people in your class actually carried out
what they wanted to do as a child? Who had the most
ambitious parents?

> Choose two different people in your class
> and write a short report about their
> ambitions and whether or not they have been
> fulfilled.

b   Present dreams and ambitions

Tell your partner what your present dreams and
ambitions are.

I hope to . . . I intend to . . . I'd like to . . . I'm . . .
I may . . . I think I'll . . . I'm definitely going to . . .
I hope I'll be able to . . . I expect I'll . . .
I won't . . . I hope I won't be . . . I'm not going to . . .

c   What were you like as a child?

> Write a few lines describing what you looked
> like when you were a small child. Don't put
> your name. Give it to your teacher.

64d d   Juster and Waiter

My mum had nicknames for me and my brother.
One of us she called Waiter
and the other she called Juster.
It started like this:
she'd say, 'Lend me a hand with the washing up
will you, you two?'
and I'd say, 'Just a minute, Mum.'
and my brother'd say
'Wait a minute, Mum.'
'There you go again' – she'd say,
'Juster and Waiter'.

Michael Rosen

64e e   What did Catherine and Stephen think of this
poem? What were they like as children?

---

65 *Language study* . . . .

What does **would** (or **'d**) mean in these sentences?

She'd say, 'Lend me a hand with the washing up . . .' (64)
And I'd say, 'Just a minute Mum.' (64)
And my brother'd say 'Wait a minute, Mum.' (64)
*On the way home, I would work out what I should
have said to the teacher.* (58)

Look at these sentences and see what other ways you
can find of expressing the same meanings.
a JM: *I hated being at school there. It was an all
    boys school and I didn't like it.*
b *When we lived in Rome, we used to go out to
    the Auburn Hills.*
c CF: *. . . I used to sit at the back . . .* (58)
d SB: *I didn't mind things like maths and English
    because I could do them . . .* (58)
e JM: *Sport . . . I hated it!* (58)
f CM: *If anybody ever asked me what I wanted to
    be, career-wise, I always said I wanted to be a lady
    doctor.* (64)
g CM: *I don't think I used to say 'Just a minute.'*

---

66 *Grammar* . . . .

Verbs in the passive: what or who was/will be/has been . . ?

Match the phrases below with those on the right to make complete sentences.

1 In Britain, people don't like
2 Catherine
3 Hadrian's Wall
4 Have your childhood dreams ever
5 One of the postcards
6 In most cases, the B & B
7 Fill in the blanks and then see which words
8 When talking to Jenny about holidays, Jeremy
9 A woman who went to a dentist in Baghdad
10 Which of these words

a was written in Ireland, by Becky's friend.
b was built in northern Britain in AD 123.
c was born in Ireland.
d being asked how old they are.
e was only allowed to ask three questions.
f been fulfilled?
g was told it would cost £30 to have a tooth out.
h will be run by the owner.
i are left over.
j can be used to describe Northumberland National
    Park?

a   Words in definitions

... is an object used for ...
a living creature found in ...
having the quality of ...
a large quantity/amount of ...
a natural material used for ...
an action which involves ...
to a large degree or extent
a part of ...

Which defining words (**object, living creature, quality, quantity/ amount, material, action, degree**) would you use in defining the following?

very	lucky
book	plenty
pen	healthy
metal	wet
quite a lot	plastic
horse	a great deal
sense of	successful
humour	highly educated
beautiful	paper
escape	foot
rat	extremely
fishing	wall

Which words have you defined as objects? What are they usually made of?

b   Words with un-

If you put **un-** on the front of these words, what will they mean?

e.g. **unhappy** = not happy, sad

happy	pleasant	fit
well	lucky	able
attractive	healthy	

Find pairs of words that are opposite in meaning.

e.g. The opposite of **unhealthy** is **fit**.

unhealthy	lucky
unusual	lovely
unattractive	fit
unpleasant	famous
unlucky	common
unable	nice
unknown	able
	well known

c   Prepositions

behind

1 *There are people behind him.*
2 *The reasons behind his action were clear.*
3 **to get behind** = to be late doing something
Oh dear – we're a bit behind – look at the time!

Where could the word **behind** fit in these sentences?

a *When driving a car you should always know what is you.*
b *I don't know what is the suggestions in his letter.*
c *I got in some subjects.*

along

Do you have the same word in your language for **along** in all these sentences?

1 *... did a lot of walking along the coast ...*
2 *... some way along there, not far.*
3 *The police came along ...*
4 *Come along, hurry up!*
5 *Bring your friends along!*
6 *We went along with his arguments.*
7 *I knew all along they had been wrong.*

away

Find which examples:
1 mean at a distance from someone or somewhere.
2 give a distance in space or time

a *He was away for quite a bit and rarely saw his family.*
b *It's about five miles away.*
c *Around twenty minutes away, by car.*
d *A: When will you be away?*
   B: The whole of July.
e *Can you put your books away now?*
f *She looked away as he spoke.*
g *They turned away and walked off.*
h *The end of term is two weeks away.*
i *He gave all his money away.*

d   Classroom language

What have the phrases in each set got in common?
When might you say them?
Read the sentences stressing one word in each. See if your partner can hear the stressed word.

1
Why don't you start?
Do you want to start or shall we?
Well, you start ...
Shall I start?
Shall we begin?
All right, I'll start, then.
Could you begin?
Let's start now.
Okay, you start off ...
It's time we started to write ...

2
Right, that's it then.
We've done ours.
Ours is done.
Have you finished?
We've done half.
I've nearly finished.
We need another two minutes.
Could we finish it later?
We've finished ours.
I've done mine, and checked it.
It's time you stopped!

3 (Guess the last word!)
Was that clear?
Did you follow his argument?
Were you able to follow what they said?
Did you get it?
Did you __d__s__n__?

e   Verb forms (past and after 'to')

Past   Which verbs have the same vowel sound in them? Divide them into four groups. Which word is left over?

After **to**   What form of each verb would be used after **to**?
e.g. *I want to grow.*

grew	said	shone
forgot	drove	dreamt
read	knew	met
wrote	woke	lost
spoke	won	spread

Important words to remember (281 so far)

attention L	definition	heart	neck	quantity	unpleasant
blood	dream	human	nose	relationship L	unusual
brain	ear	humour	object	sense L	usual
career	favourite	knee	odd L	shoulder	
chest	finger	leg	partly L	teeth	
childhood	follow L	material	physical	unable	
consequence	grow L	mathematics	push L	unhappy	
danger	happy	movement	quality	unknown	

Unit 6
What do you think's the best way of travelling?

Or boat, I suppose, but that **** doesn't take very long, does it?

I believe that's quite quick.

68 Forms of transport

a What is the longest or most complicated journey you have ever been on? Tell the class about it.

b What are the advantages and disadvantages of each of these forms of transport in the pictures?

c What could the signs be advertising?

68d **d** On the tape you will hear different sounds and announcements associated with the forms of transport on this page. Write down what places and sounds you think you hear.

SUNSHINE HOLIDAYS
BOOKING FORM
Name ....
Address ....
....

I always prefer ???? 'cause I don't like having to sort of walk too much.

You have more time to spend in Paris.

Although it was more expensive, it meant we had more time there.

HOVER*SPEED*
The Motorway to Europe

Car and Passenger Services
Dover to Calais & Boulogne

I haven't got a ???? Nor have I.

It's nice and quick.

DOVER

I suppose the cheapest way would be go to by ????

I think that would be very tiring. Horrible.

You feel exhausted when you got there.

Would you take your ????

If I had a lot of time, yes …

1st Class tickets →
Excess fares, Seasons →
⇌ Travel Centre →
Buses & Taxis →
Platforms 9 to 19
← Victoria Place-shopping
← Victoria Place-eating
Tickets →
← Gatwick tickets
← Gatwick Express

Although, early July, … it might be fairly pretty going by ????

e How many ways can you think of of travelling between London and Paris? Write them down.

Read the quotations and try to guess what means of transport are being talked about. (You will find out later whether you are right.)
Find three quotations that mention an advantage, and two that mention a disadvantage.

f Types of fuel/power

What's missing?

oil gas air steam electricity wind

You waste a lot of time.

L rate class form

35

69 London to Paris in early July

Bridget, Jenny and Danny all live and work in London. We asked them to discuss the best way of travelling to Paris.

69a **a** First Bridget asked Jenny. How many forms of transport did they mention? Did they recommend one particular way?

69b **b** Listen to their summary. Did they mention the same forms of transport as they had in their discussion?

69c **c** Next Bridget asked Danny. What advice did Danny give? How many reasons did he give?

d Now go back to section 68, and read the quotations again. Can you now say which form of transport they were about? How many did you guess right?

70 *Language study*

a **Giving advice**

Read the transcripts for section 69 carefully. Pick out seven useful phrases you might use if you were starting to give advice to someone.
e.g. *Well, I actually did that last year. We ...*

b **really**

Put the word **really** into these sentences. (There is more than one possible place in each sentence.)

It depends on the time you've got.
That would mean having a car.
It depends on how long you've got, though, doesn't it?
Well, I don't know.

70b How is the word **really** said in these sentences? What does it mean in each case?

Erm, God, this is really difficult.
I really like that one.

And how is **really** used here?

I quite like the red one but I really wanted blue.
Hi, Mike. I was really looking for Roger, but you'll do.
It's quite warm. Do you really think it'll rain?

71 From your country to ___

Decide on a country near your own that people sometimes travel to. How many ways are there of getting from your own country to the capital city of the nearby country? Write down two or three different ways of travelling there, making notes of the advantages and disadvantages of each way.

Tell people in your group what you have written. Explain the advantages and disadvantages clearly. Let them decide which way they would choose.

Tell the class about your decision.
What were the most popular forms of transport among students in other groups?

Write a short paragraph giving advice to a foreigner new to your country on how to get to another capital city from yours.

36

72 Preposition spot

a on

On can refer to:
a form of travel/transport (e.g. *on a bus/plane*)
a place where something is (e.g. *on the table*)
time (e.g. *on Sunday*)
subject or topic (e.g. *books on travel*)
On can mean continuing or going further (e.g. *go on, carry on*)
On is used with some verbs (e.g. *depend on*)
Find at least one example of each in the examples below.

a ... *no chance of promotion there, so I'm going to move on.* (2)
b ... *and we had to look on the map* ... (2)
c *We did a survey on languages we had learned.*
d *On one occasion, while on holiday in France* ...
e ... *interested in the cinema, and the theatre and so on.* (20)
f *The manager decided to keep an eye on him.* (55)
g *We're flying direct from Sydney on QF1.* (33)
h ... *if you base it on the cost of petrol and parking* ... (82)
i *Who spends the most/least money on travel?*
j *It depends on the time you've got available.*
k *I switched on the car radio.* (97)
l *He got in and I drove on.* (97)
m *'Go on then.'*

b Match phrases with similar meanings.

1 *Hold on! Hang on a minute!*	a very busy
2 *There was a policeman on duty.*	b wait a second
	c working there
3 *I can't come, I've got so much on.*	d after some time
	e please – hurry
4 *Come on!*	f most of the time
5 *Later on.*	g in the future
6 *From now on.*	
7 *It's been raining on and off all day.*	

73 Stories and a picture

a Can you guess the missing endings?

A return ticket, please
I work in a railway ticket office. One day, a man came up to my window and asked for a return ticket. After a long pause I finally said, with mounting impatience, 'To where? To where?' There was another long pause. Then, after some obvious deep thought, he replied, _____, _____.

A quick trip
One woman telephoned a travel agency and asked, 'Can you tell me how long it takes to go by plane from Paris to London?'
'Just a minute, Madam' said the employee. _____, she replied, and _____, _____.

b How does a hovercraft stay up in the air? Label the parts in both figures using words from the definition.

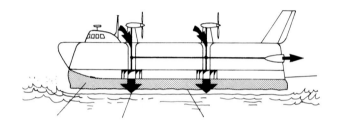

Figure 1   Hovercraft

> **Hovercraft** a vehicle that is able to travel across both land and water on a cushion of air. The cushion is produced by fans or a ring of air jets. A skirt around the base of the vehicle keeps the cushion of air in place.

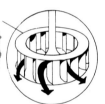

Figure 2   Airjets

74 Wordpower

way
Look up **way** in the Lexicon. Which meanings does **way** have in these examples?

(a) This word can be used in many different ways.

(b) I like the way he sings that song. It's really good.

(c) After class, or on the way home...

(d) The cheapest way would be to go by bus. (68)

(e) Sorry, is that in the way?

(f) It's interesting the way computers have changed our lives.

(g) I can remember thinking that way about teachers. (58)

(h) The American way of life is very different.

(i) I can go back the way I came.

Like a lift?

Do you ever give lifts to people, or get lifts from people? Have you ever hitch-hiked? Tell each other.

Exhausted at the end of two days filming in a small part at Pinewood Studios, I found that no transport back to London was available and began the four mile walk to Uxbridge station in the rain. Then a limousine stopped beside me.

'Like a lift into London, lady?' enquired the smiling chauffeur.
'You're very kind,' I said. 'Are you sure?'
'Just carrying out the boss's orders,' he replied. 'Every day he says to me when I've dropped him: "Don't know when I'll finish – I'll get back on my own. You just take the car and drive home anyone who's walking."'
'What's your boss's name?' I asked thankfully as the car purred softly on.
'Eh? It's Michael – Michael Caine.'

L	part
	life
	drop

?	enquired
	carry out
	boss
filming	orders
beside	softly

---

 76 ## *Grammar*

Cause and result

In the first examples, the part expressing *cause* is coloured. The other part expresses the *result*.

1 a sentence
consequently   *He was very tired.* **Consequently he fell asleep.**
as a result   *Britain is quite a small country.* **As a result travel is quick and easy.**
that's why   *... but they're ever so small.* **That's why rain is thin.**

2 a clause
because   **I don't have a journey to work** *because I work at home.* (80)
and   *John is trying to get a new job* **and is busy sending application forms all over the place.** (2)
as   **We chose to go by plane** *as it meant we had more time in Paris.* (69)
so   *There's no chance of a promotion there,* **so I'm going to move on.** (2)
so ... that   *I was so proud (that)* **I jumped up and down.** (23)
since   **I suppose that would come out the same way** *since people seem to prefer cats and dogs to snakes and spiders.* (25)

3 a phrase
as a result of   *As a result of this postcard* **I think Becky will write back.** (33)
because of   A: **Why can't you starve in the desert?**
B: **You can't starve in the desert** *because of the sand which is there.* (Can you explain this joke?)

as   *As a visitor* **you can take tax-free goods home.**
with   **Until, mad** *with energy and boredom,* **you escaped.** (26)

4 words meaning 'cause' or 'result'
make   *His pointed ears* **made him look like a rat.**
result   *Shorter periods of use* **can result in fuel bill savings.** (91)
cause   *What* **was the cause of the accident?**
lead to   *A serious illness* **led to his losing his job.**

5 no marker
I don't want that one. *It's too expensive.*
Until, *mad with energy and boredom,* **you escaped.** (26)

Look at the sentences below. Say which part expresses *cause* and which *result*.

a We had never been to Northumberland before. That's why we wanted to go. (29)
b We went by plane. As a result we had more time in Paris.
c My favourite was always English because I liked writing stories. (58)
d It's a very pleasant school, and I'd be sorry to leave it. (2)
e ... a woman ... looking a bit angry as it's one in the morning by then. (78)
f I can't see the TV with you standing in front of it!
g He worked hard and did very well as a result.
h Finally, tired out, they fell asleep.

---

77 ## *Phrase-building*

77

Think of times when you are interrupted, or when things happen while you are busy doing other things. Make up some true sentences.

| I
He | was | in the middle of
busy | cooking dinner
doing my homework
watching TV
having a meeting | when ... |
| I'll be
I'm usually | | | | |

It's true! It happened to a friend of mine...!

a Do you ever hear stories beginning 'A funny thing happened to my ... sister's boyfriend's cousin. Or somebody ...'? Do you believe in ghosts? Can people or things really vanish?
Read the first part of the story.

Dogs in the microwave, rats in the curry, murderers on car roofs and disappearing hitch-hikers all play starring roles in modern legends. They're those 'true stories' we tell each other and swear blind they happened to our best friend's sister. So how come exactly the same tales have travelled half way around the Western World? Phil Sutcliffe tells the stories – and tells us why we tell them too.

78a George: 'Something really weird happened to this friend of my sister's the other week. He lives down in Southampton and he's driving back from a Duran Duran concert when he sees this girl standing by the roadside hitching. He stops and it turns out he's going right past her door – she tells him the address, 110 Acacia Gardens or something, and off they go. She sits in the back as if she's a bit cautious maybe, but they have a nice chat. Then, when they're getting close, he can't quite remember the quickest way. He pulls up at a traffic light and turns round to ask the girl – but she's vanished.

What do you think has happened to the girl? And what does George's sister's friend do next?

▶ Plan a continuation of the story, explaining what happens to the girl. Read it to the class. ◀

78b **b** Listen to what Caroline and John think might have happened. John tells a slightly different story. How different?

78c **c** Read on.

'Of course, he's amazed, he can't think how she got out without him noticing. Anyway, he goes round to the address she's given him and a middle-aged woman in her dressing-gown answers the door, looking a bit angry as it's one in the morning by then. He stammers out what happened – feeling daft, it sounds so stupid – but the woman softens up and tells him he's the sixth person who's come along with the same story. The girl answers the description of her daughter who disappeared two years ago after telling her friends at a party that she was going to hitch-hike home!'
Tracey: 'No! I don't believe it.'
George: 'No, honestly, it's really true. The bloke told my sister ...'
Well, maybe, George. My bet is it didn't happen to your sister's friend though. I know you have to keep it simple to let a story flow along but, own up, wasn't it your sister's friend's mate's cousin ... who heard it from someone, forget who exactly, who read it in a newspaper, so it must be true?
In other words 'The Vanishing Hitch-hiker' is a modern legend. It has been told, and believed, a million times throughout Britain, America and Europe with only the place names changing. And it's complete codswallop.

Language study

Colloquial style

a Look at this version of the same story.

This happened to one of my girlfriend's best friends and her father.
They were driving along a country road on their way home from the cottage when they saw a young girl hitch-hiking. They stopped and picked her up and she got in the back seat. She told the girl and her father that ...

In what ways is the language different?

▶ Write a summary of the whole story in section 78 in the same style. ◀

b Find the colloquial words and expressions below in the text and guess what they mean. Can you find four more?

So how come ...?   *Anyway,*
really weird   *friend's mate's cousin*
this girl   *complete codswallop*

80 Transport survey

a We asked a small group of people who live in Birmingham to do a group survey on how much they spent on travelling to work, on average, per week, and how much time each person spent travelling.

Myf was the chairman. She had to fill in the form below, and check her figures afterwards.

Travel to work or place of study			
Name	Jane	Philip	Ken
Job or study area	writer	research student	lecturer
Place of work/study	home	Birmingham University	College of Further Ed
Means of transport			
Distance/time taken			
Cost per day			
Cost per week			

80a Listen to Myf doing her survey and find out which person spends the most money and takes the most time.

80b b Listen to Myf checking her figures. Is she right?

c How accurate do you think Philip's figures are for running a car? Has he included everything? Find the information given by the AA (Automobile Association) in section 82.

Ken says, 'I have a Travelcard so I don't have to pay.' What do you think he really means?

d Now do the same kind of survey in groups.

Prepare a report. Tell the class which person in your group spends the most and the least money, and who takes the most and the least time on their regular journeys. Which people in the whole class spend most/least?

---

81 *Language study*

a Verbs meaning travel of some kind

Look at the transcript from section 80a. Find thirteen or fourteen phrases with a verb, which show some kind of coming or going. What other words are there with the verb? Why?

I leave at (**at** – because it is followed by a time – 8 a.m.)
to come in (**in** = into work)

b Why does Myf change to the past tense when she does her checking through in section 80b?

c Does the word **come** always mean move or travel?

82 Travelcard

a Read these questions about the Travelcard and write four more.

1 Can you use it on trains as well as buses at no extra cost?
2 Will it still make travel cheaper, even if you own a car?
3 What if you're a student in full-time education? Can you get a cheaper rate?

▶ Tell each other what your extra questions are. Then write three more. ◀

b Read the brochure on page 41 and try to find the answers to all ten questions.

How many questions out of the ten can you now answer?
Write the answers down and compare them with other people's.

c Travel in your country

Do you have any cut-price tickets? How do the different forms of transport compare in cost and comfort? What might foreign visitors need to know about ways of travelling around your country? Discuss with your group.

▶ Write notes for a short report or talk, then tell the class. Find which country offers the cheapest/most comfortable travel. ◀

d Put the words in the column on the left in the correct phrases. Check them against the brochure itself and make sure you know what they mean.

base	*at no _____ cost*
endless	*a _____ ticket*
extra	*bus _____*
major	*For _____ if you travel ...*
charges	*if you _____ it on petrol alone*
rush	*_____ hour jams*
valid	*parking _____*
instance	*complete the _____ form*
special	*Travel _____*
Centres	*the opportunities are nearly _____*
land	*watch the planes _____ and take off*
services	*theatres and _____ sports events*
attached	*_____ all day until 11.29 pm*

TRAVELCARD

Travelcard is a special ticket – your ticket to ride cheaply on buses and trains in West Midlands county.
It can be used on all West Midlands passenger transport and most Midland Red bus services within the county. It is also valid on local and Inter-City train services within the county at no extra cost. You can hop on and off a bus and train as many times as you like with Travelcard.
And, of course, with a Travelcard you don't need to worry about having the right change. The more you use it, the cheaper it becomes.

Adult county wide travelcard

1 week	£5.00
4 weeks	£16.00
13 weeks	£46.50

ravelcards valid ALL DAY until 11.29pm

I DRIVE A CAR. HOW CAN A TRAVELCARD HELP ME?

Even if you own a car, a Travelcard can still save you time and money. For instance, if you travel 10 miles to work each day, commuting with a Travelcard could cost you as little as 4p a mile. Compare that with AA motoring mileage costs of 25p, or, if you base it on petrol and parking alone, 10p a mile.
And think of the rush hour jams, the frustration and the parking charges you'll avoid. Don't forget that many of our local rail stations have free 'park-and-ride' car parks.
Just sit on a train or bus, read your paper and arrive relaxed.

How do I get a travel card?

Just complete the attached form and take it to any of the places listed here. (For 16-18 year olds in full-time education – ask at Travel Centres for a separate form.)
You will be issued with a Photocard which costs you 35p.
Be sure and bring a passport size colour photograph of yourself (photographs may be obtained at all our Travel Centres see below). Once you have a Photocard, your Travelcard can be renewed at any of these outlets.

WHAT PLACES CAN I VISIT?

The opportunities for getting about with your Travelcard are nearly endless.
You can visit stately homes, museums and art galleries, historic buildings and cathedrals. There are leisure parks, zoos, gardens, nature centres etc.
Why not watch the planes land and take off at Birmingham's new International Airport?
You can go to theatres and major sports events, exhibition centres and on shopping trips too.
Plan an excursion to take in a country walk or picnic.
Or use it to visit friends and relations.

(leaflet published by West Midland Passenger Transport Executive)

L special services

Can you explain:
The more you use it, the cheaper it becomes.
Is it really true?

 83

Language study

Suggestions

How many suggestions does the leaflet make about places to visit, using a Travelcard? What exactly does it say about each of them?

a although

JV: *We chose to go by plane – although it was more expensive, it meant we had more time there.*
DL: *Paris? . . . I'd suggest flying. Although in early July, it might be fairly pretty going by train.*
RHT: *The only language I actually learnt was French, although I picked up English at the early age of one.*

b Agreeing or disagreeing?

A: *Very tiring . . . Horrible!* B: *Exactly!*
A: *I haven't got a car.* B: *No, no, nor have I.*
A: *It doesn't take long, does it?* B: *No, . . .*
Well, I'm not too sure.
Yes, that's true.
Yes, but . . .
What a good idea!

c neither, nor, so (to mark similarity)

A: *I don't like it!* B: *Neither do I.* C: *Nor do I.*
A: *I like that one!* B: *So do I.*
A: *I wanted that one.* B: *So did I.*

Now suggest answers for these sentences, expressing similarity/agreement.

I came early.
I wasn't late.
He never arrives on time.
She's always late.
I wouldn't buy that one.
She hasn't brought her money.

d Advising, suggesting or instructing

Talk about problems you sometimes have. Offer each other advice.

Why not	go . . .(?)
You can	ask . . .(?)
Why don't you	talk to . . .(?)

What about	
How about	going . . .?
Have you thought of	asking . . .?
Have you tried	talking to . . .?

e Verbs and nouns involving talk

Most of these words involve telling someone something, or talking about something together. Which one involves asking for information? Which one means to say something briefly or shortly?

Verbs		
discuss	suggest	enquire
explain	advise	describe
mention	decide	
inform	agree	

Do you know the nouns associated with these verbs? Notice how they are used. Can you suggest a way to complete some of the sentences?

They	gave / offered	a good description of . . .
		a quick explanation as to why . . .
		some good advice on . . .
		some clear information about . . .

They made	a good suggestion about . . .
	the right decision about . . .
	an agreement on the rates . . .
	no mention of his name at all.
	an enquiry about the train times.

We had a	good discussion on . . .
	nice chat about . . .
	long conversation about . . .
	horrible argument over . . .

A decision/agreement was finally reached.
The girl answered the description of her daughter.

Key (73a)

Which last line goes with which story?
'I see, thank you,' and hung up, satisfied.
'To here, to here!'

Important words to remember (349 so far)					
adult	cause	exhausted	lift	reduce	thought
agreement	charge	explain	major	result	throughout
aircraft	cousin	explanation	manner	role	total
airport	deep	extra	mention	services L	train
although	depend L	figure L	nor L	ship	transport
angry	discuss	gas	oil	soft	valid
associated	discussion	horrible	pause	softly	vehicle
association	drop L	include	plane	special L	watch
attach	endless	including	previous	suggest	
base	enquire	instance	properly	suggestion	
based	enquiry	journey	publish	taxi	
boss	executive	land	rate L	though	

Unit 7
I'd probably cook an omelette

Talking about food

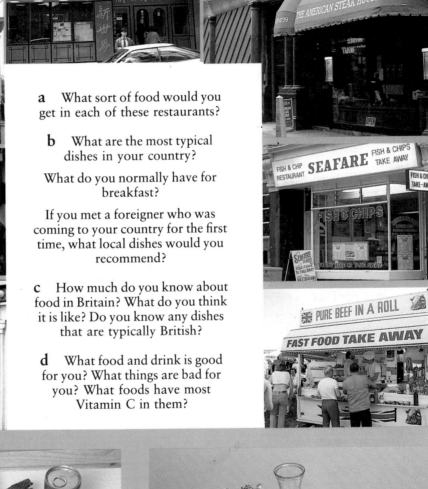

a What sort of food would you get in each of these restaurants?

b What are the most typical dishes in your country?

What do you normally have for breakfast?

If you met a foreigner who was coming to your country for the first time, what local dishes would you recommend?

c How much do you know about food in Britain? What do you think it is like? Do you know any dishes that are typically British?

d What food and drink is good for you? What things are bad for you? What foods have most Vitamin C in them?

e Think of a kind of meat, fruit or vegetable. See if your partner can guess what it is. See how many questions it takes.

f Imagine you are about to have a meal in a restaurant. What very basic thing is missing? How would you ask for it?

43

Cooking for an unexpected guest

a We asked Jenny, Bridget, David and Danny what they would cook from the fridge or store cupboard for an unexpected guest. This is what they said.

Sausages and baked beans.
A cheese flan and baked potatoes.
An omelette.
Rice and vegetables.

Which dishes do you think the men chose and which do you think the women chose?

Jenny   David

Bridget   Danny

b Find out which of these meals people in your group would like best. Take a vote to see which was the most/least popular.

c What would the people in your group cook for an unexpected guest? Explain to the class. Listen and decide whose meal you would like best. Take a vote.

86a See if you were right.

Can you summarise what they said?

A recipe

a Here is a recipe for scrambled eggs which appeared in the teenage section of a Sunday newspaper. Read the first part and work out how much you would need for three people.

Scrambled eggs for breakfast

The trick to getting nice soft scrambled eggs is to cook the eggs over a very low heat and to turn off the heat about two minutes before you think the eggs are ready. Scrambled eggs should be soft and creamy not hard and lumpy.

The seasoning given here is for one egg. To cook for more than one person, just multiply the ingredients.

You will need:

One egg per person
2 tablespoons milk
A knob of butter
¼ teaspoon salt
Shake of pepper
Saucepan
Small bowl
Fork
Large spoon

Look at the four stages for the recipe. Can you number them in the correct order?

a To get creamy scrambled eggs, be careful at this stage. As soon as the egg in the pan is thick and there is almost no liquid egg left, turn off the stove. Keep stirring to continue the cooking. The heat in the pan will cook the egg to the right consistency.

b Place the pan over the lowest heat possible and put the knob of butter in. Stir the butter around the pan.

c As soon as the butter starts to melt, pour in the egg. Keep stirring the egg in the pan with a spoon to mix the cooked egg with the uncooked part.

d Break the egg into the bowl and add the milk, salt and pepper. Beat the egg gently just to mix in the ingredients.

87a Listen and see if you got the stages in the right order.

L appeared
stage
thick

b Write a recipe for a simple dish that is popular in your country.

Tell each other about it.

Language study ·

Instructions

A recipe is a set of instructions. When giving instructions we often use these verb forms.
There are ten forms like the examples on the right in the scrambled eggs recipe. Can you find them all?

Think of a kind of fruit or vegetable.
See if your partner can guess what it is.
Listen to Jenny's summary.
Work in groups.

Your favourite cheap meal

a Jenny asked the others what they would cook for their favourite cheap meal for four people.
David chose baked potatoes with a filling of cheese and Jenny said she would do scrambled eggs on toast. Danny said he wouldn't cook anything himself. He would go out for some pie and mashed potatoes. Jenny then asked them how much it would cost to cook these things at home and how much it would cost if they went out to a café or restaurant.

 Make notes about how much each meal would cost. Compare your notes with a friend.

▷ Tell the class. ◁

 b Listen and see if you were right.

c What would members of your group cook and how much would their meals cost?

▷ Tell the class. Whose dish would be the best value for money? Take a vote. ◁

Microwave ovens

Language study

Would

a Look at the verbs in colour. What tense are they in? Do they refer to past time?

JV: Are we ready? Yes. Erm, now what would each of you cook if someone dropped in unexpectedly and stayed for a meal in the evening?

JV: What would you cook, David?
DF: Whatever vegetables happened to be there.

JV: Supposing they arrived after the restaurants had shut.

JV: But, er, and if you'd made it at home . . .

Why are they in the past tense?

b Look at these sentences. What does **would** mean? Why is it **would** not **will**?

We asked Jenny, Bridget, David and Danny what they would cook for an unexpected guest.

JV: **What** would you do, Danny?
DL: Would I have to **cook them something, because** I'd prefer **to take them out for a meal.**
JV: It says here '**What** would each of you cook?'.
DL: Erm . . .
JV: So, to summarise, Bridget would cook **sausage and beans,** Danny would cook **an omelette,** David would cook **something exotic that he'd rustled up from bits in the fridge, and** I would cook **a cheese flan.**

Vest Midlands County Council
Consumer Services Department
At Your Service
Summer 1985   Issue 8

How do they work?

Microwaves work by using a device called a magnetron to convert mains electricity into microwaves. These are short waves, rather like radio waves. They bounce off the metal sides of the oven and are absorbed by the food. The microwaves then produce heat by friction and this is caused by the water molecules in the food vibrating against each other very quickly. Several million microwaves will penetrate the food every second.

What are the advantages?

They are ideal for defrosting and reheating foods quickly. Microwaves can also reduce cooking times for certain foods quite drastically, and the shorter periods of use can result in fuel bill savings. Food cooked in a microwave oven retains more vitamins and minerals which are often lost through cooking in water or destroyed through prolonged cooking.

The safety factor

Early fears about safety have now been largely dispelled. On most modern models, the door has to be firmly shut before the oven will operate, and similarly, once the door is opened the microwaves stop being produced. Any microwave for sale in the UK must comply with Safety Regulations which include stringent tests for electrical safety and microwave leakage.* Ensure your safety by getting microwave ovens serviced regularly, and if you have any problems contact us and we'll try to help.

*Look for the BEAB label and BS 3456 approval.

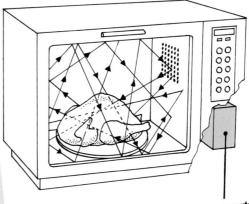

In here is a magnetron: a device which converts or changes mains electricity into microwaves.

Word study

Which of the three words below means:
a) change into   b) shake very fast
c) get right inside

penetrate
vibrate
convert

Which part of the word **microwave** means 'very small'?
What is a microcomputer? (It is often simply called a 'micro'.)

contact
fears
largely
test

▷ List the advantages and disadvantages of microwave ovens. How many in your group think that a microwave would be useful for them? If a microwave oven costs about £250, how many of you think it would be worthwhile for you to have one?

92 Wordpower

give   *an impression of being angry   good advice on....   something out   directions to someone*

Find a person here who could be giving (or be about to give):

- a speech
- a party
- a funny look
- a nice smile
- a wave
- a kiss
- a push
- a present
- something up

93 Eating out

Which story goes with this picture?

93a a Losing weight?

> Lunching at a restaurant, I ordered the special low-calorie dish. Then I ordered apple pie. The waitress told me there was none left.
> As I got up to go, I saw the same waitress serving apple pie to another table. Seeing my expression, she came over and explained, 'I just couldn't let you eat that pie after you had ordered the slimmer's lunch.'

93b b Pub food

> One evening we decided to go out to eat at a small pub, which turned out to be very busy. Noticing a woman reading the menu, I kept an eye on her until she put it down. Rushing over, I muttered, 'May I?' and brought it back to my friends. Triumphantly, I opened the menu to reveal – a photograph album!

▷ Plan how you would tell this story from the point of view of the woman with the photograph album. In groups, write her story. Read it to the other groups.

▷ Now write the first story from the waitress's point of view.

93c c Was the fast food fast?
Catherine reads a story.

93d d What was Catherine given for free?

▷ e Has anything funny ever happened to you in a restaurant, or have you ever got something for nothing? Discuss in groups, then choose the best story to tell the class.

94 Grammar

Purpose

We often use **to** and **for** to express purpose.
Keep stirring the egg in the pan ... Why? What for? ... to mix the cooked egg with the uncooked part.

I have eaten the plums which you were probably saving ... Why? What for? ... for breakfast.

Look at these sentences. Which phrases answer the question 'Why?' or 'What for?' Which of these phrases do not have **to** or **for**?

a *We gave Jeremy a set of eight questions to look at.* (29)
b *There are good facilities for other sports and pastimes.* (35)
c *But during the summer I work to make some money.* (52)
d *A woman went to a dentist in Baghdad to have a tooth out.* (45)
e *My husband stopped at his secretary's desk to see if there were any messages for him.* (55)
f *Wake me up for coffee break.* (55)
g *This is just to say I have eaten the plums.* (95)
h *They are ideal for defrosting and reheating foods quickly.* (91)
i *To cook for more than one person just multiply the ingredients.* (87)
j *The door has to be firmly shut before the oven will operate.* (91)
k *Ensure your safety by getting microwave ovens serviced regularly.* (91)
l *You'd better go to bed now or you won't wake up in the morning.*

A poem

95 **THIS IS JUST TO SAY...**

I have eaten
the plums
that were in
the icebox

and which
you were probably
saving
for breakfast.

Forgive me
they were delicious
so sweet
and so cold.

William Carlos Williams

We asked two people to say what they thought about this poem. This is what they said.

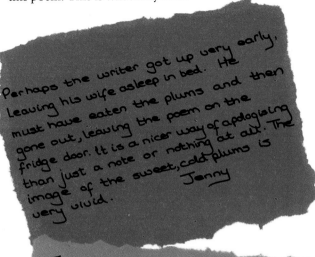

Perhaps the writer got up very early, leaving his wife asleep in bed. He must have eaten the plums and then gone out, leaving the poem on the fridge door. It is a nicer way of apologising than just a note or nothing at all. The image of the sweet, cold plums is very vivid.
Jenny

The way that this is presented as a message of apology left for someone - a lover perhaps? - is appealing. Very simple language, evocative - the plea 'forgive me' has a lot of impact but the excuse doesn't exactly exonerate him!!
Caroline

a What do you think about the writer? Would you forgive him for eating the plums?

b What do you think about the poem itself?

▶ Write a reply to his note. (It does not need to be a poem.) ◀

96 ## *Preposition spot* ....

by

1 showing who or what does something
The microwaves are absorbed by the food. (91)
B & B – in most cases it will be run by the owner. (39)

2 answering the question 'How?'
Microwaves work by using a device called a magnetron... (91)
They only deal with enquiries by letter.

3 answering the question 'When?'

By the time we got downstairs they were already halfway down the street. (178)

4 meaning 'near' or 'next to'
I would probably wait by the car. (150)

Find <u>two</u> examples for category 1, <u>three</u> for category 2 and <u>one</u> example for categories 3 and 4.
Write down the other four phrases with **by**. What do they mean?

a *I can get by in French...* (12)
b *I'm fairly interested in sport, but by no means football.* (20)
c *We went up by car.* (29)
d *She answers the door, looking a bit angry, as it's one in the morning by then.* (78)
e *He sees this girl standing by the roadside hitching.* (78)
f *They produce heat by friction...* (91)
g *Ensure your safety by getting microwave ovens serviced regularly.* (91)
h *I was driving up to London by myself.* (97)
i *There'll be a left turn followed by an immediate right.*
j *I was approached by an American mother...* (144)
k *'By the way,' I said, 'why did you lie to him?'* (161)

a Roald Dahl is a well known British writer, famous for his short stories, many of which have been dramatised and shown on television. He has written successful children's books as well as two novels.
His books have been translated into many languages and have become best-sellers all over the world.

97a

PART 1

I HAD A NEW CAR

I had a new car. It was an exciting toy, a big B.M.W. 3.3 Li, which means 3.3 litre, long wheelbase, fuel injection. It had a top speed of 129 m.p.h. and terrific acceleration. The body was pale blue. The seats inside were darker blue and they were made of leather, genuine soft leather of the finest quality. The windows were electrically operated and so was the sun-roof. The radio aerial popped up when I switched on the radio, and disappeared when I switched it off. The powerful engine growled and grunted impatiently at slow speeds, but at sixty miles an hour the growling stopped and the motor began to purr with pleasure.

I was driving up to London by myself. It was a lovely June day. They were haymaking in the fields and there were buttercups along both sides of the road. I was whispering along at seventy miles an hour, leaning back comfortably in my seat, with no more than a couple of fingers resting lightly on the wheel to keep her steady.

Ahead of me I saw a man thumbing a lift. I touched the footbrake and brought the car to a stop beside him. I always stopped for hitch-hikers. I knew just how it used to feel to be standing on the side of a country road watching the cars go by. I hated the drivers for pretending they didn't see me, especially the ones in big cars with three empty seats. The large expensive cars seldom stopped. It was always the smaller ones that offered you a lift, or the old rusty ones, or the ones that were already crammed full of children and the driver would say, "I think we can squeeze in one more."

The hitch-hiker poked his head through the open window and said, "Going to London, guv'nor?"

"Yes," I said. "Jump in."

He got in and I drove on.

b   Can you remember?

Read the first paragraph of the story very carefully. Try to remember as much as you can about the writer's car. If you want, you can ask your teacher a few questions to help you remember.

Close your books and write down what you can remember.

97b   See how much Catherine and Stephen remembered. Did they do as well as you?

c   What next?

Have three tries to see if you can guess the next question the driver asked the hitch-hiker.

97c   Make a note of the three guesses Catherine and Stephen made.

You will find out in the next Unit who was right.

97a   Now listen to the story once more.

Language study ··········

-ing

1 after part of the verb **be**
…which you were probably saving for breakfast. (95)

2 after **see, hear, watch** etc.
I saw the waitress serving apple pie. (93)

3 after **by, of, from** etc.
It is a nicer way of apologising than just a note, or nothing at all. (95)
Microwaves work by using a device called a magnetron. (91)
They are ideal for defrosting and reheating foods quickly. (91)

4 describing someone or something
It must be an interesting job. (189)

5 adding to the main part of the sentence
Perhaps the writer got up very early, leaving his wife asleep in bed. (95)
Noticing a woman reading the menu, I kept an eye on her until she put it down. (93)

6 as a noun
It was a great concert. The singing was very good.

Find words with **-ing** in the story in section 97. Which categories do they belong to?

Phrase-building ··········

a Look at the picture above. You can see:

a man waiting for a bus/standing in the rain
a woman holding an umbrella

How many phrases like this can you make about the picture?

b Memory game

99b Listen to the memory game. Can you remember some of the things they said?

Now you play the game in groups.

Cut the cake

a What is the smallest number of straight cuts you have to make with a knife in order to cut this cake into eight equal pieces?

Explain to another pair how you decided to cut the cake. Which pair got the best answer? How did they do it?

100b **b** We asked David and Jenny to do this. How many cuts did they make? How do you think they did it?

100c **c** Listen and see how they did it.

100d **d** Jenny asked Danny to see if he could do any better. How many cuts did he make?

Jenny says 'None of us had that spatial awareness where you thought of cutting it across ways.' How do you think Danny cut it? Can you draw what he drew?

> **Word study**
>
> How many meanings can you think of for the word **line**? Think of three places where you would find lines. Check in the Lexicon.

Great eaters of the world

a What do you think Michel Lotito (b.15 June 1950) of Grenoble, France, did with these things?

10 bicycles
a supermarket trolley
7 TV sets
6 chandeliers
a light aircraft

Did he buy them, sell them, cook them, steal them, make them, eat them or break them?

b Another great eater is Peter G. Dowdeswell of Earls Barton, Northamptonshire, who was born in London on 29th July 1940. He doesn't eat TV sets or bicycles but he can eat more food and eat it faster than anyone else in the world.

Which numbers do you think go in the blanks?

Peter Dowdeswell has eaten:

_____ hard-boiled eggs in 58 sec	
_____ soft-boiled eggs in 75 sec	13 14 38
_____ raw eggs in 1.0 sec	

_____ 100g hamburgers in 9 min 42 sec	
_____ 156g meat pies in 18 min 13 sec	40 22 21
_____ 15.2 × 9.5 × 1.2cm jam sandwiches in 17 min 53.9 sec	

a who, which, what

1 used to describe something or someone
 ...a foreigner who was coming to your country.
 vitamins which are often lost through cooking...
2 after words like **tell**, **ask** etc.
 See if your partner can guess what it is.
 We asked Jenny, Bridget, David and Danny what they would cook.
3 after **this is, that is**
 This is what they said.

Which category do these belong to?
a *...his short stories, many of which have been dramatised and shown on television.*
b *This is what they said.*
c *We asked Caroline and Jenny to say what they thought about this poem.*
d *Work in groups and find out which of these meals people would like best.*
e *I have eaten the plums which you were probably saving...*
f *Jenny asked the others what they would cook.*
g *...a small pub, which turned out to be very busy.*

b Cause

Heat is caused by the water molecules vibrating against each other.
Shorter periods of cooking can result in fuel bill savings.
Vitamins are often lost through cooking in water.
Once the door is opened the microwaves stop being produced.
Roald Dahl is famous for his short stories.
I always stopped for hitch-hikers. I knew just how it used to feel.
I hated the drivers for pretending they didn't see me.

Find some more expressions of cause.

c probably, perhaps

How do we show we are not quite sure of something?
How many ways can you find?
How much do you think it would cost?
I suppose it's about 50 p.
It would probably cost you four times as much as that.
About 70p I should think.
It seems that for most people their favourite cheap meal is something that is probably going to cost about a pound or so, maybe one pound fifty.
So the driver might ask him where he had come from.
I suppose he could ask him where he was going.
I would imagine that either it will be...

d To do with food

Can you divide these words into four groups?

egg	café	melt	knife	hotel
teaspoon	cook	salt	pie	mix
milk	stove	restaurant	add	pepper
pour	pan	stir	coffee	pub
fork	cheese	potatoes	cream	

e Parts of a car

Which part is which?

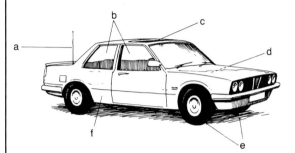

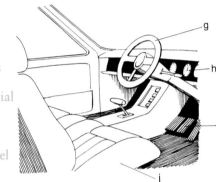

speedometer
the sun roof
the windows
the seats
the radio aerial
the engine
the body
the wheels
steering wheel
footbrake

What were they like? Which of the above can be described by these expressions?

1 *pale blue*
2 *long wheelbase*
3 *powerful*
4 *comfortable*
5 *electrically operated*
6 *top speed of 129 m.p.h.*
7 *made of leather*
8 *darker blue*
9 *of the finest quality*
10 *terrific acceleration*
11 *which popped up...*

Key (101a) He ate them!

Important words to remember (427 so far)

absorb	contact L	equal	heat	pale	stage L
advantage	conversation	excited	image	plate	sugar
among L	cook	exciting	imagine L	pleasure	terrific
appeal	cream	express L	impact	powerful L	test L
appear L	cup	expression	issue	presented	thick L
appearance L	cut	favourite	knife	restaurant	touch
beer	device	fear L	largely	rice	twice
bottle	divide	field	line L	salt	vegetable
bread	division	fork	meat	section	wave
by	driver	fruit	milk	shut	wheel
circle	egg	fuel	mix	simple L	whereas
companion	empty	genuine	mixture	speech	wine
compare	engine	genuinely	model	spoon	

Unit 8
I wish I were going with you

Has it ever happened to you?

Have you ever missed the last bus home and had to walk instead?

a Have you ever done any of these things?
Has any of these things ever happened to you?

b What should you do if you are driving and you have an accident? What information and documents should you exchange with the other driver? Who should you notify?

Has your bus or car ever broken down?

c What are the most common causes of accidents in your country?

d Can you complete this story?

> The driver of one of my firm's petrol tankers called in on his two-way radio one day: 'I'm stuck on the bypass.'
> 'What's the trouble, mate?' enquired the radio operator.

Have you ever gone to sleep on a bus or train and gone beyond your stop or station?

e What words might you use to describe an accident?

pleasant	lucky
frightening	unpleasant
embarrassing	horrible
exciting	awful
annoying	interesting
terrible	nasty

f How might you feel when you are involved in an accident?

frightened	sorry
pleased	terrible
embarrassed	unhappy
excited	angry
worried	interested
annoyed	awful

Have you ever got on the wrong bus or train by accident and not realised until it's too late?

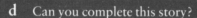

Have you ever run out of petrol?

Have you ever been involved in or witnessed an accident?

104 A frightening flight

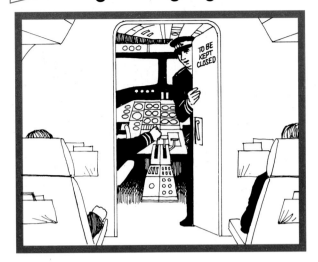

a   Which of the following can you find in the picture? the pilot/captain, the crew, the controls, the cabin, the cockpit/flight deck, the passengers, the security door, the aisle.

b   Have you ever heard a story like this before?

THE AUTO-PILOT
The flight ran several times a week taking holiday-makers to various resorts in the Mediterranean. On each flight, to reassure the passengers all was well, the captain would put the jet on to auto-pilot and he and all the crew would come aft into the cabin to greet the passengers.

Unfortunately, on this particular flight the security door between the cabin and the flight deck jammed and left the captain and crew stuck in the cabin. From that moment, in spite of the efforts to open the door, the fate of the passengers and crew was sealed.

Here is another story on the same subject. Can you think of words that would fill the gaps?

JUMBO JET PILOT
A show-off Jumbo Jet _____ put the controls on _____ in mid-flight and took his entire _____ for a stroll back down the aisle to meet the _____. He then discovered the cockpit door had _____ itself and he had _____ the key.

104b   Listen to the two stories and see if you chose the same words for the second one.

Do you think these stories are true?

Word study

Match the words or phrases on the left with the words/phrases with similar meaning on the right.

their *fate was sealed*	lost
mislaid the keys	jammed shut
then *discovered*	whole
locked itself	nothing could be done
his *entire* crew	attempts, trying
his *efforts* to open	found
---

c   Discuss in groups any frightening flight you have had or have heard about or seen on TV. Choose one story to tell the class.

104d **d**   How do Stephen and Catherine feel about flying? What does Catherine's husband think are the most dangerous parts of a flight?

e   Make a story with these words. Tell each other.

friend	air hostess	missed her connection
bad experience	frightened	back to Heathrow
home to Texas	pilot	engines on fire
noticed	window	pointed this out

104e   See if your story is the same as Stephen's. (His girlfriend lives in Texas.)

L	
controls	experience
various	suddenly
business	noticed

105 *Preposition spot* ·············

off

1   something or someone is removed from somewhere or leaves somewhere
You can hop on and off a bus or train. (82)
Do you want to take your coat off?

2   at a distance from, or quite near to
Her house is just off Western Avenue.

3   not doing a particular activity; a person or machine not working; no longer available etc.
The football match was called off.
. . . when I switched off the radio . . .
Tuesday is my day off . . .

Which categories do these examples belong to?

a   *There's this road off to the right.* (131)
b   *Turn off the heat.* (87)
c   *I'm not afraid of landing and taking off.*
d   *I fell off my bicycle.* (18)
e   *Off they go.*

Find the sentences which have phrases similar in meaning to the phrases in the box below.

f   *I tried to phone again, but we were cut off.*
g   *Oh dear – the button's come off.*
h   *Sportsday was put off until the following weekend.*
i   *The party finally went off very well.*
j   *Except that Alice went off with Janet's boyfriend.*
k   *I used to like pop music but I've gone off it now.*
l   *Phew – I'm afraid this milk has gone off.*
m   *He's fairly well off now in his new job.*

fallen off	was successful
not held	gone bad
the line went dead	don't like any more
made friends with	has enough money

'I simply didn't look'

a Have you ever been involved in an accident like one of these? Who do you think was to blame in each of these?

b Look at these sentences about what you might do in the event of an accident. Say whether you agree or disagree with each one.

You will find out later what advice a leading insurance company gives.

1 You should get the other driver's name and address.
2 You must get the name and address of an independent witness.
3 You should make a note of the make and number of the other vehicle.
4 If you are to blame you should say so.
5 You should not discuss who is to blame.
6 You must move your car to the side of the road so as not to interrupt the traffic.
7 You must report the accident to the police within 24 hours.
8 You do not have to make a report to the police but it is a good idea to do so.

9 You must report the accident to your insurance company as soon as you can.
10 If you are responsible for the accident you must fill in an Accident Report Form.

106c **c** Jenny once had a really silly accident. Listen. What happened?

106d **d** Listen to Jenny's account of it. What did Bridget say? Whose fault was it? How did she hit the other car? Which of you guessed what happened to her?

107 **Wordpower**

lead

What do the words with **lead** mean in these examples?

(a) What an interesting life you lead!

(b) There's a narrow path leading up the mountains.

(c) We set off with George in the lead.

(d) The country did well under the leadership of the new president.

(e) At the beginning of the race he led by over ten metres.

(f) He has played the leading role in many Shakespearean productions.

(g) The incident almost led to war....

Now check in the Lexicon and say which category number goes with each example of **lead/led** etc.

Yippee! Manchester's leading 3 nil!

Oh dear! I must have put the wrong lead in here.

I'll lead the way

Take us to your leader

It's Guardian Royal Exchange, a leading insurance company

What's G.R.E.?

108 After an accident

What should you do in your country after an accident? Must you tell the police? Should you take the other person's insurance certificate? What information should you obtain? Now read what an insurance company advises. Is it the same procedure in your country?

108

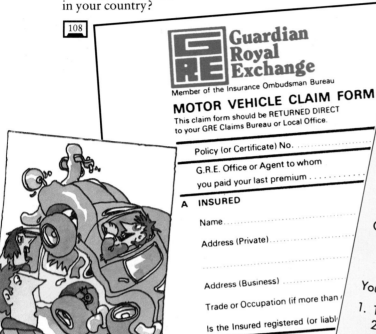

Guardian Royal Exchange
Member of the Insurance Ombudsman Bureau

MOTOR VEHICLE CLAIM FORM
This claim form should be RETURNED DIRECT to your GRE Claims Bureau or Local Office.

Policy (or Certificate) No. ....

G.R.E. Office or Agent to whom
you paid your last premium ....

A INSURED

Name..................

Address (Private)..................

....

Address (Business) ....

Trade or Occupation (if more than (

Is the Insured registered (or liabl(

B DRIVER

Name..................

Address ....

ADVICE ON ACTION TO BE TAKEN AFTER A MOTOR ACCIDENT

It is suggested that these notes be kept with your insurance certificate.

AT THE SCENE OF THE ACCIDENT

Keep calm. Do not discuss who was to blame. If there is no injury, move your car to the side of the road so as not to disrupt traffic flow.

A. Obtain the following information:

  1. Name and address of the other driver.
  2. Name and address of other driver's Insurers.
  3. Insurance Certificate Number.
  4. Name and address of independent witness.
  5. Make, owner and registration number of other vehicle.
  6. Sketch a diagram of the accident (including measurements, directions, etc.).
  7. Weather and road conditions at the time.

B. Note the date and time of the accident.

C. Provide your own particulars to anyone who has reasonable grounds for wanting them.

AFTER THE ACCIDENT

You should report to:

  1. The police as soon as possible but not later than 24 hours after the accident if there is personal injury or damage to government property. If there is no injury a police report is optional by either party, but remember that the party making an official statement is in a better position than one who does not.

  2. Your insurers as soon as possible even if you do not intend to make a claim – this is a condition of your policy.

  (a) Report any statement made at the scene of the accident by any one of the parties.
  (b) You will be required to complete an Accident Report Form, obtainable from your Insurers upon request.

L policy
make a **claim**

Word study

Match the words that are similar in meaning.
Which is the odd one out?

action	any reason
be to blame	what to do
disrupt traffic flow	in a better position
obtain	party
grounds	be in the wrong
better off	get hold of
person	must
will be required to	if you ask
upon request	tell the police
make a statement	officially what happened

109 *Language study* ....

should

1.1 used to say what it would be right to do or to have done
What should you do after an accident? (108)
Scrambled eggs should be soft and creamy. (87)
If she was working 8½ hours a day they should have paid her more than £1.20 an hour.

1.2 often used in this way to give advice
After an accident you should report to the police.
You should have reported the accident.

2.1 used to show that something is likely to happen
In early July the weather should be fairly nice. (69)

2.2 or something that was expected to happen
Bridget should have arrived at her station at about 19.50. (110)

3 often used with **think**
About 70p, I should think, for four people. (89)

ought

Ought has the same meanings, apart from 3. The difference is that **ought** is followed by **to**.

Which categories do these sentences belong to?

a *Anyone who works 8½ hours a day should receive more than just £1.20 an hour.* (42)
b *I would work out what I should have said to the teacher.* (58)
c *Jenny should have looked where she was going.*
d *We should be there by seven fifteen, I should think.*
e *Are we on the right road? We ought to have another look at the map.*
f *You shouldn't drive so fast! You'll have an accident one day.*
g *You say Jim's only 25? I should have thought he was older than that.*

Unfortunate journeys

a Bridget's family live in the village of Wadhurst in Sussex. Look at the timetable.
How long does it take by train from Charing Cross to Wadhurst? How long does it take to Hastings?

110a Listen to Bridget's story. What went wrong?

b Bridget got the 18.01 from London, Charing Cross, so she should have arrived at Wadhurst at about 19.15. Work together from the timetable to find out:
what time she got to Hastings
what train she caught back to Wadhurst
what time she got back to Wadhurst
how late she was

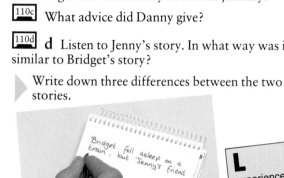

CHARING CROSS	dep	17 58		18 01h	18 45	19 45	20 45	21 45
Waterloo East	dep	18 01		18 04h	18 48	19 48	20 48	21 48
CANNON STREET	dep	17 44t			18 20			
London Bridge	dep	17 48t		18 08h	18 28t	19 22t	20 22t	——
Sevenoaks	dep	18 16t		18 36h	19 15	20 15	21 15	22 17
Tonbridge	dep	18 35		18 46h	19 24	20 24	21 25	22 27
High Brooms	dep	18 41		19 00	19 30	20 30	21 31	22 33
TUNBRIDGE WELLS	dep	18 47	18 52	19 05	19 35	20 34	21 35	22 37
Frant	dep	——	18 56	19 09	19 39	20 38	21 39	22 41
Wadhurst	dep	18 54	19 00	19 13	19 43	20 42	21 43	22 45
Stonegate	dep	——	19 06	19 20	19 49	20 48	21 49	22 51
Etchingham	dep	19 03	19 11	19 25	19 54	20 53	21 54	22 56
Robertsbridge	dep	——	19 17	19 28	19 57	20 56	21 57	22 59
Battle	dep	19 12	19 25	19 36	20 05	21 04	22 05	23 07
Crowhurst	dep	——	19 28	19 40	20 09	21 08	22 09	23 11
West St.Leonards	dep	——	19 33	19 45	20 17	21 13	22 14	23 16
St.Leonards (W.Sq)	dep	19 21	19 36	19 48	20 20	21 16	22 17	23 19
HASTINGS	arr	19 24	19 38	19 50	20 22	21 18	22 19	23 21

HASTINGS	dep		16 36	16 53	17 49	18 57	20 00	21 02	22 02
St.Leonards (W.Sq)	dep		16 38	16 55	17 51	18 59	20 02	21 04	22 04
West St.Leonards	dep		——	16 58	17 54	19 02	20 05	21 07	22 07
Crowhurst	dep		——	17 04	18 00	19 08	20 11	——	22 13
Battle	dep	16 48	17 08		18 04	19 12	20 15	21 15	22 17
Robertsbridge	dep		17 15		18 11	19 19	20 22	21 22	22 24
Etchingham	dep		17 19		18 15	19 23	20 26	21 26	22 28
Stonegate	dep		17 24		18 20	19 28	——	——	22 33
Wadhurst	dep	17 05	17 31		18 29	19 35	20 36	21 36	22 40
Frant	dep		17 35		18 33	19 39	——	——	22 44
TUNBRIDGE WELLS	arr	17 12	17 39		18 37	19 43	20 43	21 43	22 48
High Brooms	arr	17 16	17 43		18 41	19 47	20 47	21 47	22 52
Tonbridge	arr	17 21	17 43		18 46	19 52	20 52	21 52	22 57
Sevenoaks	arr	17 31	18 00		18 59	20 03	21 03	22 03	23 14t
London Bridge	arr	18 04s		18 40t	19 40t	20 43t	21 42t	22 40t	23 43t
CANNON STREET	arr	18 09							
Waterloo East	arr	18 09s		18 28	19 29	20 29	21 29	22 29	23 50t
CHARING CROSS	arr	18 12s		18 32	19 32	20 32	21 32	22 32	23 52t

What if her train had arrived in Hastings ten minutes late? She would have missed the ＿＿＿.
She would have got the ＿＿＿ and arrived back at ＿＿＿.
Then she would have been ＿＿＿ late.

▷ Tell the class what you have worked out. ◁

c Bridget also told Danny about her journey.

110c What advice did Danny give?

110d **d** Listen to Jenny's story. In what way was it similar to Bridget's story?

▷ Write down three differences between the two stories. ◁

> Bridget fell asleep on a train, but Jenny's friend

L experience
you can **imagine**
Where are you
supposed to be
going?

e Buses

Red Buses serve Central London and are a great way to see the city, you are, however, advised to get a bus map (free from bus and tube stations) before setting out. Fares are similar to tube fares.

Greenline buses run from Central London – usually from Victoria Coach Station or Regent Street – to most towns within 20 miles of London's borders, including Oxford, Cambridge, Windsor and Canterbury. Details on 222 1234.

Write down three questions that people might ask about travelling on these buses. (You should choose questions that can be answered from the information given here.)
Close your books and ask each other questions. How many can you answer?

Phrase-building

Look at these phrases with **as … as …**

John works	almost nearly almost twice	as hard as his father. as hard as his father did. as hard as his father did when he was a young man.

Can you match and complete these sentences?

a *I have lived in London for*
b *We asked him to find out*
c *I won the next year but*
d *Fill in*
e *The taxi costs*
f *You can hop on and off a bus*
g *You should report to the police*

1 *five times as much as the bus.*
2 *not as much as I'd won the first year.*
3 *as soon as possible.*
4 *almost as long as I can remember.*
5 *as much as possible about Jenny's holiday.*
6 *as many times as you like with a Travelcard.*
7 *as many boxes as you can.*

Make up some more examples yourself.

112 # No claim

a Imagine that you were driving into a car park when you bumped into a parked car and scratched it all down one side. You could not find the driver of the other car to tell him what had happened. What would you do:
if there were no witnesses?
if there were a number of witnesses?

▶ Tell the class. ◀

112b **b** Now read on and find out what one driver did when this actually happened.

> Returning to the car he had left in a nearby car park, a friend of a cousin of mine was rather perturbed to find one side of the vehicle all scratched and dinted. Seeing a note on the windscreen, he breathed a sigh of relief, for he thought that the culprit had left his name and address so, at least, he could make a claim for the damage against the other driver's insurance company. However, on opening the note, his relief turned to dismay when he read:

Dear Driver,

I have just run into your car and made a hell of a mess of it. As a crowd has gathered, I am forced to appear as if writing you this note to apologise and to leave you my name and address. As you can see, however, this I have not done.

A Well Wisher

113 # Grammar

Time

Expressions of time answer questions like 'When?', 'How long?' or 'How often?' These questions can be answered by:

1.1 a clause
I left *when I was eighteen.* (2)
I was born and lived *until I was seven in Dublin.* (2)
I spent two years in Rome *while I was still living with my family.* (17)
As soon as the butter starts to melt, **pour in the egg.** (87)
I just couldn't let you eat that pie *after you had ordered the slimmers' lunch.* (93)

1.2 with -ing
Before having the children **she worked in insurance.** (2)
I've lived in England *since leaving America.* (17)
Lunching at a restaurant I ordered the special low-calorie dish. (93)
Seeing my expression she came over and explained. (93)

2 a phrase
Mummy and Daddy went back to Ireland *some time ago.* (2)
She was born and lived *for the first seven years of her life in Ireland.* (2)
And it wasn't diagnosed *until the next day.* (18)
I've never broken any bones *so far.* (18)
I hope to see more of the world *in the next ten years.* (20)
This summer I am working for my father's publishing company. (52)

3 a word
I haven't been back *since.* (2)
But it's *still* home. (2)
I've *never* broken any bones. (18)
Once we'd been collecting firewood for a bonfire. (18)
Have you ever been to Northumberland *before?* (29)

Look at these sentences. Read out the time expressions. (You should find sixteen.)

a I was brought over here when I was seven. (2)
b She may have sneaked out while he wasn't looking or when his attention was distracted. (78)　(two expressions)
c Noticing a woman looking at the menu I kept an eye on her until she put it down. (93)　(two expressions)
d Supposing they arrived after the restaurants had shut? (86)
e Before having children I had a varied career. (20)
f I have lived in London for almost as long as I can remember. (20)
g Seeing a note on the windscreen, he breathed a sigh of relief. (112)
h He sold more during the interval than anyone had ever done before. (55)　(two expressions)
i Upon returning to his office my husband stopped at his secretary's desk. (55)
j I actually did that last year.
k Report to the police as soon as possible. (108)
l On opening the note his relief turned to dismay. (45)
m Finally he called a plumber. (45)

a Read the next part of the story and say which of these pictures is the hitch-hiker.

You made three guesses in the last Unit about what questions the driver might ask the hitch-hiker. What are they? Read and see if you were right.

PART 2

A SMALL RATTY-FACED MAN

He was a small ratty-faced man with grey teeth. His eyes were dark and quick and clever, like a rat's eyes, and his ears were slightly pointed at the top. He had a cloth cap on his head and he was wearing a greyish-coloured jacket with enormous pockets. This grey jacket, together with the quick eyes and the pointed ears, made him look more than anything like some sort of a huge human rat.

"What part of London are you headed for?" I asked him.

"I'm goin' right through London and out the other side," he said. "I'm going to Epsom, for the races. It's Derby Day today."

"So it is," I said. "I wish I were going with you. I love betting on horses."

"I never bet on horses," he said. "I don't even watch 'em run. That's a stupid silly business."

"Then why do you go?" I asked.

He didn't seem to like that question. His little ratty face went absolutely blank and he sat there staring straight ahead at the road, saying nothing.

"I expect you help to work the betting machines or something like that," I said.

"That's even sillier," he answered. "There's no fun working them lousy machines and selling tickets to mugs. Any fool could do that."

b Close your books and write down as much as you can remember about the hitch-hiker.

[114c] **c** How much did Stephen and Catherine remember? Did they do as well as you?

d Does the hitch-hiker tell the writer why he is going to Epsom?

[114d] See what Stephen and Catherine think. What do you think?

a size

How many words (or parts of words) to do with size can you find in these sentences?

He was a small ratty-faced man with grey teeth.
He was wearing a greyish-coloured jacket with enormous pockets.
... made him look like some sort of a huge human rat.
The large expensive cars seldom stopped.
A jumbo jet pilot
A microcomputer

b while

While you are in full-time education, you can get a special student travel pass.
I spent two years in Rome while I was still living with my family.

Where does the word **while** fit into these sentences?

1 *the dinner's cooking we could have a drink*
2 *I'd like to do a lot of travelling I have some money*

What other meanings does **while** have? Look in the Lexicon.

c Lexicon words

Look these words up in the Lexicon and say what they mean here.

account *Listen to Jenny's account of her accident. How much is there in your account?*

claim *You should report the accident to your insurers, even if you do not intend to make a claim.*

control *He gives us a lot of trouble. He has no self-control.*

grounds *Give your particulars to anyone who has reasonable grounds for asking for them.*

involve *I enjoy social activities which involve meeting and talking with people.*
Bridget had a similar accident involving a lorry.

machine *I expect you help to work the betting machines.*
Do you have a washing machine at home?

policy *This is a condition of your policy.*
Do you support your government's policy?

simply *I simply didn't look.*
I simply don't believe you!

supposed *Where are you supposed to be going?*
You are supposed to report the accident to your insurance company.

wish *I wish I hadn't got caught in the rain.*

d make or let?

1 *A crowd gathered and _____ him write this note to apologise to the car owner.*
2 *Did your parents _____ you stay out until midnight when you were 15?*
3 *My parents always _____ me get home by 10.30. It was awful.*
4 *The doctor's at the door. Could you _____ him in?*

e get and got

Which meanings do **get** and **got** have in these sentences (1–20)?

a have/possess   e reach/arrive at
b must/have to   f receive
c have in mind   g obtain/buy
d grow/become

How many sentences do not have any of these meanings? What do the phrases with **get** and **got** mean in these cases?

1 *She's got a daughter called Lucy Claire.*
2 *I've got absolutely no idea!*
3 *I started off as a medical student but got bored.*
4 *... Joe, who is just starting to get interesting.*
5 *Very lucky to get to the top.*
6 *When we get there, we're going to stay with my parents.*
7 *I still like to travel whenever I get the chance.*
8 *She'll be able to get us tickets to go to Jamaica.*
9 *We've got to look at a picture of a footballer.*
10 *If you get stung by a bee or a wasp ...*
11 *I think women do get less pay.*
12 *Bank manager – he must get well paid!*
13 *Women tend to get tipped more generously than men.*
14 *For a 40 hour week I get £1.20 an hour.*
15 *How do I get a Travelcard?*
16 *Do you think she actually had got out of the car?*
17 *'Jump in!' He got in and I drove on.*
18 *As I got up to go, I saw the same waitress ...*
19 *Supposing she got the 18.45 from Charing Cross, she should arrive ...*
20 *I haven't got a car.*

Important words to remember (489 so far)					
accident	connect	frightened	lead L	required	sudden
account L	connection	frightening	leader	serve	suddenly
action	control L	fun	leading	setting	supposed L
annoyed	effort	gather	machine L	several	tired
annoying	enormous	hell	measure	silly	various L
apology	entire	huge	notice L	similar	wish L
blame	fate	independent	ought	simply L	witness
captain	fault	insurance	passenger	slightly	
catch	flow	involved L	pocket	staring	
caught	flight	laugh	pointed	statement	
claim L	flying	laughter	policy L	stick	

Everything you could imagine

116 Places to buy things

a Do you have any shops like these in your country? Where would you go to buy such things?

b What other things might the joke shop sell? Has anyone ever bought you something as a joke?

c What kinds of markets do you have in your capital city? And your local town? Do you or your family ever shop in these markets?

d In Britain you can never bargain in shops, and only very occasionally in the markets. The prices are usually fixed. Do you have to bargain in your country? Talk about a bargaining experience.

All prices include VAT

Speciality SHOPS

From buttons to books, from left-handed scissors to clothes for little women, London has shops that cater for the most specialised interests. Here is a selection.

kNUTz

1 Russell Street, WC2 (Covent Garden Tube)
Open: Mon–Fri 11–8, Sat 12–8, Sun 12–6.
A sort of adult joke shop where you'll find something to annoy just about anyone you know. Exploding matches 69p each; self-lighting candles from 35p.

EXPORT DEPARTMENT

Lillywhites

24–36 Regent Street SW1 (Piccadilly Circus tube).
Open: Mon–Sat 9.30–6, Thurs 9.30.–7.
The largest sports store in London, Lillywhites looks more like a department store than a speciality shop. Whatever sports equipment or clothes you're after, they'll have them, or know where you can find them.
Shorts £9.50; running vests £4.50; tracksuits from £24.95.

I RAN THE WORLD

THE LEFT-HANDED SHOP

65 Beak Street, W1 (Oxford Circus tube).
Open: Mon–Fri 10.30–5, Sat 10–2.
When people say London can supply all your wants, no matter how bizarre, they're talking about places like this. Everything in this shop is designed to be used by people who use their left hand. You'll find scissors, tin-openers, pens – everything.
Scissors £2.75; corkscrews £1.85; tin openers from £2.

NO REFUNDS WITHOUT RECEIPTS

Street markets are a real tradition in London. They are scattered all over the city and its suburbs... Here's one of the best:

Portobello Road (Notting Hill Gate or Ladbroke Grove tube).
Open: Fri, Sat 7–5.

Always a good idea to get down the road early if you intend to snap up the bargains. Notting Hill end is antiques, the middle is fruit and veg, under the Westway there are trendy second-hand clothes and the bottom end sports gear – everything you could imagine.

59

117 Systems for paying in shops

a   We asked Bridget and David to do this task.

> In a supermarket, you choose what you want,
> put it all in a trolley or basket, then
> take it to the cashier by the exit. The
> cashier rings it up on the till, tells you
> how much it is, then takes your money. You
> pack your shopping into a box or bag, and
> that's it.
>
> In your local shop, you usually ask the
> shop assistant for what you want. He or
> she gives you your things in a paper bag,
> and takes your money.
>
> Do you know any shops with different
> systems for payment?

▶ What is the procedure for buying things in the shop nearest to your own home? ◀

David and Bridget talked about Foyles, the famous London bookshop. Foyles has an unusual system for payment. Try to put these stages in order to show how it works.

a Leave the book with the assistant and take the bill to a cashier's desk.
b Take the book to an assistant who will give you a bill.
c Take the receipted bill back to the assistant and get the book.
d Pay for the book and get your bill stamped.
e Find whatever book it is you want.

117a Now listen to David and see if you were right.

b   There are also places in Britain where you can shop from a catalogue. One of these is called Argos. Can you put these stages in order?

a Fill in the selection form, giving the catalogue number and quantity.
b Take the goods home – it's as easy as that.
c Check what you want from the master catalogue at the Selection Desk in the Showroom.
d Your purchases will be sent up from the stockroom while you make payment.
e Take your completed form to the point marked 'Service'. Our staff will be pleased to help if you need assistance.

L	marked
	post

?	goods	bill
	cash	receipt
	cashier	staff

117b Now listen to David talking about Argos and see if you are right.

▶ **c**   Prepare a short summary of both systems. ◀

117c Listen to David and Bridget summarising the systems used in Foyles and Argos. Bridget makes one mistake. What is it?

d   Have you ever bought anything from a catalogue, either in a shop like Argos or by post?

▶ Do you know of any other shops that have a different system? Can you explain what system they use? ◀

▶ How do you go about exchanging foreign money? ◀

118 *Language study*

Phrases with prepositions

a   Can you put these words in the right order to make the phrases David uses?

1 *from a catalogue you buy*
2 *the front of in the shop*
3 *a form out you fill*
4 *the number down you take*
5 *you go a cash system through*
6 *they do a computer with something*
7 *they enter into a number the computer*

b   Who is David talking about in section 117 when he says 'you' and 'they'?

Preposition spot ·······················

up

a Where could you add the word **up** in the sentences below? What difference does it make? A lot or not much?

Often the work is unpleasant – standing all day. (47)
Wake me for the coffee break. (55)
I was driving to London by myself. (97)
The waitress got the orders mixed. (93)

b What about these examples? How does the word **up** change the meaning of the verb? For instance, in the sentence: *I gave up smoking* **gave** does not mean the same as in: *I gave her a book for her birthday.*

1 *The enterprising assistant turned up the heating.*
2 *It was not a very pleasant place to grow up in . . .*
3 *Lend me a hand with the washing up, will you . . .* (65)
4 *They probably will turn up.*
5 *He pulls up at a traffic light . . .* (78)
6 *. . . the man who picks up a hitch-hiker . . .*
7 *Then he returned the book to its pocket and did up the button.*

c Find a word or phrase below which means something similar to the phrases with **up** in the examples.

a	*decide*	g	*finish*
b	*repairing*	h	*give a bed to*
c	*think of*	i	*doing* (probably
d	*introduced*		something bad!)
e	*fit and strong enough*	j	*getting better*
f	*was faced with*	k	*be quick*

1 *He brought up the subject of equal pay for women.*
2 *He came up against some huge problems.*
3 *Sure you're up to it?*
4 *Can you come up with a plan by tomorrow?*
5 *He was doing his old car up, to sell it.*
6 *Eat it up! Hurry up!*
7 *What were the kids getting up to?*
8 *Things are looking up.*
9 *Make up your mind!*
10 *Can you put me up for a night?*

120 Advertising

a What kinds of products do you think each of these is advertising?
Can you find the slogans which advertise each item here?

A finger of fudge is just enough to give your kids a treat.

12 Shredded Wheat
THE ORIGINAL BRAN/FIBRE CEREAL

PERSIL WASHES WHITER

DRINKA PINTA MILKA DAY

new system
Persil automatic
SPECIAL OFFER 10p.

HEINZ BAKED BEANS

There are two men in my life. To one I am a mother, to the other I'm a wife.

Smartie people are happy people – they smile all the while. Only Smarties have the answer.

WHOLE NUT
Cadbury's FLAKE
fudge

The dirt said HOT. The label said NOT. ARIEL gets it clean!

GO TO WORK ON AN EGG

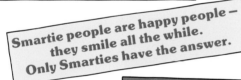
BEANZ MEANZ HEINZ

ARIEL
OUTSTANDING CLEANING EVEN AT LOWER TEMPERATURES

120b **b** Catherine, John, Stephen and Caroline try and remember some advertising jingles and slogans. They write eight on their list. Which ones?
They make these comments about four of them. Which group of comments goes with which advertisement?
What other comments do they make?

Cadbury's take 'em and they cover them with chocolate.

? housewife clean dirt label taste

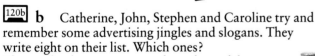
Only the crumbliest flakiest chocolate tastes like chocolate never tasted before.

CM: I think that's quite a nice one.

SB: They don't have that on TV any – still, do they?
CM: No.
CF: Erm, Yes. I saw it recently.
CM: Do they?
CF: Yes. I was very surprised.

L cover treat sense while

JM. The one that I find most irritating is [. . .]
JM: I absolutely hate it.
CF: Oh, that's awful.
JM: I'd forgotten what it's for but I remember how annoying . . .

SB: . . . which if you try and analyse it grammatically makes no sense at all.
CM: But it's quite a tongue twister.

c What is your favourite advert? Tell the class about it. As you listen to the others make a list of the products.

d What about car adverts? What kind of things do they say? Are they always truthful?

121a

PART 3

THE SECRET OF LIFE . . .

There was a long silence. I decided not to question him any more. I remembered how irritated I used to get in my hitch-hiking days when drivers kept asking *me* questions. Where are you going? Why are you going there? What's your job? Are you married? Do you have a girl-friend? What's her name? How old are you? And so on and so forth. I used to hate it.

"I'm sorry," I said. "It's none of my business what you do. The trouble is, I'm a writer, and most writers are terribly nosey parkers."

"You write books? he asked.

"Yes."

"Writin' books is okay," he said. "It's what I call a skilled trade. I'm in a skilled trade too. The folks I despise is them that spend all their lives doin' crummy old routine jobs with no skill in 'em at all. You see what I mean?"

"Yes."

"The secret of life," he said, "is to become very very good at somethin' that's very 'ard to do."

"Like you," I said.

"Exactly. You and me both."

"What makes you think that I'm any good at my job?" I asked.

"There's an awful lot of bad writers around."

"You wouldn't be drivin' about in a car like this if you weren't no good at it," he answered. "It must've cost a tidy packet, this little job."

"It wasn't cheap."

"What can she do flat out?" he asked.

"One hundred and twenty-nine miles an hour," I hold him.

"I'll bet she won't do it."

"I'll bet she will."

"All car makers is liars," he said. "You can buy any car you like and it'll never do what the makers say it will in the ads."

"This one will."

a Where is the hitch-hiker going? Do we know why he's going there? Why do you think he answered like he did?

How would you react if you were the driver? Would you keep on talking? Or leave him alone? Read on and find out how the writer reacted and why.

b Do you think the car can really do 129 miles an hour (approx 205 kmh)?

c What do you think will happen next?

121c Do you agree with what Caroline and Stephen think?

---

122 *Language study*

a Very colloquial expressions

Find phrases in the story that mean:

1 this particular car
2 want to know all about other people in detail
3 at top speed
4 a large amount of money
5 uninteresting work
6 people

b Common phrases

Find these phrases in the text and explain what is meant by them.

And so on and so forth.
The trouble is,
You see what I mean.
None of my business,
It's what I call a . . .

c The way he speaks

Look carefully at these short extracts. In what way are these extracts different from the original story?

"Writin' books is okay," he said. "It's what I call a skilled trade. I'm in a skilled trade too. The folks I despise are those who spend all their lives doin' crummy old routine jobs with no skill in 'em at all. You see what I mean?"

"You wouldn't be drivin' about in a car like this if you weren't any good at it," he answered. "It must've cost a tidy packet, this little job."

"All car makers are liars."

121a Listen to the story again, and pay attention to the way the hitch-hiker speaks. What does this tell you about him?

122c What do Caroline and Stephen feel about this?

case

Look up **case** in the Lexicon.

Try to explain exactly what situation the word case refers to in each example.

(a) If you buy from Argos, you can only see things in the catalogue, but this is not the case with Comet; in Comet you can see the goods on the shelves and try them first.

(b) 'My house isn't on fire, officer.' 'In that case,' he said, 'you've got yourself into a nasty mess!' (147)

(c) Daughter: Sorry if I woke you up by ringing so late. Mother: It doesn't matter. In any case, you should always phone if you are going to be back late.

(d) It's not likely to rain. But I suppose I'd better take this just in case it does.

(e) A: Africa? It'll be terribly hot. B: I don't care whether it's hot or cold. I'm going in any case.

(f) We asked a lot of people about cutting a round cake into eight pieces with the smallest number of cuts. In every case except one, they answered four. What about cutting a square cake into eight pieces? Would it be the same answer in this case?

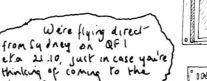
"IN THE CASE OF A POWER CUT DO NOT USE LIFTS."

THE CASE AGAINST NUCLEAR ARMS TUESDAY JUNE 23RD. ALL WELCOME

We're flying direct from Sydney on QF1 e.t.a. 21.10, just in case you're thinking of coming to the airport.

IN CASE OF EMERGENCY BREAK GLASS

---

[124] **Song**

[124] Sing the song and then discuss what you think the *pom pom pom* was.

I discovered a pom pom pom...

As I was walking down the beach
One bright and sunny day,
I saw a great big wooden box
Afloating in the bay.
I pulled it in
I opened it up
And much to my surprise
I discovered a pom pom pom
Right before my eyes.

▶ What do you think he did next? Decide, then tell the class. ◀

[125] **Phrase-building**

As I was...

Look at the first two lines of the song. This is a very traditional opening to a song or a story. Can you think of other ways you could start a story, based on the same pattern?

As I was... (action)...(place)...(time)

or

...(time) *as I was...* (action)...(place)

I saw
I heard...,...(name and description of a person)
I met

Write the beginning of the story and then ask someone else in the class to carry on.

Tax-free shopping

126

a Although you can find bargains in London it's not generally a very cheap place to shop. But if you know how to get tax relief you will be able to save some money. Even if you can't actually go to Britain yourself, you can always get things by mail order, by writing direct to the shops concerned.

This extract from a tourist newspaper explains how to buy things tax-free if you are not living in Britain. In what ways could it help you, or someone you know?

In Britain, Value Added Tax (VAT) is charged on most goods at a standard rate of 15%. Some stores offer relief from VAT under the Retail Export Scheme. This means that, provided you export what you have bought, you can have the VAT amount refunded to you.

These are the ways to obtain relief from VAT:

a Many London stores are able to send goods direct to an overseas address, free of VAT.

b Under the Personal Export Scheme, you may, as a visitor, have goods which you have bought in Britain delivered, free of tax, direct to the port by which you are leaving the country, for exportation as baggage. (This scheme does not apply to visitors leaving by air.)

c The Over-the-counter Export Scheme, also known as Retail Export Scheme. There is a form that must be filled in by the shopkeeper and shown, together with the goods, to the Customs Officer at the airport when you leave UK. This scheme is only for things that can be carried on the plane as hand luggage.

It is advisable to tell the shop that you want to claim refund of VAT before making your purchase. You will need to show your passport, so don't forget to take it with you when you go shopping.

64 A VAT reclaim desk in a London store

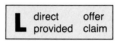 **FOR TOURISTS**

b True or false?

1 *You can't buy things free of VAT unless you live outside the UK.*
2 *You are not allowed to use the 'Over-the-counter' Export Scheme unless you can carry the goods on to the plane as hand luggage.*
3 *Many London stores are able to send things direct to your home address overseas, but not unless you have actually been to the store yourself.*
4 *You may not use the 'Over-the-counter' Export Scheme unless you are leaving by sea.*

L direct | offer
provided | claim

? goods | export
mail order | scheme
personal | over-the-counter

c Imagine you want to make the following purchases in London. Say whether it would be worth reclaiming VAT and if so under which scheme assuming:

1 that you were leaving Britain by sea
2 that you were leaving by air

Work it out then tell the class what your group thinks.

127 *Language study*

Have things done for you

Have you had your hair done? It looks great.
When did you last have your house painted? It looks terrible!

Find phrases with **get** or **have** which mean:

a there is no need to do it yourself,
b you can't/don't do it yourself.

Under the Personal Export Scheme, you may have goods delivered direct to the port by which you are leaving the country.

You take the bill to a special cash desk, pay, and get it stamped.

...under the Retail Export Scheme. This means that, provided you export what you've bought, you can have the VAT refunded.

If you live overseas, you can order things by post and have them sent directly to your home address, free of VAT.

If you ever go to London, you can have a suit made at Moss Bros. You could get your hair cut and styled at Vidal Sassoon. You could even have your fortune told by Madame Sharp in Rupert Street.

Favourite colours

a Without talking, write down your own favourite colour(s). What used to be your favourite colour as a child? Was there any particular reason? If so, write one sentence saying why.

Look around the class. Without asking anyone, try to guess four or five other people's favourite colours, and write them down.

Then write down what you think is the most popular colour for clothes. (If you saw a large crowd of people together, what colour would the majority be wearing?)

128b **b** Listen and find out what Stephen and Catherine's favourites are.

c Go round and ask the four or five people in your class what their favourite colours are.

128d **d** Listen again carefully to the conversation. What words have been missed out of these extracts?

CM: And I don't know why I like _____, except it's – I think it's probably the most _____ colour for . . . a _____ of the population.
CM: Well, If you look at any group of people together, like _____ in a football stadium or _____ like that . . .
CM: If you go shopping do you not particularly choose _____, a blue shirt _____ a pink shirt?
SB: . . . most clothes I buy _____ to be khaki or olive or grey, and then I have things with _____ colours to go _____ them so – and it's very much a _____ of mood . . .

---

129 *Grammar* •

Conditional sentences

a Conditions are often introduced by **if**.

If you met a foreigner who was coming to your country for the first time, what local dishes would you recommend?
If I had a lot of time, yes, that might be quite a good idea. (69)
If we get sunshine that's just a bonus. (38)

But how many other ways of introducing a condition can you find?

1 *Imagine you are going to London. Make a list of the people for whom you would buy presents.*
2 *Provided you export what you have bought, you can have the VAT amount refunded to you. (127)*
3 *Under which system would you claim VAT assuming you were leaving Britain by sea?*
4 *In the case of a power cut do not use the lifts.*
5 *You can see everything from outside providing you are willing to walk. (157)*
6 *Supposing they arrived after the restaurants had shut. (86)*

7 *You can't buy things free of VAT unless you live outside the UK. (126)*
8 *You can get a 'Cheap Day Return' ticket as long as you start your journey after 9.30.*
9 *As long as you are not living in Britain, you can buy things free of tax.*

b How many occurrences of **would** can you find in the passage below? How many past tenses? Why do we have **would** and the past tense here?

Imagine you were applying to a computer dating agency to find a partner. Tell the person with you what you would say about yourself.
JM: *First thing on my list would be that I have a sense of humour. I would need to meet somebody who also had a sense of humour. I'd want to meet somebody who was interested in the cinema, and the theatre and so on. And, somebody who read a lot . . . because I do. And who wasn't terribly interested in sport, because I absolutely hate sport. (20)*

a Lexicon words

Choose the appropriate words to complete the sentences. (Some words are used more than once.) Then look them up in the Lexicon. Say which categories they belong to as they are used here.

cover, direct, marked, matter, show, supply, treat

1 Take your completed form to the point ____ Service.
2 When you ____ that you have paid you can take whatever it is you want to buy and leave with it.
3 Have you got enough money to ____ the hotel bill?
4 People say that London can ____ all your needs, no ____ how bizarre.
5 Cadbury's take them and they ____ them with chocolate.
6 A finger of fudge is just enough to give your kids a ____.
7 ... then I have things with bright colours to go with them, so it's very much a ____ of mood.
8 Some London stores are able to send goods ____ to an overseas address.

offer, post, provided, show, shown, trade

9 Some stores ____ relief from VAT under the Retail Export Scheme.
10 This means ____ you export what you have bought, you can have the VAT amount refunded to you.
11 A form that must be filled in by the shopkeeper and ____ to the Customs Officer at the airport.
12 You will need to ____ your passport.
13 Writing books is what I call a skilled ____. I'm in a very skilled ____ too.
14 Using a mail order catalogue you can buy things through the ____ without even going to the shop.
15 ____ Unions try to improve working conditions for their members.
16 Britain does quite a lot of ____ with Eastern Europe.

b any more/further/longer

Make some sentences.

We decided not to We don't intend to I don't think I'll I'd rather not	go on discuss the matter write watch TV	any more. any further any longer.
Being 65 she's unable to go jogging		

c What are the missing words?

1 What makes you think I'm any ____ at my job?
2 Imagine you want to make the ____ purchases in London.
3 Even ____ you do not intend to make a claim you should notify your insurance company.
4 Make a list of people for ____ you might buy presents.
5 Your purchases will be ____ up from the stockroom while you make payment.
6 The poem makes a good point about people ____ dogs.

7 What make of ____ was the writer of the hitch-hiker story driving?

What word appears in all these sentences? What other phrases do you know with this word? Check in the Lexicon.

d Odd word out?

Find the word or phrase whose meaning is quite different from the other words in these sets. Explain.

1 smell, sight, taste, hearing, running, touch
2 gets it clean, that's awful, how annoying it is, most irritating, I absolutely hate it
3 the most popular, very fashionable, liked by the majority, trendy, traditional
4 staff, cashier, shopkeeper, trade union leader, equipment, boss, master
5 abroad, airport, overseas, another country, foreign country
6 bill, cash, change, receipt, goods, payment, postbox
7 very few, hardly any, not many, quite a lot

Important words to remember (551 so far)					
ability	clean	forth	passport	skill	uneducated
abroad	cover L	goods	popular	staff	unless
advertising	design	intend	port	store	whatever
analysis	direct L	kids	post L	suit	whom
bargain	economy	mail	product	supply	wind
basically L	enter	majority	receipt	taste	wonderful
bill	equipment	make L	recognise	tax	
box	exit	mark L	save	trade L	
case	export	master	scheme	tradition	
cash	fashion	mood	self	traditional	
catalogue	fill	offer L	silence	treat L	

131 Map reading

a From Caldwell

Look at this map and work out how to get from Caldwell to Middleton-in-Teesdale. Make a list of the roads you would use and any towns or villages you would go through.

131a Did Catherine give the same route as you?

Listen again and make a note when Stephen repeats Catherine's words.

b ... to Middleton-in-Teesdale

Work out directions for the rest of the journey.

▶ Tell the class and together decide on the best route. ◀

131b Listen and check. Did Catherine choose the same route as you?

c What other route could she have chosen? Why do you think she chose the route she did?

131c Listen and check.

d Plan and give directions for a journey in your own country.

132 *Language study*

a actually, only, immediately, eventually

Use these words to complete the four sentences below.

1 *And the B6279 _____ runs into the B6278.*
2 *The 6278 _____ comes in from the left and you're coming down from the right.*
3 *When you say left in Eggleston, is there _____ one road?*
4 *I want you to turn left and then _____ right onto the B6282.*

b Instructions

132b Match these parts of sentences to give instructions.

I want you to	*go straight across there.*
You just	*come to a little village.*
I want you to	*a little town.*
You come to	*head north on the B6274.*
You should immediately	*turn left in Eggleston.*

133 What's it like?

Look at the map of Middleton with your partner. Do you think it's flat or hilly? Nice scenery or industrial? What do you think it looks like? Write down five things about it.

Compare your list with another pair.

▶ Tell the class what you have written. ◀

133 Did you get the same as Stephen?

67

134 How does it compare?

How does Middleton compare with Barnard Castle?

> BARNARD CASTLE 5,016 Co.Durham Map40NZ01 EcThu Md Wed/alt Tue Alston 32 Brough 18 London 244 Middlesbrough 31 Newcastle upon Tyne 45 Scotch Corner 5 **King's Head 12/14 Market Pl Tel Teesdale (0833) 38365 rm20 bath no dogs 25P B&B(c)(d)

Write five sentences, three of which are true, and two of which are false. Read them to your partner.

What can you write about Middleton from this entry in the *AA Member's Handbook*?

> MIDDLETON-IN-TEESDALE 1,200 Co Durham Map 40NY92 EcWed Md cattle alt Tue Alston 22 Barnard Castle 10 Kendal 44 London 254
> **Teesdale Market Pl Tel Teesdale (0833) 40264 rm14 (7bath)P B&B(b)

135 *Grammar*

Cause, purpose, time, condition

In the last four units we have looked at words, clauses and phrases expressing:

1 cause *There's no chance of a promotion there,* **so I'm going to move on.** (result)
2 purpose **We gave Jeremy a set of eight questions** *to look at.*
3 time *Before having the children* **she worked in insurance.**
4 condition *Provided you export what you have bought* **you can have the VAT amount refunded to you.**

Cause / result because ...	There's no chance of promotion there,
Purpose in order to ...	to look at
Condition if ...	Provided you export what you have bought
Time when / how long etc	Before having the children

Find more examples in the sentences on the right. Which of the coloured expressions belong in which part of the table?

a *The A688 goes through Staindrop and* then *at the end there's this road off to the right.* (133)
b *The 6279 fades out* at this stage *and the 6278 takes over.* (133)
c As long as you keep to the speed limit *you'll be all right.*
d *You can buy things VAT free* since you are not living in Britain.
e *There are lots of camping-sites around,* so it must be quite scenic. (134)
f In ten seconds or so *we were doing ninety.* (136)
g If I look up somewhere on a map to find out where I'm going, *I can work out what I'm supposed to be doing and so I don't worry about that. And* when I came here *I looked it up in the A–Z* before leaving home, and then I checked the map *in the underground station* when I got off, *and had no trouble at all.* (140)
h *He saw a man hitching a lift and,* remembering the days when he used to do the same, *he stopped.*
i Finally, after some time, *he told the writer he was in a skilled trade.* (136)
j *I heard a police siren.* It was so loud *it seemed to be right inside the car.*
k *The policeman raised his hand* to order them to stop.
l *The ratty-faced man was going to Epsom* for the races. (136)
m *Catherine couldn't sleep* for the pain in her shoulder.

The Hitch-hiker

a The story so far

Can you spot three mistakes?

The writer had just bought a new car – a smart grey BMW – and he was driving up to London on a nice summer day.

On the way he saw a man hitching a lift, and, remembering the days when he used to do the same, he stopped, asked the man where he was going, and offered him a lift.

The passenger was a 'small ratty-faced man'; he was wearing a greyish jacket and hat. He said he was going right through London to Epsom for the races, since it was Derby Day.

When the writer asked him why he went to the races he said he wasn't going to bet, he just went to watch the horses run. Then he just sat and said nothing until the writer asked him what work he did. Finally, after some time, he told the writer he was in a 'skilled trade' but he still didn't say what work it was.

They started talking about the car, and the passenger asked the writer if it would really go as fast as the manufacturers said it would in the adverts . . .

136b **b** Now read on . . .

c Without looking back, summarise what happened. Had you guessed?

136c Did Stephen and Catherine guess?

d What do you think will happen next? Will the driver stop, or will he drive on even faster? What would *you* have done in that situation?

> Tell the class, and make a list of other students' suggestions.

136d Did you say the same as Stephen and Catherine?

e If the policeman orders the driver to stop, what will he say to him?

> Make a list of what he might say and tell the class.

136e Compare your ideas with Stephen's and Catherine's.

PART 4

'GO ON! GET 'ER UP TO ONE-TWO-NINE'

"What can she do flat out?"

"One hundred and twenty-nine miles an hour," I told him.

"I'll bet she won't do it."

"I'll bet she will."

"All car makers is liars," he said. "You can buy any car you like and it'll never do what makers say it will in the ads."

"This one will."

"Open 'er up then and prove it," he said. "Go on, guv'nor, open 'er right up and let's see what she'll do."

There is a roundabout at Chalfont St Peter and immediately beyond it there's a long straight section of dual carriage-way. We came out of the roundabout on to the carriage-way and I pressed my foot hard down on the accelerator. The big car leaped forward as though she'd been stung. In ten seconds or so, we were doing ninety.

"Lovely!" he cried. "Beautiful! Keep goin'!"

I had the accelerator jammed right down against the floor and I held it there.

"One hundred!" he shouted . . . "A hundred and five! . . . A hundred and ten! . . . A hundred and fifteen! Go on! Don't slack off!"

I was in the outside lane and we flashed past several cars as though they were standing still – a green Mini, a big cream-coloured Citroën, a white Land-Rover, a huge truck with a container on the back, an orange-coloured Volkswagen Minibus . . .

"A hundred and twenty!" my passenger shouted, jumping up and down. "Go on! Go on! Get 'er up to one-two-nine!"

At that moment, I heard the scream of a police siren. It was so loud it seemed to be right inside the car, and then a policeman on a motor-cycle loomed up alongside us on the inside lane and went past us and raised a hand for us to stop.

"Oh, my sainted aunt!" I said. "That's torn it!"

L | beyond

?	prove	as though
	pressed	cried
	flashed	shouted

137 *Phrase-building* ··

Starting and ending a discussion or report

a Find the phrases from the box below which complete what Stephen and Catherine actually said.

a	. . . 'Can I see your licence?'
b	. . . came into his mind.
c	. . . 'Do you know what speed you were doing . . .?'
d	. . . ask to see the driver's licence.

SB: I think the first thing he will do is . . .
CM: Or I think the first thing he might say is . . .
CM: And then he might say . . .
CM: And anything else that . . .

What phrase started their discussion?

b Look at the sets of phrases and sentences in boxes A-D. Which sets do you think would come near the beginning, and which near the end of a discussion or report? Complete four phrases in C.

B	
We have	three main points in our report: . . .
We've got	two things to say: . . .
We thought of	three things: . . .

C	
The first thing	is . . .
	was . . .
	he'll do is . . .
	he did was . . .
	we want to say is . . .
	to do is . . .

A	
I don't think	there's anything else.
	there's anything else we wanted to say.
	we've missed anything out.
	there's anything else to add, is there?
I think	that's all. Okay?
	we've covered every point, haven't we?

D			
Is Was	there anything else to	say? add?	I think that was all. Oh – the point about the . . .
Have we covered	everything? most things?		I think so. I would have thought so.

138 Useful notices

Where might you see these? Make a list. Choose five of these places, and imagine a conversation you might have there.

e.g. Cashier: Do you have any change?
Customer: Hang on . . . I might have. Let me see.

SMALL ADS

In case of FIRE

CASHIER

NO REFUNDS WITHOUT RECEIPTS

ELECTRICAL GOODS

One piece of hand luggage only

ECONOMY TRAVEL

CUT PRICE OFFERS!

UK Passport Holders Only ➡

Next showing 8.30

← EEC Passports

CUSTOMS OFFICER

VAT REFUNDS

PAY HERE

BOX OFFICE

TRADITIONAL BRITISH FOOD

139 A Cockney song

Which of these words go best in the gaps?

> like/love
> think of/talk about
> a kind of/funny
> since/because

Maybe it's because I'm a Londoner

Maybe it's because I'm a Londoner, that I _____ London so.
Maybe it's because I'm a Londoner, that I _____ her wherever I go.
I get a _____ feeling inside me when I'm walking up and down,
That maybe it's _____ I'm a Londoner, that I love London town.

139 Listen and check.

Do you feel the same way about your town or city?

140 A good sense of direction

Do you have a good sense of direction, or do you get lost? What do you do if you lose your way? Have you ever been totally lost?
Tell each other.

140 What about Catherine and Stephen?

141 *Language study*

a   More words ending in -ly

Put these words in the first three sentences.

> fairly   totally   really   probably   utterly

1 *Well, it looks like a _____ small village at the foot of a valley. So it's _____ very scenic with Middleton Common behind it.* (133)
2 *Have I ever been lost? Well, not _____ and _____ lost.* (140)
3 *It sounds _____ weird, but in the middle of a city would look for the sun and follow that.* (140)

And these in the last four.

> usually (2) certainly   suddenly
> obviously probably

4 *But _____ there are landmarks and you _____ realise that . . . maybe you're heading the wrong way.* (140)
5 *He's _____ . . . a man, who is _____ well within the law.* (136)
6 *I _____ wouldn't have gone at 120 miles an hour.* (136)
7 *If there was a policeman beside me, telling me to pull over or flagging me down, I would _____ pull over.* (136)

b   ever

ever = at any time (no matter when . . .)

If you ever go to London, you could have a suit made at Moss Bros.
Do you ever shop in your local markets in your country?
Have you ever been totally lost?
A: *Have you ever had an accident?*
B: *No, touch wood, never.*

Where could you put the word **ever** in these sentences?

1 *Do you say 'Just a moment?'* (64)
2 *Have you been involved in an accident like one of these?* (106)

3 *When I was very young, if anybody asked me what I wanted to be I always said a doctor.* (64)
4 *You can save a lot of money if you go to London.*
5 *I don't think we'll be able to go.*
6 *When you were a child, did you stay away from school?*

In these two sentences **ever** means 'always'. Where does it go?

7 *My parents came to live in England and I've lived there since.*
8 *Children's stories often end: 'And they lived happily after.'*

71

a whatever, wherever, whenever, however

1 in place of what, where, when or how
You choose what/whatever you want.
You can go where/wherever you like.
We save money how/however we can.
I visit her when/whenever I can.

The **-ever** form is emphatic (it doesn't matter what/where/when/how).

With this meaning **whatever** is often followed by a noun.
A: *What would you cook?*
B: *Whatever vegetables happened to be in the fridge.*

2 introducing a separate clause meaning 'It doesn't matter what/who/when/how/where . . .'
She'll never agree, whatever you say.
You'll still be late, however you go.
Wherever they are, we'll never find them.
I think he's a fool, whoever he is.

3 when you are not sure who, where, when
They've just bought a new house or flat or whatever.
If she's still in Singapore . . . or wherever . . .
I'll be round about seven or whenever . . .

4 whatever is often used to emphasise a negative sentence or a sentence with the word any
There was no reason whatever for them to behave like that.
There is no time whatever for playing games.
You can ask about any subject whatever.

Which category do these sentences go in?

a *We had no time whatever to enjoy ourselves.*
b *You can, you know, bulk buy or whatever it is.*
c *Whatever you do, don't forget your ticket.*
d *Maybe it's because I'm a Londoner that I think of her wherever I go.*
e *I read whatever books I could find.*
f *You can't get a free ticket, whoever you are.*
g *The hitch-hiker was ready to accept a lift from whoever happened to be passing.*
h *We never managed to do anything, however hard we tried.*

b above, against, behind, below, beneath, beyond

Find five sentences where the words in red refer to place. What do you think the other sentences mean?

1 *Middleton is a few miles beyond Egglestone.*
2 *Just sign your name beneath mine.*
3 *You can't drive a car in Britain below the age of seventeen.*
4 *Is there anybody down below?*
5 *You can see Middleton in the valley, and the hills behind it.*
6 *They are behaving very strangely. I wonder what's behind it.*

c come

Look at these uses of the word **come**. In which sentences does **come** involve moving from one place to another? What does it mean in the other sentences?

He comes from Warrington.   *This came to 25p a mile.*
(not movement = was born/brought up in; his family lived there)   (not movement = works out at, the solution is)

1 *There are holes in the sky where the rain comes in.*
2 *We'll do the word 'mind' when we come to Unit 15.*
3 *Sorry you couldn't come to the airport.*
4 *What ambitions do you have? How far have they come true?*
5 *I try to come in a little bit ahead of most of the traffic.*
6 *We'll deal with that problem when it comes up.*
7 *So how come exactly the same tales have travelled halfway round the Western world?*
8 *The pilot and crew would come into the cabin to greet the passengers.*
9 *I had to wait for another train to come back again.*
10 *But if you know them, why not? If they come to mind.*
11 *The B6278 comes in from the left.*
12 *I don't think anything else came into his mind.*
13 *Can you guess what's going to come next?*

7 *It's on that shelf, above the dictionary.*
8 *I don't understand it – it's totally beyond me.*
9 *He was against the idea of driving through the town centre.*

Important words to remember (589 so far)					
against L	camp	fast	onto	step L	whichever
ahead L	castle	flash	press	totally	whoever
below L	challenge	guy	prove	towards L	within
beneath	continue	immediately L	respect	turning	
beside	cross	motor	shout	upon	
beyond L	distance	obvious	sing	whenever	
branch	eventually L	obviously L	spot	wherever	

Unit 11
I would have let his tyres down

GIVE WAY

NO TROLLEYS Fine up to £200

NO DOGS ALLOWED

The Police Force was founded in Britain by Robert Peel

143 The cops are coming!

Watch out! The cops are coming!

What's up!

The law! Quick! This way!

ROAD CLOSED

LOOK BOTH WAYS

One way

143a **a** **Cop** is a slang word for 'police'. How many words do you have meaning 'police' in your language? Do you hear these words a lot on TV? What image do they give of the police in each case? Do they all have exactly the same meaning?

b What image do you get of the police from popular television programmes?

c Look on this page and find three slang words in English, meaning police. Do you know how they originated?

d Would you like to be/have been a police officer?

No right turn ahead except buses

P ← Pay at machine Display ticket inside windscreen Every day 9am - 6pm

Maximum speed 20 REDUCE SPEED NOW

METROPOLITAN AREA POLICE STATION PLEASE REPORT TO THE OFFICER ON DUTY

WANTED

bobby: a policeman (*fr.* Robert Peel, the founder of the modern police force).

Dual carriageway ahead

DANGER KEEP CLEAR

Waiting limited to 10 minutes on Railway business only

No Parking Motorists failing to comply with parking restrictions on Railway property are liable to prosecution under Byelaw 25

9.30 BBC
Cagney and Lacey
The two first ladies of the New York Police Department. Starring **Sharon Gless** as Christine Cagney and **Tyne Daly** as Mary Beth Lacey

Traffic rules and regulations

e What are the speed limits in your country? What fines are you likely to get if you go over them and get caught?

f Look at the road signs and notices on this page. Can you explain what they mean?

Look, there's a bobby on the corner. Why don't you ask him?

COUNTY COURT

and I look forward to seeing you on the 5th as we discussed on the phone.

Yours sincerely,

Bobby

Robert Green

rozzer: a policeman (possibly *fr.* Romany *roozlo*, strong).

copper (cop): a policeman (*fr.* cop: to catch, arrest *ca.* 1700).

g Have you ever had a parking ticket? Or been in a vehicle that has been stopped for speeding? What happened?

h Do you know anyone who has been charged with a traffic offence and has had to go to court, or been fined, or lost his/her licence?

144 Cops or bobbies?

a Humour in uniform...

As a police officer in the Cotswold village of Broadway, I come across large numbers of tourists. On duty one day, I was approached by an American mother and her four-year-old son. She asked whether I would pose for a photograph with the boy and, in the interests of good public relations, I naturally agreed. As I took the child's hand, however, he looked distinctly apprehensive. Noticing this, his mother said, 'Now don't worry, son. This is not a real cop. This is an English bobby.'

Why do you think the child was worried?

? duty
approached
relations

144a Before you listen, guess which words will be stressed. Then listen and see how it is read.

b

Look carefully at the picture above. Imagine that just after this photo was taken, the man coming out of the shop discovered that his wallet was missing from his pocket.

Discuss what might have happened. Write down three ideas.

e.g. *He might have dropped it while visiting the village.*

145 What's your excuse?

What excuses might you make if you were stopped for speeding? Write down two that are not on the list below.

▶ Tell the class whose are the best. ◀

*I'm on my way to hospital where my _____ is seriously ill...
I didn't realise there was a speed limit on this road.
I have to post an urgent letter.
My house is on fire and I've got to get there fast.
My wife/sister/friend is having a baby.
I was just trying out the car to see if it would do 129 miles an hour like the manufacturers said.
I'm not used to this car and I didn't realise it was going so fast.*

? urgent
not used to
realise

146 *Preposition spot* ··········

over, into

*... there's one over there.
Like a lift into London, lady?* (75)
Place the pan over the lowest heat possible... (87)

Find four sentences that need **over** and four which need **into**.

a *... we spent _____ an hour there...*
b *I don't think anything else came _____ his mind.*
c *... telling me to pull _____.* (136)
d *That's 50 miles an hour _____ the limit!* (147)
e *... to convert mains electricity _____ microwaves.* (91)
f *Rushing _____, I muttered, 'May I?'* (93)
g *I once backed _____ my neighbour's car.* (106)
h *... and the B6279 eventually runs _____ the B6278.* (131)

Find phrases below which express a similar idea to one of the phrases in the box.

1 *It's a good book once you get into it.*
2 *They're both really into Yoga.*
3 *The company's being taken over by...*
4 *Go into the plans very carefully.*
5 *Their age doesn't come into it...*

like a lot / love	examine in detail
have started	has nothing to do with it
change ownership	normal

a Which of these pictures of policemen do you think is the most accurate?

PART 5

'THIS IS REAL TROUBLE...'

The policeman must have been doing about a hundred and thirty when he passed us, and he took plenty of time slowing down. Finally, he pulled into the side of the road and I pulled in behind him. "I didn't know police motor-cycles could go as fast as that," I said rather lamely.

"That one can," my passenger said. "It's the same make as yours. It's a B.M.W. R90S. Fastest bike on the road. That's what they're usin' nowadays."

The policeman got off his motor-cycle and leaned the machine sideways on to its prop stand. Then he took off his gloves and placed them carefully on the seat. He was in no hurry now. He had us where he wanted us and he knew it.

"This is real trouble," I said. "I don't like it one bit."

"Don't talk to 'im any more than is necessary, you understand," my companion said. "Just sit tight and keep mum."

Like an executioner approaching his victim, the policeman came strolling slowly towards us. He was a big meaty man with a belly, and his blue breeches were skin-tight around his enormous thighs. His goggles were pulled up on to the helmet, showing a smouldering red face with wide cheeks.

We sat there like guilty schoolboys, waiting for him to arrive.

"Watch out for this man," my passenger whispered. "'Ee looks mean as the devil."

The policeman came round to my open window and placed one meaty hand on the sill. "What's the hurry?" he said.

"No hurry, officer," I answered.

"Perhaps there's a woman in the back having a baby and you're rushing her to hospital? Is that it?"

"No, officer."

"Or perhaps your house is on fire and you're dashing home to rescue the family from upstairs?" His voice was dangerously soft and mocking.

"My house isn't on fire, officer."

"In that case," he said, "you've got yourself into a nasty mess, haven't you? Do you know what the speed limit is in this country?"

"Seventy," I said.

"And do you mind telling me exactly what speed you were doing just now?"

I shrugged and didn't say anything.

When he spoke next, he raised his voice so loud that I jumped. "*One hundred and twenty miles per hour!*" he barked. "That's *fifty* miles an hour over the limit!"

L	pull raise voice

?	stroll meaty guilty

147b **b** What sort of person is the policeman? Do you like his voice? Listen for the advice the hitch-hiker gave the driver.

Do you think the hitch-hiker's advice was good?
If you had been the driver, would you have stayed sitting in the car?

▶ Tell other groups how you would have handled the situation. ◀

147c **c** How many details did Stephen and Caroline remember about how the policeman looked?

d Is he the kind of policeman who might be very reasonable, and say 'Well, never mind' and let the driver off? Or is he likely to take him to court?

147e **e** See what Caroline and Stephen think about his character.

▶ Summarise this episode in three sentences. ◀

148 Wordpower

go/going

What about these? In your language do you use the word **go** in these situations? When does **go** mean to move from one place to another? When does it not?

I'm going to let his tyres down!

Ssssss!

(a) A: Wow! this price has gone up! We should go into this with the agent. B: Well, you don't expect prices to go down, do you?

(b) Who's that going by?

(c) Once you've started you must go through with it.

(d) But there are still two years to go!

(e) How are things going? How's it going?

The television's gone wrong!

(f) A few seconds went by, then he said....

(g) A: How did that story go? B: Shall I tell you? A: Yes. Go ahead!

(h) They went to sleep.

(i) She went out with her first boyfriend for years.

(j) Oh dear – the milk's gone off! It's so warm.

(k) She's going to University in October.

(l) I've really got to go now. Bye!

(m) A: I've gone off the idea. B: Yeah – I don't like it now, either.

149 Phrase-building

When speaking, we sometimes start explaining something like this:

| Well what | I
you
she | did
said
thought
told X
meant to do
should have done
should have said
could have done
would have done | was, ... |

Find some ways of introducing these phrases:

a ... *go to work by bus and save the petrol money.*
b ... *'Don't waste money on clothes.'*
c ... *took/take/taken the kids to school first, then ...*
d ... *'Come half an hour earlier.'*
e ... *get/got less money out of the bank.*
f ... *have lunch around 12, then ...*
g ... *you could borrow the car and drive to ...*

| Well, what I | normally do
always say
'm always telling her
think | is, ... |

Now think of some more examples like these.

Well, what I usually do is, have lunch around 12 ...
Well, what she should have done was, take less money out of the bank.

Parking problems

a

A plumber who had parked on a double yellow line placed a note reading 'Plumber working inside' under a windscreen wiper of his car. When he returned, he found a parking ticket under the other wiper with a note: 'Traffic Warden working outside.'

What should he have done in the circumstances?

b Read about this parking problem and discuss what you would have done in the circumstances.

A friend of ours had a garage that opened directly on to a side-street near a main road in the centre of town. One morning he found that someone had parked in front of his garage door so that he couldn't get his car out. He left a polite note explaining the situation, and went to work by bus. Next day the same car was parked in the same place. Our friend left a less polite note. The same thing happened the next day. This time our friend left a warning note. But next day exactly the same thing happened again.

What do you think our friend did?
What would you have done?

> Tell each other:
>
> what the police can do in such circumstances as these?
> what you would have done, if you had been the person blocked in?

 Did Stephen and Catherine have similar ideas to yours? What was Catherine going to say after 'Surely, surely not unless...'?
Make notes of the three things they each suggested.

L allowed	**?** surely legal legally

Do you have parking problems anywhere in your country? If so tell each other and try to suggest solutions.

> Write out a statement of the problems, and possible solutions.

Language study

would/could have

a Find the verb phrases with **have**. Do they refer to the past, present or future? Do they refer to something that actually happened?

b The phrases in colour have one meaning in common. What?

1 *What would you have done in that situation?* (136)
2 *'I would have stopped.'* (147)
3 *'If you had been the driver, would you have stayed sitting in the car?'* (147)
4 *'If it was me, I would have let his tyres down.'* (150)
5 *'I probably wouldn't have waited for four days.'* (150)
6 *'I would also have told the local police.'* (150)
7 *'He could have got the police to tow it away...'* (150)
8 *'I wouldn't have done any damage like smash the windscreen.'* (150)

9 *'I would have sought advice from some friend who could have given me the legal bits of it...'* (150)
10 *'Then I would have let the police know, and then, I think, had they not done anything, I would have...'* (150)
11 *He was going to let the tyres down, but he realised that then the car couldn't have moved.*
12 *'I probably wouldn't have gone at 120 miles per hour.'* (136)

What about these?

13 *The policeman must have been doing about a hundred and thirty.* (147)
14 *He must have eaten the plums and then gone out.* (95)
15 *She's late. I suppose she might have missed her train.*

152 The Hitch-hiker

a While reading, stop at a few points and discuss how the writer must be feeling.

PART 6
'ME? WHAT'VE I DONE WRONG?'

He turned his head and spat out a big gob of spit. It landed on the wing of my car and started sliding down over my beautiful blue paint. Then he turned back again and stared hard at my passenger. "And who are you?" he asked sharply.

"He's a hitch-hiker," I said. "I'm giving him a lift."

"I didn't ask you," he said. "I asked him."

"'Ave I done somethin' wrong?" my passenger asked. His voice was as soft and oily as haircream.

"That's more than likely," the policeman answered. "Anyway, you're a witness. I'll deal with you in a minute. Driving-licence," he snapped, holding out his hand.

I gave him my driving-licence.

He unbuttoned the left-hand breast-pocket of his tunic and brought out the dreaded book of tickets. Carefully, he copied the name and address from my licence. Then he gave it back to me. He strolled round to the front of the car and read the number from the number-plate and wrote that down as well. He filled in the date, the time and the details of my offence. Then he tore out the top copy of the ticket. But before handing it to me, he checked that all the information had come through clearly on his own carbon copy. Finally, he replaced the book in his tunic pocket and fastened the button.

"Now you," he said to my passenger, and he walked around to the other side of the car. From the other breast-pocket he produced a small black notebook. "Name?" he snapped.

"Michael Fish," my passenger said.

"Address?"

"Fourteen, Windsor Lane, Luton."

"Show me something to prove this is your real name and address," the policeman said.

My passenger fished in his pockets and came out with a driving-licence of his own. The policeman checked the name and address and handed it back to him. "What's your job?" he asked sharply.

"I'm an 'od carrier."

"A *what*?"

"An 'od carrier."

"Spell it."

"H-O-D C-A-..."

"That'll do. And what's a hod carrier, may I ask?"

"An 'od carrier, officer, is a person, 'oo carries the cement up the ladder to the bricklayer. And the 'od is what 'ee carries it in. It's got a long 'andle, and on the top you've got two bits of wood set at an angle..."

"All right, all right. Who's your employer?"

"Don't 'ave one. I'm unemployed."

The policeman wrote all this down in the black notebook. Then he returned the book to its pocket and did up the button.

"When I get back to the station I'm going to do a little checking up on you," he said to my passenger.

"Me? What've I done wrong?" the rat-faced man asked.

"I don't like your face, that's all," the policeman said. "And we just might have a picture of it somewhere in our files." He strolled round the car and returned to my window.

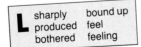

sharply   bound up
produced   feel
bothered   feeling

?

snapped
unbuttoned
replaced
wonder
strike

152b b Listen to the story being read. Try to remember everything the policeman did.

c Memory test!
What details did the policeman write down, and where did he write them? Then what did he do?

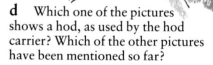

152c Which of the two, Caroline or Stephen, remembered best? Write notes of the details they remembered.

d Which one of the pictures shows a hod, as used by the hod carrier? Which of the other pictures have been mentioned so far?

e Do you think the passenger really is a hod carrier? Would that count as a 'skilled trade'?

152e See what Stephen and Caroline think.

▷ Summarise how you think the driver and the hitch-hiker are probably feeling. ◁

152f f What do Caroline and Stephen say about how the characters feel?

Choose five situations from a-h. What excuses could you use in these circumstances? Think of two or three for each one. Be as polite as is appropriate – you mustn't cause offence!

a *You forget an invitation to a friend's birthday party. They ring you the next day to ask why you didn't turn up.*
b *You arrive twenty minutes late for an important meeting because you got up too late.*
c *You turn up for a meeting on the wrong day.*
d *You do the wrong exercise for homework.*
e *You forget to do your homework.*
f *You don't want to accept an invitation (personal reasons)*
   a: *to a rather formal dinner.*
   b: *to a friendly dinner.*
g *Someone asks you to help them prepare food for a party. You don't really like the person concerned . . .*
h *You're asked – at the last minute – to attend an urgent meeting but you have something else (personal) planned, although it is in work time . . .*

In groups, decide on the best excuse for each circumstance.

Read these extracts from the transcript of 152c and notice where they stop (−), change their minds, and start again. Write down what you think they had been going to say.

SB: What details did the policeman write down, and where did he write them?
CM: He wrote down . . . – well, where he wrote them was in his, his notebook.
SB: But he wrote down . . . the passenger's name, address, occupation, and the fact that he's –
CM: occupation, and the fact that he's unemployed.
SB: in his notebook.
CM: Yes, and he's going to check them on his – when he gets back to the station.
SB: Yeah.
CM: Where did he put it – did – and he returned his notebook to his pocket and he did up the button didn't he?
SB: To his pocket. Yeah.

This is Peter's father. Peter's too ill to come to school today...

Ways of saying 'but . . .'

Can you match these parts?

a *This time our friend left a warning note.*
b *She asked whether I would pose for a photograph with the boy and I naturally agreed.*
c *We chose to go by plane because, although it was more expensive*
d *Coach services are frequent*
e *In a restaurant it would probably cost twice as much,*
f *People usually like mammals better than reptiles or insects.*
g *Despite losing their way there*

1 *Mind you, rats are mammals.*
2 *whereas Danny's meal would probably cost more to make at home.* (89)
3 *it meant we had more time.*
4 *though the travelling time is longer than by train.*
5 *As I took the child's hand, however, he looked distinctly apprehensive.* (144)
6 *But the next day exactly the same thing happened again.* (150)
7 *they still arrived on time.*

What about these?

a *I would have let his tyres down*
b *I am forced to appear as if writing you this note to apologise and to leave you my name and address.*
c *I enjoy living on my own*
d *'It's really true. This bloke told my sister.' Well, maybe, George.*
e *The weather was hot*
f *I have pink and blue shirts*
g *I won the next year*
h *In spite of the efforts to open the door*

1 *but not as much as I'd won the first year.* (23)
2 *As you can see, however, this I have not done.*
3 *My bet is it didn't happen to your sister's friend though.* (78)
4 *although I love to be with friends.* (20)
5 *not green.* (128)
6 *yet rainy and unpleasant.*
7 *but I probably wouldn't have waited four days.* (150)
8 *the fate of the passengers and crew was sealed.* (104)

How many ways are there of saying **but**?

a Odd one out

1 skilled worker, holidaymaker, officer, driver, passenger, builder, building site, employee, policeman
2 sunny, cool, cold, warm, hot, personal
3 enormous, fat, huge, large, big, dangerous
4 at top speed, fast, slowly, in a hurry, rush, quick, urgently

b Match the opposites

Check the words marked (L) in the Lexicon for their other meanings.

sharply (L)	safe
slowly	against the law
urgent	push (L)
pull (L)	tiny
enormous	warm
dangerous	softly, kindly
legal	not important
reasonable	fast/quickly
cool	relaxed
bothered	dropped (L)/lowered
raised (L)	placed carefully
threw carelessly	unreasonable

c Where might you see or hear these notices?

Only five standing passengers allowed.

DANGER

URGENT

PUSH

These seats are meant for elderly and handicapped.

Lifejacket under your seat

PULL

The driver is not allowed to talk to passengers.

Sorry, credit cards not accepted.

. . . found guilty of driving under the influence of alcohol.

£1 coins not accepted.

Smoking is not allowed during take-off or landing.

Speed limit 25 mph

Produced by Waver Products Ltd, G.B.

This machine accepts 5p, 10p, 20p, 50p coins.

Standard size 46p Large size 50p

Please produce passport or means of identification.

L allowed pull
push produced

d What word can fit all these gaps?

I would have _____ his tyres down.
He was going to _____ all the air out of his tyres.
Then I would have _____ the police know.
Do you think they'll get _____ off?
I just couldn't _____ you eat that pie.
_____'s turn the page.
_____'s find out who it is.
_____ him go .
Please would you _____ me go early today?
Did your parents _____ you stay out after midnight when you were just sixteen?

Saying: _____ *bygones be bygones.*
In which three sentences could you use the word 'allow to' to give the same meaning? Notice we say 'Allow X to . . .'

e Word forms

employ	employment	employee
employer	unemployed	unemployment

Which form fits where?

1 *The company used to provide _____ for over 200 workers.*
2 *They now _____ only 120, of whom 12 are new _____*
3 *So there are now 92 more people in the village _____, and looking for jobs.*
4 *Other local _____ are also cutting back on labour costs.*
5 *The official figures for _____ are rising daily.*

Important words to remember (656 so far)

accept	confident	finally	officer	replace	suspicious
allow L	cool	formal	official	rule	throw
approach	copy	guilty	overseas	return	ticket
block	count	influence	personal	safe	unemployed
bothered	countless	invite	polite	seat	urgent
bound L	damage	jump	produce L	sharp L	voice L
breast (pocket)	duty	lean	pull L	sink	wood
brick	employ	legal	raise L	site	
careful	excuse	licence	real	slowly	
careless	exercise	limit	realise	speed	
circumstances	fat	minor	reasonable	standard	
confidence	feelings L	offence	relations	surely	

Things for free, or almost free

MUSEUMS AND ART GALLERIES

157 Free – or almost

a Imagine you are in a big city on holiday. What can you do for free or almost free? Make a list.

b All the pictures here are of people and places in London. Compare your list with what you can do in London.

ENTERTAINMENT

RUPERT STREET THEATRE, Rupert Street, W1 (Oxford Circus tube). Tel 485 6224. A small theatre run by an actor's co-operative who just ask that you pay what you can afford. Comedy, avant-garde, musicals.

BUSKERS. Not strictly legal, but can still be found in many a tube station (Leicester Square, Piccadilly, South Kensington, Green Park and Bond Street) or street corner (Leicester Square, Shaftesbury Avenue). For organised street entertainment, Covent Garden Piazza is a must.

SPEAKER'S CORNER. Hyde Park W1, (Marble Arch tube). Since 1972, people have travelled from far and wide to give vent to their views on politics, the price of butter, religion, anything, and they're still doing it on Saturdays and Sunday afternoons.

GUILDHALL SCHOOL OF MUSIC AND DRAMA. Barbican EC2. Tel 628 2577. Recitals to the public lunchtimes and evenings. Call in at the main entrance in Silk Street for a free programme of events. Open: Mon–Fri 8–9, Sat 8–3.

TV SHOWS. Ever wondered how all that laughter gets in the can?* Yes, it's real live audiences and if you'd like to be part of one apply (well in advance) to the following addresses. Specify your preferred programmes, but you have to take what comes, usually comedy shows, game shows and sitcoms.

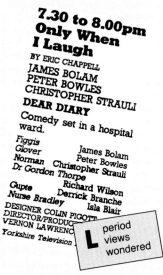

7.30 to 8.00pm Only When I Laugh
BY ERIC CHAPPELL
JAMES BOLAM
PETER BOWLES
CHRISTOPHER STRAULI
DEAR DIARY Comedy set in a hospital ward.
Figgis   James Bolam
Glover
Norman   Peter Bowles
Dr Gordon Thorpe Christopher Strauli
Gupte   Richard Wilson
Nurse Bradley Derrick Branche
              Isla Blair
DESIGNER COLIN PIGOTT
DIRECTOR/PRODUCER
VERNON LAWRENCE
Yorkshire Television

L period views wondered

Enclose an sae. Ticket Unit, BBC, Broadcasting House W1; Ticket Unit, Thames Television, 149 Tottenham Court Road W1 . . .

* on to the TV film recording (the film is kept in a 'can')

BRITISH MUSEUM. Great Russell Street WC1 (Russell Square or Tottenham Court Road tube). Tel: 635 1555. Mummies from Egypt and sculptures from Greece are but a few of the millions of treasures housed here. Details on noticeboard inside main door. Open: Mon–Sat 10–5, Sun 2.30–6.

TATE GALLERY. Millbank SW1 (Pimlico tube). Tel: 821 1313. Major collections of British paintings of all periods and an important collection of foreign sculpture, prints and printings. Open: Mon–Sat 10–5.50, Sun 2–5.50.

THE DESIGN CENTRE. 28 Haymarket SW1 (Piccadilly Circus tube). Tel 839 8000. The best of modern British design in fascinating and frequently changed exhibitions. Open: Mon, Tues 10–6, Wed–Sat 10–8, Sun 1–6.

THE TATE GALLERY
MODERN MASTERS
on permanent display

? in advance audience call in

c Which of these things do you like? Where might you choose to go?

theatre	play	paintings
art collections	zoo	concert hall
comedy show	art gallery	exhibition hall
design exhibition	music	fashion show
exhibitions	museum	animals

d Look at the words above. Choose the three things you like best.

157e **e** Which places and things did Stephen and Catherine suggest? Any of the same things as you thought of? Any of the places on this page? Make a neat list of their suggestions.

f Which of the things listed in section 157c are free or almost free in your country?

158 Language study

Feed the pigeons in Trafalgar Square.

Look at the transcript for section 157e.

a In the transcript which words or phrases come before **do it, sit, go to, walk around, see, eat, go to, get a, walk along, walk down, to walk, take a bus** (1–4 words)? How do these words affect the meaning?

b Look at the part of the transcript in square brackets [ ]. Who do the words **they, them** and **you** refer to?

c Which words follow the word **I**?

159 Free in your country?

a Choose a town that you know and think of how you might spend a day there without spending much money.

▶ Tell the class about it. ◀

Listen to the other groups and take notes.

> Write about your suggestion. Then choose two things the other groups told you about, and write descriptions of those, too. (Look at the way things are described on the first page of this unit.)

b Describe a picture
From memory, say a sentence describing one of the pictures in 157. Can someone in your class tell which picture it is?

c Plan a page of a brochure intended for one of these two audiences:

either fairly well-off tourists or businesspeople on expenses
or penniless students or hard-up travellers.

In groups produce a page of a colour brochure (similar to the first page of this unit) about a town or city other than London. Suggest three or four places or activities suitable for the audience you have chosen. Plan the page design carefully so that it will look attractive to your readers.

Decide exactly what pictures you would want, then write a description of each one so that an artist could draw it, or so that a picture researcher could find a photograph as close as possible to what you want.

160 Preposition spot

of

1 with quantity (to answer the question 'How many?' or 'How much?')
There's an awful lot of bad writers around. (121)
. . . a packet of cigarette papers . . . (167)
It's none of my business what you do. (121)

Can you think of some other words like **lot, packet** and **none** to complete these phrases?

. . . a _____ of people . . .
. . . a _____ of water . . .
. . . _____ of the people . . .

2 with part of a whole (to answer the question 'What part?')
. . . along the edge of the paper . . . (167)
. . . watching him out of the corner of one eye. (167)
. . . a small village at the foot of the valley.

Can you think of other words to complete these phrases?

. . . _____ of the story
. . . _____ of the page
. . . _____ of the day
. . . _____ of the garden

3 after some adjectives
Is it something you're ashamed of? (167)
I'm about as proud of it as anyone could be. (167)
We're all being very suspicious of him. (167)
You can always be sure of finding comfortable accommodation. (38)

Can you think of anything the driver and the hitch-hiker in *The Hitch-Hiker* might be ashamed / proud / suspicious / afraid / frightened / jealous of?

4 in phrases like these
. . . a sense of
. . . a result of
. . . in spite of
. . . a means/way of

Can you complete these sentences?

a *Do you _____ direction?* (140)
b *I haven't had to use Joe as _____ jumping queues.* (165)
c *From that moment, _____ the efforts to open the door, the fate of the passengers was sealed.* (104)

The Hitch-hiker

a Do you remember what the policeman did after he had stopped the writer for driving at 120 m.p.h. on the motorway?

What punishment or penalty do you think the driver will get? (Do you think he'll have to pay a fine? If so, how much? Will he lose his driving licence altogether? Or even go to prison?)

What might the police find out about the passenger from their files?

Tell each other what you think.

161a What did Stephen and Catherine think? The same as you?

161b **b** Read on and see how well you guessed.

> **L** you're in **serious** trouble
> into **position**
> out of **sight**
> You mustn't **believe** what he said . . .

c What lie was the driver talking about? Why do you think the hitch-hiker lied?

So what punishment do you think he will get?

What do you think he will say to his solicitor? Make a list of points he will probably include.

161c Did Catherine and Stephen think the same as you? Did they remember the hitch-hiker's name and address correctly?

> **?** I'm **positive**
> You **mean** prison?
> his **lips**
> behind the **bars**
> criminals who **break** the law
> **pleased** about that
> see you in **court**

Find the words or phrases from Words to look up and Words to guess which mean:

very sure or absolutely certain
happy
so they could no longer see him
very bad
in prison
it's not true

PART 7

'IN SERIOUS TROUBLE'

"I suppose you know you're in serious trouble," he said to me.

"Yes, officer."

"You won't be driving this fancy car of yours again for a very long time, not after *we've* finished with you. You won't be driving *any* car again come to that for several years. And a good thing, too. I hope they lock you up for a spell into the bargain."

"You mean prison?" I asked, alarmed.

"Absolutely," he said, smacking his lips. "In the clink. Behind the bars. Along with all the other criminals who break the law. *And* a hefty fine into the bargain. Nobody will be more pleased about that than me. I'll see you in court, both of you. You'll be getting a summons to appear."

He turned away and walked over to his motor-cycle. He flipped the prop stand back into position with his foot and swung his leg over the saddle. Then he kicked the starter and roared off up the road out of sight.

"Phew!" I gasped. "That's done it."

"We was caught," my passenger said. "We was caught good and proper."

"I was caught, you mean."

"That's right," he said. "What you goin' to do now, guv'nor?"

"I'm going straight up to London to talk to my solicitor," I said. I started the car and drove on.

"You mustn't believe what 'ee said to about goin' to prison," my passenger said. "They don't put nobody in the clink for just speedin'."

"Are you sure of that?" I asked.

"I'm positive," he answered. "They can take your licence away and they can give you a whoppin' big fine, but that'll be the end of it."

I felt tremendously relieved.

"By the way," I said, "why did you lie to him?"

> **Word study**
>
> Match the phrases in the left-hand column with the one in the right-hand column which has a similar meaning.
>
> 1 *come to that*   a *for a short time*
> 2 *into the bargain* b *if we are going to talk about that*
> 3 *for a spell*   c *in addition to everything else*
>
> Find three more phrases with 'for'.

162 Cheap accommodation in town

a What advice would you give to a stranger in your capital city about finding a reasonably priced room for the night?

What range of accommodation is there available in your capital city?

In groups decide which town or city to write about.

▶ Prepare a short report giving suitable advice both for a visiting student and for a reasonably well-off tourist.

Find out from others in your class what advice they have given.

b Compare the advice you gave with the advice given here about London. What kind of person is this advice aimed at?

c Find someone in your class who has stayed (or who knows someone else who has stayed) in one of these types of accommodation.

| a luxury hotel | a guest house |
| a cheap hotel | a hostel |

Find out what it was like.

Hotels in London are pretty pricey and you get what you pay for. Cheap hotels (£20 and under per night) are all too often not 'nice' places to be in at all. But if you have no choice, or are set on booking in, here are some general guidelines to follow:

* Book in advance.

* Ask the advice and opinions of friends who've stayed or lived in London. [ ]

THE LONDON TOURIST BOARD will provide invaluable information and advice, but only deal with enquiries by letter. Write to them at 26 Grosvenor Gardens SW1. They also give a free advance booking service.

* Be prepared to pay up to £40 a night.

* Remember, sharing a room brings the cost down, so plan your trip with a friend. [ ]

EMERGENCIES If you do find yourself in London with no place to stay, ring one of the following:

THE PICCADILLY ADVICE CENTRE on 930 0066 or the **HOUSING ADVICE SWITCHBOARD** on 434 2522 and they will put you in touch with a night shelter or ... [ ]

▶ When you have enough details, write a short critical report of it. Your last paragraph should give would-be travellers advice on whether or not to stay there. ◀

Show your report to the person you interviewed, and ask if it is a fair report.

Finally, read each other's reports. Take a vote on the two best and the two worst places to stay.

163 *Language study* ·····················

do, did etc

Find all the examples of **do, don't, does, doesn't, did** and **didn't**. All the extracts are from this unit.

Which ones can you miss out? Which ones can you shorten when you write or speak? Which ones would you need to say in full? Why?

a *If you do find yourself in London with no place to stay ...*
b *So, there's really quite a lot to do.*
c *But they can still do it for nothing or next-to-nothing!*
d *It doesn't cost that much to get a bus pass ...*
e *Well no ... I don't think people get sent to prison.*
f *Don't you get fined something like a pound an hour?*
g *'Phew!' I gasped. 'That's done it.'*
h *'By the way,' I said, 'why did you lie to him?'*
i *What job do you think he does?*
j *'So what do you do?' I asked him.*
k *Doesn't strike me really as a surgeon.*
l *'Do I look like a copper?' 'No,' he said. 'You don't.'*
m *'I don't really care one way or the other.' 'I think you do care,' he said.*
n *I didn't like the way he read my thoughts.*
o *Didn't he say that?*
p *'Well, what do you think?' he asked.*
q *Yes, that was how they did it.*
r *How do you think it ends?*

163 Now listen to a–r.

Babies can be useful ...

a Read this story about the couple and their baby, who was called Johnny. How do you think it ends? Write down two different endings. Show each other.

> A couple took their three-month-old son to the cinema with them. On the way in, the usher said they would have to leave if the baby cried. 'But we'll refund your money,' he added.
>
> After watching the film for half an hour, the husband turned to his wife. 'Well, what do you think?' he asked.
>
> 'It's the worst thing I've ever seen!'
>
> ....
> ....

164b **b** How do John and Monica think the story will end?

What does John say about his son Joe? Is he usually badly behaved?
What does John say about some relatives of his who travelled a lot with their two sons?

Listen carefully as they read the last line of the story. How does it end?

c Have you ever had an embarrassing or funny experience with a small child?

▶ Tell the class about it. Who had the most embarrassing or funniest experience? ◀

Language study

Useful words

a Can you find where the words and phrases below fit in John and Monica's conversation? Look up the words with (L) by them in the Lexicon.

around (L)	as a means (L) of
behaved (L)	poor
causing	shake / shook
enable (L)	as a source (L) of

JM: Er ... Yes, they can be useful _____ disruption, I suppose, babies.
MJ: Do you find?
JM: Well, erm, I haven't had to use Joe _____ jumping queues but I'm sure if I got Joe to be really, erm, badly _____ I could get him to sort of make people leave the room and, er, _____ me to get to the front of queues in waiting rooms I suppose. This is apparently what erm, some relatives of ours used to do all the time. They had two sons and they used to make them run _____ and they'd get boarded onto planes or onto boats more quickly because they were _____ so much fuss.
MJ: Gosh, yes. Let's have a look and see. '_____ little Johnny.' Yes. That was how they did it. They _____ him and he cried.
JM: Mhm.
MJ: _____ little Johnny.
JM: Yes. Right.

164b **b** Listen again and check.

Phrase-building

Say these phrases quickly.

The best film	I have ever seen ...
	I have seen this year ...
	I saw last year ...
	I saw as a child ...

One of the best / worst	films ...
	books ...
	stories ...
	journeys ...
	things ...

How many sentences can you make?

The worst	**film**		seen
The best	**meal**		had
The nicest	**book**		heard of
The silliest	**song**		been to
The longest	**food**	I've ever	read
The most interesting	**story**		eaten
The most expensive	**person**		heard
	journey		bought
	day out		met

is ...
is called ...
is about ...
was ...

167 The Hitch-hiker

a   Read on. Stop after a few lines (it says *Stop here*) and discuss what trade the hitch-hiker could be in.

c   Later, you will find that some words have been blacked out. Can you guess what the words were? Talk together and decide what words they could be, or what they might mean.

167d **d**   What words did Stephen and Catherine think went in the blanks?

e   Now what job do you think the hitch-hiker does? What jobs need skilled hands? Can you think of four? If you don't know the word, try to describe what the person actually does.

167e   Do you agree with Stephen and Catherine? Do you think the hitch-hiker was in a 'crooked' trade too? Or was he simply an unemployed hod-carrier on his way to the races?

167d 167e **f**   Listen carefully for the words from the list that Stephen and Catherine use, and try to catch the word or phrase that goes with them.

kind	disappeared
quite	altogether (L)
plain (L)	strike (L)
edge	not the point (L)
appeared	

Word study

Check all the possible meanings of the words marked (L) in the Lexicon. Which meaning do they have in the transcript?

What do these words and phrases have in common?

went	told him
asked	answered
cried	

---

g   Can you say what the hitch-hiker did so that someone else can act while listening to you?

h   In groups, rewrite the dialogue between the driver and the hitch-hiker so that both the hitch-hiker and the driver sound very educated.

167

PART 8

'IT WAS QUITE FANTASTIC'

"Who, me?" he said. "What makes you think I lied?"

"You told him you were an unemployed hod carrier. But you told *me* you were in a highly skilled trade."

"So I am," he said. "But it don't pay to tell everythin' to a copper."

"So what *do* you do?" I asked him.

"Ah," he said slyly. "That'd be tellin', wouldn't it?"

"Is it something you're ashamed of?"

"Ashamed?" he cried. "Me, ashamed of my job? I'm about as proud of it as anybody could be in the entire world!"

"Then why won't you tell me?"

Stop here   167b **b**   Discuss what trade he could be in. Do you agree with what Stephen thinks? Could the hitch-hiker be proud of a job that is illegal? Do you think that's why he wouldn't be willing to tell the police about it?

"You writers really is nosey parkers, aren't you?" he said. "And you ain't goin' to be 'appy, I don't think, until you've found out exactly what the answer is?"

"I don't really care one way or the other," I told him, lying.

He gave me a crafty little ratty look out of the sides of his eyes. "I think you do care," he said. "I can see it on your face that you think I'm in some kind of a very ███████ trade and you're just achin' to know what it is."

I didn't like the way he read my thoughts. I kept quiet and stared at the road ahead.

"You'd be right, too," he went on. "I *am* in a very ███████ trade. I'm in the ███████ ███████ trade of 'em all."

I waited for him to go on.

"That's why I 'as to be extra careful 'oo I'm talkin' to, you see. 'Ow am I to know, for instance, you're not another ███████ in plain clothes?"

"Do I look like a ███████?"

"No," he said. "You don't. And you ain't. Any fool could tell that."

He took from his pocket a tin of tobacco and a packet of cigarette papers and started to ███████ a cigarette. I was watching him out of the corner of one eye, and the speed with which he performed this rather difficult operation was incredible. The cigarette was rolled and ready in about five seconds. He ran his tongue along the edge of the paper, stuck it down and ███████ the cigarette between his lips. Then, as if from nowhere, a lighter appeared in his hand. The lighter flamed. The cigarette was lit. The lighter ███████. It was altogether a ███████ performance.

"I've never seen anyone roll a cigarette as fast as that," I said.

"Ah," he said, taking a deep suck of smoke. "So you noticed."

"Of course I noticed. It was quite fantastic."

He sat back and smiled. It pleased him very much that I had noticed how quickly he could roll a cigarette.

i   What kinds of dialects do you have in your country? Try to describe some of the features of one of them to the class.

e.g. *They don't say the -ing on the ends of words properly. They tend to drop their Hs at the beginning of words. Some people from London say a V sound instead of a TH sound.*

Wordpower

break

Think of three things that break easily.
Have you broken anything recently?
What time do you normally have a break?

The *Collins COBUILD English Language Dictionary* defines **break**'s first meaning like this.

break/ / breaks, breaking, broke, broken
1 When an object breaks, or when you break it, it splits into pieces as a result of an accident, for example because you have dropped it or hit it too hard. EG *He has broken a window with a ball ... She stepped backwards onto a coffee cup and saucer, which broke into several pieces ...*

What do you think is meant by **break** in these examples?

(a) She comes from a broken home.

(b) He's broken up with his girlfriend.

(c) She broke down and cried.

(d) When does your school break up for the summer?

(e) War broke out in Europe in 1914.

(f) The house next door was broken into and everything of value was taken.

(g) I'm sorry, I can't come out. I'm broke.

(h) An outbreak of...
   (Is this likely to be good or bad?)

(i) He broke out of prison in broad daylight.

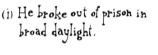

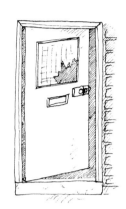

Now look up **break** in the Lexicon and read the examples there. Some come from this book and some from the *Collins COBUILD English Language Dictionary*. Did you guess the meanings?

Grammar

Descriptions

See how these descriptive sentences are made up.

It was a pale blue car with electrically operated windows and dark blue seats made of leather.

The car was pale blue.
It had windows.
The windows were electrically operated.
It had dark blue seats.
The seats were made of leather.

Can you make up one long descriptive sentence from these short sentences?

1 *John is a teacher.*
   He teaches English.
   He teaches at a Catholic school.
   The school is in London.

2 *I was born in Warrington.*
   Warrington is in Lancashire.
   Warrington is a small town.
   It is an industrial town.
   It is in the north of England.

How many ways of describing can you find in your sentences?

Ahead of me I saw a small, ratty-faced man in a greyish jacket, who was thumbing a lift.

Ahead of me I saw a man.
He was small.
He was ratty-faced.
He was wearing a greyish jacket.
He was thumbing a lift.

3 *The Hovercraft is a vehicle.*
   It is able to travel across land.
   It is able to travel across water.
   It travels on a cushion of air.

4 *Rupert Street Theatre is small.*
   It is run by an actors' cooperative.
   They just ask that you pay what you can afford.

a down (and opposites)

In which sentences can you use one of these phrases, instead of the phrase with **down**, to make it mean the OPPOSITE?

push . . . up	been repaired
pick . . . up	up
speeding up	put some air into . . .
	makes it more expensive

. . . she put the menu down.
Has your bus or car ever broken down on a motorway?
. . . it helps them to keep down crime.
. . . I would have let his tyres down but . . .
He took plenty of time slowing down.
Sharing a room brings the cost down . . .
. . . they were already half way down the street.

b Ways of saying 'said', 'asked'

Which of these words could you put into each space?

added	wanted to know	asked
agreed	told me	explained
replied	wondered	answered
nodded	smiled	
pointed out	went on	

'Tomorrow's a good day for me. All right, then. I'll do it,' he _____.
'Difficult to tell her age. How old could she be?' he _____.
'Terrific! It must be because of the warm weather,' she _____.

c Getting/making/enabling people (to) do things

Which of these verbs must be followed by 'to' when it has this meaning?

If I got Joe to be really badly behaved . . .
I could get him to make people leave the room . . .
. . . and to enable me to get to the front of queues . . .
They had two sons and they used to make them run around . . .
Did your parents make you get home by midnight?

d give

Find phrases with **give** where it means 'say something', 'write', 'hand', 'stop', 'look at'. Which phrases are left over? What do they mean?

1 Staying in a B & B gives you the chance to make friends.
2 What advice did Danny give?
3 How many reasons did he give?
4 If you'll just give me a sheet of paper . . .
5 She should give up smoking.
6 The seasoning given here is for 1 egg.
7 You haven't given me any idea of how long this is.
8 He gave me a crafty little ratty look out of the sides of his eyes.
9 He gave me one of his sly little ratty smiles.
10 Give as many details as you can.
11 He gave the impression he was afraid of us.
12 Give it a kick!

e Lexicon words

Look up these words in the Lexicon and then find which sentence you could use them in, and what form of the word is appropriate. Use some words twice.

believe	operation	plain	serious	view
due	period	point	sight	

1 Listen, it's not funny – I'm quite _____ about this matter.
2 It's an important _____ and one which must be taken seriously.
3 That motorway accident was _____ to careless driving.
4 All in all he spent a _____ of five weeks in hospital after his _____.
5 If you take a tourist bus, you can see many of the _____ of London for free, and you get a good _____ if you go upstairs.
6 I like the man, – he's got a lot of good _____ , but I shall never agree with his _____ on politics.
7 I like _____ colours for carpets – not flowery designs .
8 She's 87? I don't _____ it! She only looks about 50.
9 Your local travel agent may be a good _____ of information.

Important words to remember (721 so far)

add	believe L	evidence	performance	religion	unit
addition	break L	exhibition	period L	religious	view
additional	care	feed	plain L	remarkable	visitor
advance	collection	file	pleased	serious L	willing
advice	comedy	film	politics	seriously	wonder L
altogether	court	frequently	poor	shake	
arts	disappear	lie	position L	sight L	
artist	due L	lip	positive	signal	
audience	edge	memory	prepare	smile	
bar	enable L	museum	pride	source L	
behave	encourage	operation L	prison	strike	
belief L	event	painting	programme	theatre	

How did you do that? I never saw you

171 Jokes and tricks

In Vienna, we lived next door to a young couple. One evening the wife, white as a sheet, called me over to her flat saying that it had been burgled. All the cupboards and drawers were open, with the contents scattered about the floor. She wanted to call the police, but I advised her first to inform her husband. And thus the case was solved: . . .

a Have you ever watched (or performed) any conjuring tricks? Describe some.

b Find some practical jokes on this page and say what you think is about to happen.

c Read the story about the room that's in a mess. What could have happened? How will the story end?

d Do you have a day like April Fool's Day?

e Do you know the answer to the question the Hodja is asked? What do you think he might say? What reason could he give?

f How could the trick with the banana have been done?

g Why did the Hodja give his friend the small pot?

h Do you know any card tricks? How are they done?

WATCH OUT, THERE'S A SPIDER ON YOUR BACK

EEK!

APRIL FOOL!

The Sun or the Moon

One day someone asked the Hodja which was more useful, the sun or the moon. The Hodja thought for a moment then answered '. . .

The Hodja and the Pots

One day the Hodja borrowed a big cooking pot from one of his friends. After a while he took it back to his friend's house and gave it back to his friend together with a small pot. 'Thank you very much,' said his friend. 'But what about this small pot? It doesn't belong to me.'
    'Oh, yes,' said the Hodja. 'When you lent me the big pot it was pregnant and the little pot is the baby, so it does belong to you.'
    'Well thank you very much,' said his friend and took both pots.

NOW SEE THIS MAGIC BANANA ALREADY IN FOUR PIECES FOR FOUR CHILDREN HERE!

172 # What was the trick?

a The Hodja's pots

Summarise what you think the Hodja will do next. Exchange ideas with your friends.

Rearrange these paragraphs to complete the story.

1 Excuse me, but could I have my big pot back?' he asked.

2 But after three weeks the Hodja had still not returned the big pot, so the friend went round to the Hodja's house.

3 Next day the Hodja asked if he could borrow the big pot again. Of course his friend agreed, hoping that he would get another small pot.

4 The Hodja shook his head sadly. 'But of course pots die,' he said. 'You believed me when I said your pot was pregnant, and if pots can get pregnant they can certainly die.'

5 'What do you mean?' said his friend. 'Pots don't die. I don't believe you. I want my pot back.'

6 'Oh dear,' said the Hodja. 'I'm afraid I have some very bad news for you. Your big pot is dead.'

L dead
die

b April Fool

172b John told Monica about a joke they played once, when he was at university. Which picture in section 171 illustrates this tale?

Can you complete this sentence of John's?

JM: . . . she said 'I didn't know _____ to sort of _____ through it like jumping out of a hoop, you know, _____ a hoop, or, erm, _____ to ignore it and just sort of calmly, erm, tear it _____.'

c The Magic Banana

Did you work out how the banana trick could be done?
If not, here are some clues to help you.

All you need is a needle and some relatively strong thread.
Choose a fairly ripe banana.
Thread the needle.
Carefully push . . .

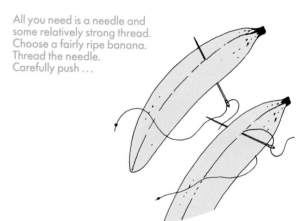

▶ Work out and write the rest of the instructions. Exchange ideas with the rest of the class.

d What had happened in Vienna? What guesses did you make? Were you right?

. . . her husband had dropped in briefly while she was out, to look for his driving licence.

173 ## *Language study* . . . .

had

a In each example below there are two or more things that happened. Which thing took place first?

1 *One evening the wife, white as a sheet, called me over to her flat saying that it had been burgled.*
2 *Her husband had dropped in briefly while she was out (before she got back), to look for his driving licence.*

Now what about these sentences from other units?

3 *The assistant sold more ice-cream in the interval than anyone had ever done before.* (55)
4 *And I won the next year but not as much as I'd won the first year.*
5 *. . . they arrived after the restaurants had shut.* (86)
6 *The pilot then discovered the cockpit door had locked itself and he'd mislaid the key.* (104)
7 *One morning he found that someone had parked in front of his garage door.* (150)

b In what ways are **had** or **'d** used in the story below?

173b

SB: Well, my girlfriend's very frightened of flying, and she had a bad experience. [Describes how plane engine caught fire.] And they had to take the plane back to Heathrow.
CM: Does that mean that nobody else had noticed?
SB: I think maybe the pilots had noticed, but certainly nobody else on board had noticed, [ ] so they drugged her up with [ ] valium for the next flight, by when she'd missed her connection in New York to Texas and so she had to go on . . .

a What kind of work did you think the hitch-hiker might do? Summarise the ideas you had after reading the last episode. See if you thought of any of the jobs the writer guesses at here.

b As you read, you will notice that some of the words in this episode have been blacked out. Discuss what meaning you think they have.

c Where did he get the belt from? What do *you* think?
Was it really the driver's belt?
Was there a bag or suitcase of clothes in the car that the hitch-hiker had managed to open?
Had the driver taken his belt off, before he'd picked up the hitch-hiker, so as to be more comfortable when driving?
Or what?

d What did you think the missing words meant? Write down as many ideas for each one as you can. Tell each other.

174d Listen to Stephen and Catherine. Did they mention any of the words you thought of?

174e **e** Listen and see how many words:
they managed to guess right
you managed to guess

Then compare the meanings. Find out which ones are too colloquial for you to use.

174f **f** Listen to the episode being read.

PART 9
'ANY *** CAN LEARN TO DO THAT!'

"You want to know what makes me able to do it?" he asked.
"Go on then."
"It's because I've got fantastic fingers. These fingers of mine," he said, holding up both hands high in front of him, "are quicker and cleverer than the fingers of the best piano player in the world!"
"Are you a piano player?"
"Don't be daft," he said. "Do I look like a piano player?"
I glanced at his fingers. They were so beautifully shaped, so slim and long and ▮▮▮▮▮▮, they didn't seem to belong to the rest of him at all. They looked more like the fingers of a brain surgeon or a watchmaker.
"My job," he went on, "is a hundred times more difficult than playin' the piano. Any ▮▮▮▮▮ can learn to do that. There's ▮▮▮▮▮▮▮ little kids learnin' to play the piano in almost any 'ouse you go into these days. That's right, ain't it?"
"More or less," I said.
"Of course it's right. But there's not one person in ten million can learn to do what I do. Not one in ten million! 'Ow about that?"
"Amazing," I said.
"You're darn right it's amazin'," he said.
"I think I know what you do," I said. "You do ▮▮▮▮▮▮ ▮▮▮▮▮▮. You're a ▮▮▮▮▮▮."
"Me?" he snorted. "A ▮▮▮▮▮▮? Can you picture me goin' round ▮▮▮▮▮▮ kids' parties makin' rabbits come out of top 'ats?"
"Then you're a card player. You get people into card games and you deal yourself ▮▮▮▮▮▮ hands."
"Me! A rotten ▮▮▮▮▮▮!" he cried. "That's a miserable ▮▮▮▮▮ if ever there was one."
"All right. I give up."
I was taking the car along slowly now, at no more than forty miles an hour, to make quite sure I wasn't stopped again. We had come on to the main London–Oxford road and were running down the hill toward Denham.
Suddenly, my passenger was holding up a black leather belt in his hand. "Ever seen this before?" he asked. The belt had a brass buckle of unusual design.
"Hey!" I said. "That's mine, isn't it? It *is* mine! Where did you get it?"

175 | Preposition spot

from

1 a starting point in time or space; the place or person where something or someone originates
So you come from Ireland . . .
Water from the river.
From 10 to 2p.m.

2 the idea of separation, leaving, being away or apart or removed from (in place or time)
My first job, straight from school.
The money was taken from her bag.
Some stores offer relief from VAT under the . . .

Look at these examples. Which phrases with **from** refer to a place? Which to a time? What do the others mean?

a *. . . fourteen miles from the centre of London.*
b *JM: You're Irish. CM: You've guessed from my accent!* (9)
c *. . . can't think of anywhere where it's different from here.* (117)
d *Track-suits from £24.99.*
e *I like green, I'm not too keen on yellow, but apart from that, red, blue, . . .* (128)
f *He copied the name and address from my licence.* (152)
g *. . . he was suspicious of him from the very beginning . . .* (152)
h *Huge collection of art, dating from 1300 to 1900.*
i *The police try to prevent people from breaking into houses.*
j *It isn't expensive – far from it . . .*
k *He caught a cold from walking home in the rain.*

176 | Survey

How safe is your property?

This is taken from the Community Pages of a Local Directory from an area just north of London, where many new roads have been built and where crime is on the increase.

THOMSON LOCAL DIRECTORY
COMMUNITY PAGES WITH AA MAPS AND Post Office POSTCODES
THE MAIN DIRECTORY
NAMES & NUMBERS AND INDEX
ISLINGTON-HARINGEY AREA
1987-88

Read the advice, then work in groups to copy and complete the questions on the questionnaire. (Don't write in any answers.)

Then give the questionnaire to another group to fill in.

Finally exchange questionnaires and read each other's. Which group seems to have the safest homes? Which was the best questionnaire?

Fight Crime and Protect your Home

Do you support a burglar? Your home could be a criminal's wages for the day. You don't have to be rich or own a lot of possessions to be worth a thief's attention, and we all have things of sentimental value, even if they are worth little or nothing in hard cash.

You should be able to answer "yes" to all the questions listed under General Precautions. If you can't, take immediate steps to put things right. And remember, when in doubt, ask at your police station for your Crime Prevention Officer. His advice is free.

GENERAL PRECAUTIONS

	YES	NO
1 Do you tell your newsagent when you're going to be . . . .?	☐	☐
2 Do you always lock the garage door when you . . . .?	☐	☐
3 When you're out for the evening, do you . . . .?	☐	☐
4 When you go out, ...?	☐	☐
5 If you go on holiday, do you ask . . . .?	☐	☐
6 Do you tell the police when . . . . . .?	☐	☐

YOUR PROPERTY

7 Have you photographed . . . .?	☐	☐
8 Have you made a note of the serial numbers of . . . .?	☐	☐
9 . . . your bicycle or car when you . . . .?	☐	☐
10 . . . .?	☐	☐

L protect
steps
support

?
crime
criminal
rich
hard cash
in doubt
crime prevention

Word study

Match words and phrases with similar meanings.

1 precautions	a if you're not sure
2 don't have to	b safety measures
3 when in doubt	c pay for someone's food, drink, clothes . . .
4 protect	d needn't
5 support	e not valuable
6 worth little	f make it safe

177 | If you lost your . . .

a If you lost your purse or wallet could you describe it?

Think of something that you have with you today. Describe it in great detail to your partner, so that they can write a good description of it.

REWARD
ANSWERS TO NAME PRINCE
POST CARD
LOST
A black leather wallet
High St Area
REWARD OFFERED TEL 62910
POST CARD
WANTED

b Decide what a good description should generally contain. Add two more things to those below to make a list.

the material it is made of

size or measurements

177c **c** How well does Caroline describe her purse?

What information does she give that is not relevant?

a Which are these likely to be – true or false?

1 *The crime rate is generally on the increase.*
2 *It cannot happen to me – my house is secure enough.*
3 *It's up to the police to improve matters; it's not my affair.*
4 *A thief needs only two or three minutes to break in, take what he wants, and leave your house again.*
5 *Most burglaries are carefully planned.*
6 *Crime prevention concerns everyone.*

Now read the text below and discuss which of the above statements are true and which are not.
Which point from above sums up the message of the text best?

> Whether we like it or not, the fact is that the crime rate is going up in almost all areas. The Police are doing their part to keep it down – but there is more that can be done to assist them – BY US ALL.
>
> It is negative to take the attitude that "It cannot happen to me" or "It is not my affair".
>
> It is important to realise that most robberies, especially in homes, are opportunist and take place in a few minutes.

Close and lock ALL windows and doors.
Make certain that your home is really secure, cancel milk and newspapers.
Take care with your handbag and luggage.

Which of these do not apply?

b Speed reading

Read the list below through, once, quickly, and try and remember any points which were not covered in your version of the questionnaire in section 176.

Check with your partner.

Read for a second time and take note only of the advice that you hadn't thought of previously.

> *Please take note of these points:*
>
> 1 Make certain that your home is really secure, even when you are only away for a short period. Close and lock ALL windows and doors. Get proper locks. Secure all outbuildings.
>
> 2 Tell the Police, milkman, newsvendor and neighbours when you will be on holiday and cancel milk and newspapers.
>
> 3 Keep your garage door closed and locked and secure any ladders.
>
> 4 Do ALWAYS lock your car, or other vehicle, and hide valuable items or goods in the boot. Ensure that nothing is visible.
>
> 5 Take care with your handbag and luggage.
>
> 6 Take all precautions when answering the door. DO NOT allow strangers into your home without proper authority. If you are in any doubt, inform the Police.
>
> 7 Make certain you do not part with any cash for goods delivered to your house without being absolutely certain you are getting what you pay for.
>
> 8 Report to the Police any questionable telephone calls.
>
> 9 Contact the Police when you see or hear anything suspicious. Dial 999.
>
> 10 Contact the Crime Prevention Officer at your local Police Station for any free Crime Prevention advice you think you might need.
>
> *Written with the assistance of Police Crime Prevention Officers.*

?
attitude
make certain
proper locks
proper authority
part with . . .
valuable
visible
questionable

Word study
Find five phrases with the word take on this page.

c Monica and her husband Kas had two break-ins, one after another, and also one attempted burglary.

178c Listen and find the answers to the questions.

	1st	2nd	Attempted
What was stolen?			
Were they in the house at the time?			
What time did it happen?			
Who phoned the police?			
What damage was done?			
Did they catch the burglars?			
Did they know who did it?			

Have your family or any friends of yours ever had anything stolen? Find someone in your class who has, and ask them questions about it, so you can write a report about what happened. What should they have done to prevent such a thing happening?

179 **The Hitch-hiker**

a If the hitch-hiker had got the driver's belt, what other things might he have got, and how? Think of four things.

179a What things do you think Stephen and Catherine will say? Guess, and then listen.

179b **b** Had you guessed correctly? What things had he taken? Does he give a reason for doing this? Now listen to the episode being read.

179c **c** 'The question is, why's he doing this?' Listen and fill in the blanks.

to _____ the other guy.
to _____ him what he can do.
to answer his _____ about what sort of job he does.
Well, he's a _____.

L reached

?	nodded
	impossible
	around here
grinned	trust
gently	glad

Word study

Match the colloquial words in the column on the left with their meanings in the column on the right.

catch on	good-quality thing
guy	steal
flog	man
nick	friend
pal	sell, give away
nice bit of stuff	realise, understand
get rid of	sell

PART 10

'NICE BIT OF STUFF, THIS'

1 He grinned and waved the belt gently from side to side. "Where d'you think I got it?" he said. "Off the top of your trousers, of course."

2 I reached down and felt for my belt. It was gone.

3 "You mean you took if off me while we've been driving along?" I asked, flabbergasted.

4 He nodded, watching me all the time with those little black ratty eyes.

5 "That's impossible," I said. "You'd have had to undo the buckle and slide the whole thing out through the loops all the way round. I'd have seen you doing it. And even if I hadn't seen you, I'd have felt it."

6 "Ah, but you didn't, did you?" he said, triumphant. He dropped the belt on his lap, and now all at once there was a brown shoelace dangling from his fingers. "And what about this, then?" he exclaimed, waving the shoelace.

7 "What about it?" I said.

8 "Anyone around 'ere missin' a shoelace?" he asked, grinning.

9 I glanced down at my shoes. The lace of one of them was missing. "Good grief!" I said. "How did you do that? I never saw you bending down."

10 "You never saw nothin'," he said proudly. "You never even saw me move an inch. And you know why?"

11 "Yes," I said. "Because you've got fantastic fingers."

12 "Exactly right!" he cried. "You catch on pretty quick, don't you?" He sat back and sucked away at his home-made cigarette, blowing the smoke out in a thin stream against the windshield. He knew he had impressed me greatly with those two tricks, and this made him very happy. "I don't want to be late," he said. "What time is it?"

13 "There's a clock in front of you," I told him.

14 "I don't trust car clocks," he said. "What does your watch say?"

15 I hitched up my sleeve to look at the watch on my wrist. It wasn't there. I looked at the man. He looked back at me, grinning.

16 "You've taken that, too," I said.

17 He held out his hand and there was my watch lying in his palm. "Nice bit of stuff, this," he said. "Superior quality. Eighteen-carat gold. Easy to flog, too. It's never any trouble gettin' rid of quality goods."

18 "I'd like it back, if you don't mind," I said rather huffily.

19 He placed the watch carefully on the leather tray in front of him. "I wouldn't nick anything from you, guv'nor," he said. "You're my pal. You're givin' me a lift."

20 "I'm glad to hear it," I said.

21 "All I'm doin' is answerin' your question," he went on. "You asked me what I did for a livin' and I'm showin' you."

180 *Language study*

a **Phrases with 'all/whole'**

Which meaning does each have? (Para. = paragraph)

1	*the whole thing* Para.5	a	suddenly
2	*all the way round* Para.5	b	the belt
3	*now all at once* Para.6	c	I'm simply...
4	*All I'm doin' is...* Para.21	d	right round

b **-ing**

There are 17 verbs ending in **-ing** in Part Ten. (But remember the hitch-hiker pronounces most of his ing- endings as **-in'**.) Can you find 12 and say exactly who or what they refer to? How many can you find with a comma (,) in front? (e.g. *He nodded, grinning.*)

Phrase-building ··············

Make up a sentence, then imagine a situation where you might need to say something similar, and think of what might come next.

'You never saw anything – you never even saw me move an inch...'

I	didn't see	anything	at all.
We	never saw	anyone	like it/that/him/her.
They	never heard	a thing	, not a single person/thing.

I	never even	saw/see	anyone	walk by/past...
We	didn't even	heard/hear	anybody	come in...
They	certainly didn't	noticed/notice		talking to...

They		realised that	somebody had come/opened/taken...	So...
We		remembered that	somebody was/had been waiting/standing...	
He	suddenly	noticed that		
She		saw that		
You		told me that		

How observant are you?

a What order were these photos taken in? Say why you think so. Close your books and see how much your partner noticed about the people in the picture.

b Imagine that you were one of the people in the picture. Close the book and say what you noticed happening around you just as the photo was taken.

c Write a description of what was happening around you just as the photo was taken.

Grammar ··············

Saying, thinking etc.

After verbs of *saying* and *thinking* we often have a report of what was said or thought. This is sometimes, but not often, introduced by the word **that**.

He'll say that the man encouraged him to do it. (161)
The policeman said (that) he was going to check on him. (152)
I think (that) I know what you do. (174)
I thought that the driver might have taken the challenge. (136)

There are many other verbs that work in the same way as **say** and **think**, e.g. **know, remembered, showed, found, realised, was sure**...

Read these sentences and find other verbs like these. How many sentences do not have **that**?

a *The Jumbo Jet pilot discovered the cockpit door had locked itself.* (104)
b *I expect you help to work the betting machines or something like that.* (114)
c *My husband ... tells me that the most dangerous time on a plane is take-off.* (104)
d *She suddenly saw that one of the engines was on fire.* (104)
e *This means ... that you can have the VAT amount refunded to you.* (126)
f *He finally told the writer he was in a skilled trade.* (121)
g *One morning he found that someone had parked in front of his garage door.* (150)
h *That doesn't mean he's not a hod carrier.* (152)
i *I would imagine that's one of the more menial jobs on a building site.* (152)
j *It is important to realise that most robberies ... take place in a few minutes.* (178)
k *Make certain that your home is really secure.* (178)
l *I was taking the car along slowly ... to make sure I wasn't stopped again.* (174)
m *He knew he had impressed me greatly with those two tricks.* (179).

a whether

Read on and see whether you guessed right.
He couldn't have known whether or not he was lying.
Whether we like it or not, the fact is that the crime rate is going up.

Put the word **whether** into these sentences:

She asked I would pose for a photograph with the boy.
There's always something going on in London, it's day or night.
I didn't know to sort of jump through it or to ignore it. (twice)
We never did get to find out the car could do 129 m.p.h.
I can't remember his jacket was black or dark blue.

b The passive

Notice the forms in the verb phrases.

. . . saying her flat had been burgled.
She didn't say whether anything of value had been taken.
Both times the video was stolen.
The dogs don't get burnt because they jump through the hoops so fast.
The banana was already cut into four pieces . . .
. . . taking the car along slowly, to make sure I wasn't stopped again.
Caroline didn't get paid for about four months.
Phone numbers of local police stations will be listed in the local press.

Now put these words and phrases into the right order to make sentences.

1 *We twice in the burgled last few months were*
2 *The were videos both rented*
3 *What order taken photographs were in the ?*
4 *got never thieves caught The*
5 *Listen to read the being episode*
6 *Have you burnt ever got cooking while a meal ?*

c Odd words out

1 grinned, nodded, laughed, joked, smiled
2 looked, glanced, stared, caught
3 in doubt, unsure, impossible, uncertain, doubtful, questionable
4 crowded, lonely, alone, on your own
5 burning, on fire, strong, hot
6 prevent, try, attempt
7 things, stuff, security, personal property, contents
8 valuable, gold, leather, plastic
9 fantastic, terrific, marvellous, terrible, great
10 glad, happy, pleased, shocked

d ????

The same word (but different forms of it) is missing from each sentence.

It is negative to _____ the attitude that 'It cannot happen to me.'
Please _____ note of these points.
_____ all precautions when answering the door.
Most burglaries _____ place in a few minutes.
Watching . . . and even _____ part in sport.
You must _____ a decision quickly.
I've sometimes _____ the wrong turning.
They broke the window and they came in and _____ the video.
It _____ me about twenty minutes I suppose to come in.
I was _____ the car along slowly now.

e Lexicon words

Look up the words below, and see which sentences they fit.

around	question	step	stuffed
burning	round	strong	support

1 *The first _____ is to look in the papers for job adverts.*
2 *Then go _____ all the job centres and ask.*
3 *No point in just sitting _____.*
4 *He was out of work, but still had to _____ his daughter.*
5 *She was very tall and easily _____ enough to do the job.*
6 *The _____ was, how did the fire start?*
7 *There was no-one _____ at the time.*
8 *It had been a _____ hot day, though.*
9 *She _____ the things quickly into the bag.*

Important words to remember (779 so far)					
affair	corridor	fool	locked	prevent	strong L
area	crime	gentle	marvellous	proper	stuff
around	criminal	gently	mess	property	support L
attempt	die	glad	moon	protect	tears
attitude	doubt	gold	negative	protect	thus
authority	doubtful	greatest	nod	questionable	trust
belong	elegant	ignore	possibility	relevant	undo
bend	ensure	impossible	possibly	round L	valuable
burn L	fantastic	lend	pregnant	security L	
contents	fight L	local	precaution	shock	

And he told me I was going to win

185 Do you believe it?

a Find the following things on this page:

some things that are supposed to be lucky
some things that are supposed to be unlucky
some things that you believe in
some things that you don't believe in

b How many ways of telling fortunes can you think of?

c What things are considered lucky or unlucky in your country?

d In Britain some people think it is unlucky to light three cigarettes from one match? Can you think why? Do you know the explanations for any other superstitions?

97

186 New Year's resolutions

a In most societies there are many traditions, beliefs and superstitions associated with the New Year. Often they are to do with making a new start. In many parts of Britain, for example, we welcome the first visitor of the new year as a bringer of good luck for the whole year. In some countries they clean out the house at the end of the year to sweep out the bad luck and make a fresh start. In many countries people make 'New Year's Resolutions' – they resolve to give up the bad habits of the old year and to do everything better in the future.

Here is a list of possible resolutions. See if you can choose one for yourself, one that would be good for another member of your family and one for a friend.

Give up smoking.	Answer letters promptly.
Go on a diet.	Get up early in the mornings.
Spend less money.	Try not to lose your temper.
Be tidier.	Drive more carefully.
Watch less television.	Try not to worry too much.

b Catherine wrote down three resolutions for herself and three for her husband.

For Peter (husband)
1) Be tidier – hang up clothes.
2) Be more assertive with the children.
3) Try to be more sociable.

Me
1) Be more relaxed.
2) Be stricter about keeping up with personal correspondence.
3) Find some occupation away from the home.

Stephen wrote down three for his flatmate.

1) Give up smoking. After all, it is making me unhealthy too.
2) Stop dieting. A 19 inch waist is small enough and malnutrition makes illness even more likely.
3) Stop worrying about the rent. We both get a monthly cheque from the university to pay for it.

And Caroline wrote three for a close friend.

1) Give up smoking
2) Have more self-confidence
3) Lose some weight

Look carefully at the resolutions above. Which of the four people:

is not very friendly?
needs to lose weight?
is slim, but wants to lose more weight?
is bad at answering letters?
is not strict enough with the children?
smokes too much?
worries too much?

The first visitor of the New Year in Scotland

c Monica thought of three resolutions for her husband, Kas. She told Caroline about the first two she made and her reasons for them.

MJ: Mm. Well, for Kas I've got, er, I will try not to –
CF: Who's Kas?
MJ: Kas is my husband.
CF: Right.
MJ: I will try not to finish everything at the eleventh hour. He always finishes everything at the absolute last minute. Like at the moment he's finishing off an MA thesis he's been doing for four years, and we're leaving the country, erm, Friday week, and he's in Cambridge at the moment, erm, reading through the, erm, the computer script for it. He still needs to get it corrected and bound and submitted. Erm, I will always reply to letters within two weeks of receiving them. In fact he never replies to letters at all normally. I have to reply to his letters.

Who is Monica actually talking about each time she says 'I...'? Herself or her husband Kas?

What were the first two resolutions?

186c Now listen to all three resolutions. What was the third one?

186d **d** Monica then gave three resolutions for herself.

▶ Write down as much as you can about Monica from this recording. ◀

e Close your books and see how much you can remember about the people who have made resolutions, or had resolutions made for them.

Preposition spot

out

1 away from the inside, or away from home or work
We decided to go out to eat at a small pub. (93)

2 extended away from its usual place
He held out his hand, and there was my watch lying in his palm. (174)

3 used to complete or intensify the meaning of a verb
We never did get to find out whether the car could do 129 miles an hour. (193)

4 together with a verb to produce a new meaning
Have you ever run out of petrol? (103)

What categories do these examples belong to?

a *We went out in a boat one day and saw seals and things.* (29)

b *You can work it out roughly from the information he gives on the tape.*

c *He stops and it turns out he's going right past her door.* (78)

d *She called over an air hostess and pointed this out . . .* (104)

e *The first shop assistant writes out the bill . . .* (117)

f *Fill out a form for it . . .* (117)

g *Watch out for this man.* (147)

h *Out jumped two policemen.*

---

188 Fortune-telling

a Read this account of Caroline having her fortune told.

Caroline had her fortune told in Delhi, in India. It cost her about 200 rupees, which she thought was very cheap. She was told that she would go back to India and that she would be married soon. She was also told that she would win £400,000 in a lottery. None of this came true, and Caroline realised that the fortune teller was a rogue when she met a friend in New Zealand who had been to Delhi and had been told exactly the same things.

188a Listen to Caroline talking about having her fortune told. This is what she actually said. There are three mistakes in the paragraph above. Can you find them?

JM: Have you ever erm . . . had your fortune told?
CF: Mm. Yes. In India.
JM: Oh yes.
CF: Mm. In Delhi. A very plausible rogue. Accosted me in the street and took me off to this little carpet shop. And he was so charming, as only Indian men can be.
JM: Mm.
CF: Erm. He persuaded me to part with – I can't remember how many rupees now. I think it was about 200, which is quite a lot of money. And then proceeded to tell me all sorts of wonderful things. He told me, by this time next year – this was last year, I think it was in June actually – I would be married.
JM: Are you?
CF: And back in India. No, no, no. And I liked the idea of being back in India very much. And he told me I was going to win forty thousand pounds in a lottery, and various other things.
JM: Did anything come true?
CF: Absolutely nothing. I then went back to the hotel and found a New Zealander who'd had the – exactly the same story.

b Do you know any stories concerned with fortune-telling? Talk in a group and try to find one case where a fortune came true and one where it didn't.

▷ Write down the best story and read it to the class. ◁

188c **c** Caroline also had her fortune read in the tea leaves. What was she told? Did it come true? What did John say about palm reading?

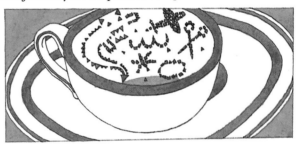

Look at this tea cup. Can you see any significant shapes in it? What do you think they might mean?

188d **d** Madame Wawanda

Mme. Wawanda tapped her crystal ball nervously and began to speak. 'You soon will meet a tall, handsome man who looks something like Mayor John Lindsay,' she told the young woman. 'He owns 94 producing oil wells, two square blocks in downtown Minneapolis, and a yacht with a crew of 34. He will marry you and you'll be happy forever after.'

'Sensational!' breathed her ecstatic customer. 'But tell me just one more thing: . . .'

Can you put these words in order to complete the story?

about   and   do   do   husband   I   kids   my   the three   what   ?

e What did different people (e.g. your teachers at school, your parents, your friends) say about your future when you were younger? What did *you* think you would do?

▷ Write some sentences about what people told you about your future. ◁

189 The Hitch-hiker

a Summarise the things the hitch-hiker has taken from the driver. What else might he have got? Now what do you think his trade is?

189a Make a list of the things Stephen and Catherine mention. How many of them are things that the hitch-hiker has already taken?

189b **b** How do you think the driver is feeling now? How would you be feeling in such a situation?

c The next episode is the final episode. How do you think the story will end? Think for a moment then tell each other any ideas you have. Can you think of two possible (alternative) endings?

PART 11
A FINGERSMITH

1   "What else have you got of mine?"
2   He smiled again, and now he started to take from the pocket of his jacket one thing after another that belonged to me – my driving-licence, a key-ring with four keys on it, some pound notes, a few coins, a letter from my publishers, my diary, a stubby old pencil, a cigarette-lighter, and last of all, a beautiful old sapphire ring with pearls around it belonging to my wife. I was taking the ring up to the jeweller in London because one of the pearls was missing.
3   "Now *there's* another lovely piece of goods," he said, turning the ring over in his fingers. "That's eighteenth century, if I'm not mistaken, from the reign of King George the Third."
4   "You're right," I said, impressed. "You're absolutely right."
5   He put the ring on the leather tray with the other items.
6   "So you're a pickpocket," I said.
7   "I don't like that word," he answered. "It's a coarse and vulgar word. Pickpockets is coarse and vulgar people who only do easy little amateur jobs. They lift money from blind old ladies."
8   "What do you call yourself, then?"
9   "Me? I'm a fingersmith. I'm a professional fingersmith." He spoke the words solemnly and proudly, as though he were telling me he was the President of the Royal College of Surgeons or the Archbishop of Canterbury.
10 "I've never heard that word before," I said. "Did you invent it?"
11 "Of course I didn't invent it," he replied. "It's the name given to them who's risen to the very top of the profession. You've 'eard of a goldsmith and a silversmith, for instance. They're experts with gold and silver. I'm an expert with my fingers, so I'm a fingersmith."
12 "It must be an interesting job."
13 "It's a marvellous job," he answered. "It's lovely."
14 "And that's why you go to the races?"
15 "Race meetings is easy meat," he said. "You just stand around after the race, watchin' for the lucky ones to queue up and draw their money. And when you see someone collectin' a big bundle of notes, you simply follows after 'im and 'elps yourself. But don't get me wrong, guv'nor. I never takes nothin' from a loser. Nor from poor people neither. I only go after them as can afford it, the winners and the rich."
16 "That's very thoughtful of you," I said. "How often do you get caught?"
17 "Caught?" he cried, disgusted. "*Me* get caught! It's only pickpockets get caught. Fingersmiths never. Listen, I could take the false teeth out of your mouth if I wanted to and you wouldn't even catch me!"
18 "I don't have false teeth," I said.
19 "I know you don't," he answered. "Otherwise I'd 'ave 'ad 'em out long ago!"
20 I believed him. Those long slim fingers of his seemed able to do anything.
21 We drove on for a while without talking.

190 *Language study*

What should the hitch-hiker have said? Correct the coloured words.

e.g: *Pickpockets is coarse and vulgar people.* (are)

1   *It's the name given to them who's risen to the top.*
2   *You simply follows after 'im and 'elps yourself.*
3   *I never takes nothin' from a loser.*
4   *I only go after them as can afford it.*
5   *It's only pickpockets ... get caught.*

191a

a

Ring, a ring o' roses,
A pocketful o' posies,
Hish-a, hish-a
All fall down.

This is the first song many English children learn. They play a game in which they hold hands in a circle and dance round, until the last line, when they all fall down – usually with lots of shouting and laughter.

Not many children know the origins of this song, and they might not play so happily if they did. It was first sung over three hundred years ago during the Great Plague, an epidemic which swept across Europe, killing millions of people. The first line:

Ring a ring o'roses

refers to the red circles on the skin. These first signs of the disease looked like rings of red roses. The second line:

A pocketful o' posies

refers to the fact that people carried pockets of flowers with them in the belief that these would protect them against the plague. But most people caught the disease and as it took hold they developed a sneezing cough:

Hish-a, hish-a.

And the last line, of course, describes how they all fall down – dead.

191b **b**

The big ship sailed on the Ally-Ally-O
The Ally-Ally-O, the Ally-Ally-O.
The big ship sailed on the Ally-Ally-O
On the last day of September.

The big ship sank to the bottom of the sea,
The bottom of the sea, the bottom of the sea.
The big ship sank to the bottom of the sea
On the last day of September.

This is another children's dancing song, and this too has special meaning. The Ally-O is the Atlantic Ocean. This song was first sung over seventy years ago. Can you think of a big ship that sank to the bottom of the Atlantic Ocean?

What songs did you sing as a child? Were there any which had unusual origins like the two above? Although *The Ally-Ally-O* has a cheery tune and is a children's dancing song it is about something quite tragic – a ship being sunk and all the people drowned. Did you have any cheery songs about sad events?

192 *Grammar*

Probability and possibility

Look at these 22 sentences. Can you find 6 where the speaker or writer feel sure of what they are saying?

How many ways can you find of expressing uncertainty?

What do sentences b, d, m, q, s and t have in common?

a A: *Who do you think is the healthiest?*
   B: *Certainly not me!*

b *I suppose she may have sneaked out while he wasn't looking.* (78)

c *Perhaps the writer got up early …* (95)

d *He must have eaten the plums and then gone out, leaving his wife asleep in bed.* (95)

e *Think of three things the driver might ask the hitch-hiker next.* (95)

f *Maybe he is a pickpocket.* (114)

g *Maybe the pilots had noticed, …*

h *… but certainly nobody else on board had noticed.* (104)

i *It's probably very scenic with Middleton behind it.* (133)

j *I would certainly pull over.* (136)

k *Perhaps there's a woman having a baby.* (147)

l *Perhaps your house is on fire and you're dashing home to rescue the family from upstairs.* (147)

m *He may have had experience as a hod carrier.* (152)

n *He could be a thief that's proud of his trade.* (167)

o *He'll probably get a fine and an endorsement on his licence.* (161)

p *The lie must be about being an 'od-carrier.* (161)

q *What else might he have got?* (189)

r *You're probably quite right.*

s *I wonder what could have happened.*

t *The policeman must have been doing 130.*

u *Maybe it's because I'm a Londoner, that I love London so.* (139)

The Hitch-hiker

a How do you think the driver is feeling now?

193b **b** Before you listen, choose three of the words and phrases that you think Stephen and Catherine might use to describe how the driver is feeling:

excited	sort of frightened
nervous	impressed
pleased	very angry
a bit of a fool	

c Compare the endings you thought of in section 189c. Which two do you think are the most likely?

193c Did you think of the same as Stephen and Catherine?

193d **d** Now listen to the story.

PART 12

'IT'S ALWAYS NICE TO BE APPRECIATED'

"That policeman's going to check up on you pretty thoroughly," I said. "Doesn't that worry you a bit?"

"Nobody's checkin' up on me, he said.

"Of course they are. He's got your name and address written down most carefully in his black book."

The man gave me another of his sly, ratty little smiles. "Ah," he said. "So 'ee 'as. But I'll bet 'ee ain't got it all written down in 'is memory as well. I've never know a copper yet with a decent memory. Some of 'em can't even remember their own names."

"What's memory got to do with it?" I asked. "It's written down in his book, isn't it?"

"Yes, guv'nor, it is. But the trouble is, 'ee's lost the book. 'Ee's lost both books, the one with my name in it *and* the one with yours."

In the long delicate fingers of his right hand, the man was holding up in triumph the two books he had taken from the policeman's pockets. "Easiest job I ever done," he announced proudly.

I nearly swerved the car into a milk-truck, I was so excited.

"That copper's got nothin' on either of us now," he said.

"You're a genius!" I cried.

"'Ee's got no names, no addresses, no car number, no nothin'," he said.

"You're brilliant!"

"I think you'd better pull in off this main road as soon as possible," he said. "Then we'd better build a little bonfire and burn these books."

"You're a fantastic fellow," I exclaimed.

"Thank you, guv'nor," he said. "It's always nice to be appreciated."

Language study ··

a ask

The writer asked him why he went to the races. (136)
The passenger asked the writer if it would really go as fast as the manufacturers said. (136)
We then asked him to find out as much as possible about Jenny's last holiday. (29)

Look at these sentences. What words like **to, why** and **if** come after **ask**?

1 *I suppose he could ask him what he was doing.* (97)
2 *The driver might ask him where he'd just come from.* (97)
3 *I think the first thing he will do is ask to see the driver's licence.* (136)
4 *Jenny then asked them how much it would cost to cook these things at home.* (89)
5 *She asked whether I would pose for a photograph with the boy.* (144)

b tell

You told me that it was you and the two children who went on holiday. (29)
She rings it up on the till, tells you how much it is, then takes your money. (117)

What words come after **tell**?

1 *If there was a policeman beside me, telling me to pull over, I would certainly pull over.* (136)
2 *I'm sure you told me where you stayed, but I can't for the life of me remember where.* (29)
3 *Phil Sutcliffe tells the stories – and tells us why we tell them too.* (78)
4 *She was told that she would go back to India.* (188)
5 *He told me I was going to win forty thousand pounds.* (188)

Wordpower ·······································

thing

1 replacing another word or phrase

She likes to eat sweet things.
Think of three things the driver might ask
the hitch-hiker next. (97)

2 referring to the situation in general or life in general

Hi! How are things with you?
Business is bad. Things don't look good.

3.1 introducing an idea that you want to develop

But tell me just one more thing: what do I
do about my husband and the three kids? (188)
I think the first thing he might say is 'Do
you know what speed you were doing?'
(136)

3.2 highlighting the importance or the important aspect of what you are saying

The thing is, he has a skilled job.
The silly thing is, the car was parked
at the time.

Look at these phrases using the word **thing**. Do they belong to category 1, 2 or 3?

(a) The news is bad today. Things are very worrying.
(b) We went out in a boat one day and saw seals and things. (29)
(c) Has any of these things ever happened to you? (103)
(d) The important thing is you must report the accident.
(e) Could you bring it first thing tomorrow?

(f) The awful thing is, I had totally forgotten her name.

(g) I'm afraid I've got no time. Things are very busy at present.

Phrase-building ···························

Here are some other words which are used in the same way as **thing** category 3 (see section 195).

a Make up five sentences and try to remember them.

b Now make up some similar sentences about things in your country.

The	fact point trouble problem	is	living in London is more expensive. transport's easy in Central London. it's difficult to park your car. shopping is such fun, you spend too much. you can find whatever you want.
The	question trouble problem	is	how to get home after 11 o'clock. where to park. what to eat and where.

a   ask, tell, know

Look at these sentences with **ask**, **tell** and **know**.

1 *He told him (that) he was a hod carrier.*
2 *He asked him why he was going to London.*
3 *The policeman told him to move over.*
4 *The driver knew (that) he was speeding.*
5 *He knew where he was going.*

The words below can be used in sentences like those above, as shown in brackets. For example **inform** can be used in sentences 1 and 2, but not 3, 4 or 5, **remember** can be used in 4 and 5, but not 1, 2 or 3.

Read the sentences above once or twice, but instead of the verbs in colour, try out some of the different verbs from below. Think about what your new sentences now mean.

inform (1, 2)	think (4)	know (4)
tell (1, 2, 3)	believe (4)	learn (4, 5)
ask (2, 3, 5)	mean (4)	remember (4, 5)
advise (3)	explain (4, 5)	notice (4, 5)
invite (3)	guess (4, 5)	say (4, 5)
order (3)	find (4, 5)	see (4, 5)
want (3)	hear (4, 5)	understand (4, 5)
agree (4)	imagine (4, 5)	wonder (5)

Complete these sentences. (Try using two different verbs in each.)

a *He stopped the car and _____ the hitch-hiker to get in.*
b *The driver _____ why the hitch-hiker was going to the races.*
c *The driver _____ his passenger that he was a writer.*
d *The driver _____ (that) he was a writer.*
e *The hitch-hiker _____ the writer what job he did.*
f *They _____ that the policeman was a dangerous looking man.*

b   He told me I was going to . . .

Caroline says:

He he told me I was going to win 40,000 pounds.
He told me by this time next year I would be married.

Which of these things did Madame Wawanda *not* tell her customer?

1 *Madame Wawanda told her she was going to meet a tall handsome man.*
2 *He would marry her.*
3 *They were going to have four children.*
4 *They would live happily forever after.*

c   after

1 later, during the period of time following the time or event mentioned
   She likes to eat sweet things after lunch.
   After my return home I wrote him a short letter every week.
   The day after tomorrow.

2 if you are after someone or something you want them or it for some reason
   I think the police are after him.

3 if you go after someone you follow them
   She ran after him as quickly as she could.

4 with a verb to make a new meaning
   Who's looking after the baby?

Which of the following sentences belong to which categories?

a *I only go after those who can afford it.*
b *Supposing they arrived after the restaurants had shut.*
c *He started to take out of his pocket one thing after another.*
d *She's a clever girl. She takes after her mother.*
e *He will marry you and you will be happy forever after.*
f *Give up smoking, after all, it is making me unhealthy too.*

d   Lexicon words

Use your Lexicon to say what the words and phrases in colour mean. In what sense are they used here?

1 *She is a dear friend of mine.*
2 *He has been picked for the Olympic Games.*
3 *That's all right as far as I am concerned.*
4 *I like to eat cakes, but they're very rich.*
5 *This one is cheap. The other is much dearer.*
6 *In fact the song is concerned with the Plague.*
7 *That glass holds just over a litre.*
8 *We are all very concerned about unemployment.*
9 *Newspapers seldom give all the facts.*
10 *Get hold of it!*
11 *The only way to get rich is by working for yourself.*
12 *Somehow he managed to pick the policeman's pocket.*
13 *This is a bargain I picked up in the sale.*
14 *The government ought to tax the rich more heavily.*

Important words to remember (830 so far)					
announce	cry	fortune	normal	relief	sweep
ball	dear L	habit	occupation	rent	temper
blind	diet	handsome	origin	resolution	washing
brilliant	dirty	impress	palm	resolve	weight
breath	ending	invent	persuade	rich L	welcome
breathe	expert	jacket	pick L	rise	worry
closely	false	leather	president	sail	
concern L	fellow	match	proud	somehow L	
correct	final	nervous	queue	strict	

198 **Talking and writing about people**

a Can you make these into one sentence?

Sir Robert Peel was born in 1788.
He was born in Bury.
Bury is in Lancashire.
Bury is a small industrial town in the north of England.

And these?

He was a politician.
He was famous
He is still well known.
The police force he created still exists today.

b Here are some notes about the author of *The Hitch-hiker*.

Roald Dahl, writer (short stories, e.g. *Kiss Kiss*; children's books, e.g. *Charlie and the Chocolate Factory*). B. 1916, Llandaff, South Wales, M. Patricia Neal, actress (3d., Is.). Lives Buckinghamshire, SE England.

▶ Write a short paragraph about Roald Dahl. ◀

c Study this picture carefully. How many things can you say about the people? Begin with a simple sentence and then add to it. For example:

The man on the left is wearing a brown jacket.
The man on the left in the brown jacket has fair hair.
The man on the left in a brown jacket with fair hair is reading a newspaper.

199 **Talking about places**

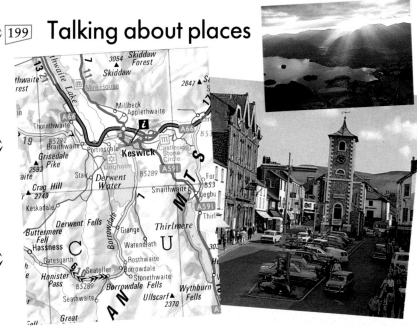

KESWICK 5,635 Cumbria (STD0596) Map 39NY22 EcWedMdSat
Carlisle 31, Kendal 30, London 304, Penrith 18, Windermere 22
***Derwentwater Portinscale (IH) Tel 72538 43rm (33 bath) 60P B&B(c)
***Keswick Station Road (THF) Tel 72020 C64 bath 50P B&B(e)

Here are some pictures and a map of Keswick, together with the entry from the *AA Member's Handbook*. Use this information to write a short description of the place.

▶ Write a short description of a place you know. Leave out the name and see if anyone else in the class can recognise the place. ◀

105

200 The Hitch-hiker

A dramatisation

Here is a brief dramatisation of the first three parts of the story. (See sections 97, 114 and 121.)

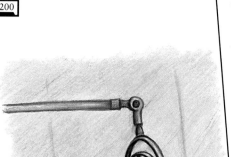

Driver (*to audience*):   I was driving up to London one day in my new BMW when I saw a man by the side of the road thumbing a lift. I always stop for hitch-hikers, because I used to do a lot of it myself, so I came to a stop and offered him a lift . . .

[Sound of a powerful car engine dying down as the car comes to a halt]

Hitch-hiker: Going to London, guv'nor?
Driver: Yes, jump in.
HH: Thanks.

○   [The car sets off again]

D: What part of London are you heading for?
HH: I'm goin' right through London. I'm goin' to Epsom for the races – the Derby.
D: Great. I love racing.
HH: I don't. It's a waste of time.
D: Why do you go then?
HH   Ah well . . . I just do.
D: I see, it's part of your job is it? Do you mind me asking what you do? I'm very curious, I'm afraid.
○   Perhaps it's because I'm a writer.
HH: You must be a good writer if you're drivin' round in a car like this. Writing's a skilled trade like mine. How fast will this car go anyway?
D: One hundred and twenty-nine miles an hour.
HH: I bet it won't. All car makers are liars. They always say they'll go faster than they really will. Go on. Open 'er up. I bet she won't do a hundred and twenty-nine.

Choose one other episode and write a dramatised version. Decide what sound effects you might need, and include them in the script in square brackets [ ].

201 Song

In English, people often talk about life in the same way as a journey.

. . . *as you go through life* . . .
. . . *when you reach the age of twenty* . . .
. . . *you meet a lot of troubles on the way*.
. . . *he is approaching middle age* . . .
etc.

Do you talk about life as a journey in your language?

This is an old music hall song that was first sung by a famous Scottish comedian, Harry Lauder, during the First World War. Harry Lauder was so popular that before he died he was knighted and became *Sir* Harry Lauder.

Keep right on to the end of the road

Every road through life is a long, long road,
Filled with joys and sorrows too,
As you journey on how your heart will yearn
For the things most dear to you,
With wealth and love 'tis so
But onward we must go

Keep right on to the end of the road,
Keep right on to the end.
Though the way be long let your heart be strong,
Keep right on round the bend.
Though you're tired and weary, still journey on
Till you come to your happy abode,
Where all you love and you're dreaming of
Will be there at the end of the road.

Telling stories and summarising

202a **a** In section 178 we heard Monica talking to Caroline about her two burglaries. This is a slightly different account of the same story. Listen carefully.

b Look at this summary. There are two mistakes in it. Can you spot them?

Monica told Caroline that her house had been burgled twice, once when she was living in Cambridge and once in Bristol. The first time the thieves got in by breaking a window while Monica and her husband were out. The second time the thieves got in by battering the door down. On each occasion a video was stolen. Monica found the second occasion more frightening because they were at home when it took place.

> Choose one of the transcripts you have studied. Write a summary of it which includes two mistakes. Give your summary to another group and see if they can spot the two mistakes.

203 *Wordpower* ·······························

mind

Your **mind** (noun) is:

1 where your thoughts are. People often use the word **mind** as if it is a box that thoughts come into or go out of. When something is 'in your mind', you are thinking about it. If you say 'Her name has gone right out of my mind' you mean that you have forgotten her name.

2 your ability to think, your intellectual ability

You have a good mind.

Anne's got a scientific mind.

He's now 82 and very absent minded. (= he forgets a lot)

Find the phrases with **mind** in these examples. Then find phrases in the boxes below each set which express similar meanings to the phrases.

a He went over it in his mind.
b The little talk took our minds off the awful things that were happening.
c That place just sticks in my mind.
d It was a weight off my mind.

> 1 thought about it carefully
> 2 I stopped worrying about it.
> 3 helped us forget
> 4 I can't forget

e Make your mind up! Which do you want?
f He's always changing his mind at the last minute.
g He must have read my mind.
h She's in two minds about it.
i It's a stupid plan. She must be out of her mind!

> 5 to be uncertain, unsure what to do
> 6 to make a decision, to decide one way or another
> 7 to be crazy
> 8 to change a decision, or make different plans
> 9 He knew what I was thinking.

What about **mind** as a verb?

204 How to do things

a Divide into A students and B students. A's look at the *X-ray vision* trick opposite. B's look at the *Magic birthday* trick on page 110. When you have practised these tricks you can try them out on each other.

Preparation

Take a telephone directory and memorise the tenth name on page 89. Have the directory with you when you do the trick.

X-ray vision *A students*

1 Tell your audience that you have X-ray vision.
2 Ask someone to think of a three figure number, for example 329.
3 Ask them to reverse the number and to subtract the smaller from the larger:
$$923 - 329 = 594$$
4 Ask if the resulting combination has three digits. If not ask them to put 0 in front of it. If, for example, they have thought of 322, then $322 - 223 = 99$, so they must put 099.
5 Ask them to reverse this number and add the two together:
or $$594 + 495 = 1089$$
$$099 + 990 = 1089$$
6 Pick up the telephone directory and stare at it saying 'I am trying to read the 10th name on page 89. Yes, yes . . . I think I have it. Yes, it's . . .

b Another magic banana

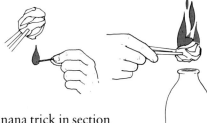

Do you remember the magic banana trick in section 171? Well here's another banana trick. The banana in section 171 cut itself into a number of pieces. The banana in this trick will peel itself. Try to work out from the pictures how to do the trick.

> When you have worked it out write numbered instructions for the trick.

> How do you think it works? Write a short explanation.

205 Stating your case

Say whether you agree or disagree with the following statements. If possible relate something from your own experience, or that of someone you know, which supports your opinion. For example:

You should always lock up carefully when you go out.
Monica left a window open and that's how someone got into her house and stole a video recorder.

a *You should always lock the house up carefully when you go out.*
b *Fines for parking in the wrong place ought to be much higher.*
c *Television programmes give a very bad impression of the police.*
d *Parents should be much stricter with their children.*
e *Men work harder than women.*
f *Tourist brochures often give the wrong impression of a place.*

Warnings and anecdotes

Personal security

a Prepare to discuss these questions.

1 What kind of areas are the most risky? Make a list.
2 Which people in this picture are most at risk? What ought they to do in order to lessen the risk of having a bag or money stolen?

3 Do you know anything about the methods that pickpockets use? Tell each other.
4 Have you ever been pickpocketed or had any money etc. stolen?

▷ Find another pair and compare notes and stories. ◁

What would you do if you saw a pickpocket or a shoplifter at work?

206b **b** Monica and Caroline exchange stories. Which of them came off worst? Who do you feel most sympathy with?
What should they have done to avoid this kind of misfortune?

206c **c** This is what one English magazine wrote for a teenage audience, the majority of whom may never have been to London. Read it quickly and say which advice Monica and Caroline ignored.

PREVENTION IS BETTER THAN CURE

Here are some general warnings

■ Never carry your purse in your back pocket or in an open handbag. High risk areas are at bus stops, in the crush in the underground and in crowded markets or shops, so be sure you know exactly where your purse is in any of these situations, and don't carry vast amounts of cash with you. Take enough to cover the day's needs plus an extra £5 to cover emergencies.

■ London, as capitals go, is relatively safe, but don't walk alone at night in lonely places like parks and commons.

LOSS OR THEFT

Report all losses or thefts to the police; this will validate your insurance claim should you later make one. Phone numbers of local police stations will be listed in the local press, or ring directory enquiries on 142 and ask for the nearest one to you. Don't ring 999 unless you were attacked at the time of the theft.

Watch out!

There's a thief about

If you see anything suspicious, dial 999

Lock it or lose it

Help fight crime... dial 999

If you see anything suspicious – call the police immediately.

---

207 *Grammar* ••

Possibility, probability and certainty

Which three of these words and phrases express *certainty*, and which express *uncertainty*?

I suppose	maybe
certainly	definitely
perhaps	probably
might (have)	may (have)
must (have)	could (have)

Which words fit where?

a _____ the writer got up early, leaving his wife sleeping in bed. (95)
b *Think of three things the driver* _____ *ask the hitch-hiker next.* (97)
c _____ *he is a pickpocket.* (114)
d _____ *the pilots had noticed, but certainly nobody else on board had noticed.* (104)

e *It's* _____ *very scenic with Middleton Moor behind it.* (133)
f *I would* _____ *pull over.* (136)
g _____ *there's a woman in the back having a baby.* (147)
h _____ *your house is on fire and you're dashing home to rescue the family from upstairs.* (147)
i *He* _____ *had experience as a hod carrier.* (152)
j *Discuss what trade he* _____ *be in.* (161)
k *He* _____ *be a thief that's proud of his trade.* (167)
l *He'll* _____ *get a fine and an endorsement on his licence.* (161)
m *The lie* _____ *be about being an 'od carrier.* (161)
n *I'll try not to worry about things that* _____ *never happen.* (186)
o *The policeman* _____ *have been doing 130.* (147)
p _____ *it's because I'm a Londoner, that I love London so.* (139)

Unit 15

208 How to do things

a Magic birthday

B students

1 Ask someone to think of the day of the month on which they were born. If they were born on the 17th September, for example, they will think of the number 17.
2 Ask them to multiply this number by 3.
$$17 \times 3 = 51$$
3 Ask them to multiply this number by 3.
$$51 \times 3 = 153$$
4 Ask them to add up the digits of this number.
$$1 + 5 + 3 = 9$$
5 Ask them if the answer is an odd number or an even number. If it is an even number ask them to divide it by 2. The answer at this stage is *always* 9.
6 Ask them to add this number to the date of their birthday and tell you the answer.
$$9 + 17 = 26$$
7 All you have to do now is take away 9 from the number you are given to find the person's birth date.
$$26 - 9 = 17$$

How do you think the trick works?

210 *Evaluation*

Have you enjoyed your English course? What have you learned that is particularly useful?

Write down ten questions which could be used in a questionnaire to give a student's evaluation of the course and also to find out what parts they enjoyed most, what they found boring, and so on.

209 Giving advice

How best to learn English

We asked some students from a language school in the south of England to give some advice to other students of English from abroad. Read what they wrote.
Which four pieces of advice do you think are the best?
Write a few sentences giving advice to other students from your country who are about to start an English course.

You should try to speak to British people as much as you can.
It's a good idea to have an English friend who you can spend a lot of time with.
Emiko Suzuki

Spend a holiday at a language school in England.
Have you tried getting an English pen-friend?
Listen to English or American radio.
Joachim Burbiel, Germany

If I were you, I'd read some English books.
Listen to English tapes.
Have you tried looking at a newspaper?
Live with an English family.
Go to an English language school.
Judith Lenz, Germany

If I were you, I'd go to England.
Find an English girlfriend.
Practice speaking English all the time.
Tong (Thailand)

Listen to English radio programmes.
Make friends with English people.
Chidori Asakawa, Japan

Read something written in English every day.
It is best to go to England.
Nasako Eder (Japan)

You shouldn't speak your own language in class.
Have an English boyfriend!
Harumi

Listen as much as possible to English on the radio or T.V. and practise listening and speaking it with native speakers or people like you who are also learning. Use it at every opportunity.
Munling Shields

Important words to remember (850)				
attack	dreadful	minus	practice	risk
being	exchange	multiply	practise	sympathy
brochure	lonely	occasion	preparation	warning
curious	method	plus	relatively	wealth

This 15-page *Lexicon* appendix contains information on selected words from the Level 2 syllabus. All the words featured here are marked 'L' in the *Wordlist* on pages 126–128.

These Lexicon entries are not necessarily comprehensive. They focus on the important meanings of a word. Most of the categories given in an entry include one or more examples, which illustrate the particular meaning that has been described. Many of the examples are drawn directly from the Student's Book material, and a cross-reference to the section where each occurs is given in brackets after the example.

Numbers after headings give the Student's Book Unit(s) where a Lexicon word is referred to or practised. Additional exercise material relating to the Lexicon is included in the *Practice Book* for Level 2.

about 1

1 If you talk or write **about** a particular thing, you talk or write on that subject. EG *Catherine wrote about John.* (2)
2 Characteristic of. EG *What I like about him is his sense of humour.* (4)
3 Approximately. EG *Parking for about 200 cars.* (7)
4 That's all, it's finished. EG *... that's about it.*
5 Referring to the future. EG *We're about to start the lesson.*
6 With some verbs: **bring about** means make happen; **go about** means start, do. EG *Excuse me – I'm not sure how to go about this!*
7 Around. EG *They sat about doing nothing.*

above 10

1 In a position that is higher and directly over something. EG *The sky above us.*
2 Earlier in a text or on a page. EG *Which of the pictures above do you think might be part of the story?*
3 Higher in rank. EG *He's a senior manager, above me.*
4 More than. EG *It cost above a hundred pounds.*

account 8

1 An **account** is a written or spoken report which gives you all the details of something that has happened.
EG *The police did not accept his account of the accident.*
1.1 When you say that something is the case **by all accounts**, you mean that everyone says that it is so.
2 **Accounts** are a detailed record of the money that a person or organisation receives and spends. EG *He had to submit accounts of his expenditure.* 2.1 If you have an **account** with a bank or a similar institution you leave money with them and ask for it when you need it. EG *How much is there in my account please?* 2.2 If you have an **account** with a shop you can buy goods there and pay for them at a later date. EG *Could you put it on my account please?*
3 If you say '**On no account** go home alone', you mean 'whatever you do do not go home alone'.

4 If you say 'He was not sent to jail **on account of** his youth', you mean 'because of his youth he was not sent to jail'.
5 **account for.** If you say you can **account for** something you mean you can explain it.

against 10

1 In opposition to. EG *In their first match against Manchester United ... Make a claim for damage against the other driver's insurance company.* (112) *I'd advise him against doing that.*
2 Referring to objects that may be touching each other or pressing each other. EG *... the water molecules in the food vibrating against each other.* (91) *I had the accelerator jammed right down against the floor and I held it there.* (136)
3 Used when expressing contrast or comparison, often with reference to a visual background. EG *You could see the trees against the sky ... If you go shopping, do you not particularly choose, say, a blue shirt against a pink shirt?* (128)

ahead 10

1 In front. EG *Up ahead I see the lights of the town.*
2 Leading. EG *Two people were ahead of us, and travelling fast.*
3 Winning, in the lead. EG *Liverpool were ahead by two goals.*
4 If someone goes on **ahead**, they go first and you follow. EG *The rest of the family went on ahead.*
5 In the future. EG *I see a lot of trouble ahead.*

allow, allowed 11

1 Permitted to do something. EG *You're not legally allowed to park.* (150)
2 To make something possible. EG *Railways allow quick travel from place to place.*
3 With time, space, distance etc. EG *I'm allowed a half hour break ...* (47) *Allow one centimetre between each line.*

among 7

1 When someone or something is **among** a group of people or things, they are in the middle of them. EG *We were occupying a small table in among many other tables.*
2 When something is **among** a group or collection of things, it is one of them, it is part of the group or collection. EG *I found a photograph of Peter among her things.*
3 If you say something is one example **among** others, you are saying that there are many other examples you could have mentioned. EG *Your father was, among other things, a very private person.*
4 If something is divided **among** two or more people, it is divided between them, usually so that they all have an equal share. EG *Half a chicken among four won't go very far.*
5 If you talk, argue etc **among** yourselves, you are talking together as a group. EG *They talked quietly among themselves at the far end of the room.*

apart 1

1 Separated, not together. EG *Their chairs were two metres apart ... He stood with his legs apart.*
2 Separated in time. EG *Our birthdays are just one month apart.*
3 **apart from** means except for. EG *Well, apart from English and American, which is similar, I can get by in French ....* (12)

appear 7

1 When you can see something for the first time, you say it has **appeared**. EG *Two men suddenly appeared at the top of the hill ... Then, as if from nowhere, a lighter appeared in his hand.* (167)
2 In a newspaper or magazine. EG *Here is a recipe for scrambled eggs which appeared in the teenager's section of a Sunday newspaper.* (87)
3 To be seen in public on stage or in a film or in court. EG *He has appeared in more than twenty films ... You will have to appear in court.*
4 To seem. EG *The baby appears to be hungry ... I am forced to appear as if writing you this note to apologise.* (112)

appearance 7

1 The **appearance** of someone or something in a place is their arrival, often sudden. EG *The sudden appearance of two men at the top of the hill ...*
2 An **appearance** on television, or in a play.
3 The way you look. EG *... a good appearance ... The two girls are very alike in appearance.*
4 To **put in an appearance** means to be somewhere for a short time. EG *I must put in an appearance at work.*

attention 5

1 If you give a subject or activity your **attention**, you look at it, listen to it, or think about it carefully. EG *He was finding it a strain to hold his students' attention ... Please pay attention!*
2 **Attention** to something is the act of dealing with it or caring for it. EG *The children are crying – they need my attention.*

back 2

1 In the opposite direction. EG *... he stepped back.*
2 To **go back** means to return to a place where you've been before. EG *Do you remember Ireland at all? Oh, I go back there every year ...* (9)
3 Used with words that describe positions. EG *Stand back from the edge ... The house is set back from the road ... She pushed her hair back from her face ... He sat back and smiled.* (167)
4 Used to say that something or someone is once again in the state or situation in which they were before. EG *He went back to sleep ... ... back to work ... You'll get the money back ... She put it back on the shelf ...*
5 Earlier in time. EG *... way back when I was a paperboy.* (46)
6 In reply (writing, telephoning, etc). EG *I shall call you back ...*
7 The part of your body which goes from your neck to your bottom. EG *We lay on our backs under the tree.*
8 Not the front. EG *... the back of her hand ... ... at the back of the book ... ... the back of the building ... The back door ... ... in the back of the police car.*

background 2

1 Personal details and experience. EG *The background of the person you talked to.*
2 The **background** to an important event or situation is the conditions behind it. EG *The economic background to the present political crisis ...*
3 The scenery behind an activity or object. EG *With the sea for a background, you can play golf ...* (35) *There were some lovely trees in the background.*

basic 4

1 Main or general. EG *... the basic problem is ... For my basic 40 hour week, I get £1.20 an hour.* (47)
2 Simple or essential. EG *... basic English ... ... basic food ... It's very basic ...*

basically 9

To show the most important feature or point. EG *... to tell the Willises about the holiday and basically to suggest that they pick them up.* (33)

behaviour 12

The way people or animals generally act. EG *... the behaviour of certain types of animal ... ... bad behaviour ...*

behind 10

1 At the back of, on the other side of. EG *The sun went behind a cloud.*
2 The events **behind** something are the cause of it. EG *Nobody knew what was behind his strange behaviour.*
3 The person **behind** something is the person responsible for it. EG *We know that there was a lot of trouble, but we don't know who was behind it.*

belief 12

The feeling that something is true. EG *... belief in God.*

believe 12

1 If you **believe** something is the case, you have that idea or opinion. EG *people used to believe the earth was flat.*
2 If you **believe** someone, you accept that they are telling the truth. EG *You mustn't believe what 'ee said to you about goin' to prison.* (161)
3 To think (if you are not completely sure). EG *Paris by train – I believe that's quite quick.* (6)
4 To show surprise. EG *I don't believe it!* (78)
5 **believe in.** EG *Fortune telling? Don't you believe in it?* (14)

below 10

1 In a lower position. EG *From the hills you can see the town below.*
2 Underneath. EG *The author's name was written below the title.*
3 In a text or on a page. EG *Look at the list of jobs below.* (43)
4 Less than. EG *The temperature was below zero.*

beyond 10

1 On the other side of, further than. EG *He pointed to the house and the street beyond it. . . . going beyond my destination.* (110)
2 Except for. EG *I'm very tired. Beyond that I have nothing to say.*
3 Later than. EG *Few children stay at school beyond 16.*
4 If you say something is **beyond** you, you mean you do not understand it or you cannot do it. EG *I'm afraid the mathematics is beyond me.*

bit 2

1 A small amount, piece or part (often of something larger); used mainly in informal spoken English. EG *I know a tiny bit of Italian . . . Would you like a bit of cake?*
2 To a small degree or extent; used mainly in informal spoken English. EG *. . . he looks a bit like Clive Sinclair. . . . looking a bit angry . . .*
3 For a short length of time. EG *. . . we stopped to walk for a bit.* (29)
4 To quite a large extent or degree. EG *. . . quite a bit of money . . . I have to reply to his letters. Well, that's a bit rough!*
5 Used with a negative, to mean 'not at all'. EG *You haven't changed a bit! . . . Are you hungry? Not a bit.*
6 A particular part, section or area. EG *The crowded bits of Spain.*
7 In computing, a **bit** is the smallest amount of information that is held in the computer's memory.
8 The past tense of the verb 'bite'. EG *. . . the dog bit her.*

board 3

1 A flat, thin, rectangular object made of wood, cardboard, plastic or similar material. **Boards** are made in a wide variety of sizes and can be used for many purposes. EG *Bread board . . . . . . the blackboard . . .*
1.1 **The board** is also used when referring to something which has 'board' as part of its name, for example 'diving board', 'notice board', 'blackboard'. EG *Look at the board, please.* 1.2 A **board game** is a game such as chess or ludo, which people play by moving small objects around on a board.
2 The **board** of a company or organisation is the group of people who control it and direct it. EG *The London Tourist Board . . . The Milk Marketing Board.*
3 If you **board** a train, ship or aircraft, you get on to it in order to travel somewhere. EG *. . . as you board the bus . . . I've already boarded this flight five times.* (34)
3.1 When you are **on board**, you are on or in a train, ship, or aircraft. 3.2 If you **take on board** an idea, knowledge, etc, you understand or accept it; an informal expression.
4 If you **board with** someone, you stay in their home for a period of time, usually in return for payment. EG *He boarded with an Italian family.* 4.1 **Board and lodging** is food and a place to sleep. (Full board – with all meals. Half board – with some meals.) 4.2 A **boarding school** is a school where some or all of the pupils live at the school during term time.
5 If you **board up** a door or window, you fasten boards over it so that it is covered.

bound 11

1 Sure to. EG *He's bound to come late.*
2 Obligation. EG *He's bound by law to pay the money.*
3 Concerned, worried. EG *The driver is so bound up with the fact that he's being booked for speeding.* (152)
4 To travel in the direction of. EG *He was bound for New York.*

break 12

1 When something **breaks** or when you **break** it, it splits into pieces. EG *They broke the window . . .* (184) *I've never broken any bones so far . . .* (18) *Break the eggs into the bowl.* (87)
2 If you **break** a law, you do something that is wrong. EG *Along with all the other criminals who break the law.* (161)
3 A **break** is a short period of time when you stop what you are doing in order to have a rest. EG *Wake me up for coffee break . . .* (55) *Mums get a good break from the kitchen . . . I'm taking a break.*
4 **break down.** EG *Has your car ever broken down on a motorway?*
5 **break in.** If someone **breaks in** or **breaks into** a building, they get into it by force. EG *My home has been broken into.*
6 **break into.** 'He broke into a run' means 'he started running'.
7 **break off** means to stop or put an end to. EG *I've broken off my engagement*
8 **break up. 8.1** If you **break up** with your girlfriend, boyfriend etc, your relationship with that person ends. EG *Tim and I broke up . . . Their marriage is breaking up.* **8.2** To put an end to something, to stop it. EG *The police broke up the fight.* **8.3** To finish school for the holidays.

bring 1

1 To come with something. EG *Bring your books with you . . . Be sure and bring a passport size colour photograph of yourself.* (82)
2 **bring up.** When you **bring up** a child, you look after it until it is grown up. EG *She brought up two children alone.*
3 **bring down** can mean reduce. EG *. . . brings the cost down.* (162)

burn 13

1 To be on fire. EG *The dogs jumped through burning hoops.* (171)
2 To set on fire, destroy. EG *We burnt all the papers.*
3 To injure (yourself). EG *I burnt myself while lighting the gas.*
4 To spoil food by cooking it too much. EG *It's a pity she burnt the cake.*

business 8

1 Work relating to the production, buying, or selling of goods or services. EG *He had made a lot of money in business.*
2 A **business** is a company or organisation that sells goods or services. EG *. . . someone whose office or business is in Central London.*
3 Work that you do as part of your job, often contrasted with pleasure. EG *Are you in London on business or pleasure?*
4 The **business** you are in is the field in which you work in order to make money. EG *My brother is in the travel business.*
5 Something that concerns you personally and that other people have no right to ask or advise you about. EG *It's none of my business what you do.* (121)
6 You describe a task, activity or event as a **business** when you find it difficult, annoying or boring. EG *It's a dreadful business.*

case 9

1 Used in phrases, meaning 'in X's situation', 'as far as X is concerned'. EG *Bed and Breakfast: In most cases it will be run by the owner ...* (39) *We asked a group of people to talk about their journeys to work. In Myf's case, this was difficult, because she didn't go out to work.* 1.1 As part of a phrase with the verb 'be' to show that something is true. EG *Is that still the case today?*
2 **In any case** can mean 'Anyway ...' and is often used to mark a closing point in a conversation, or a new stage in a story or meeting. EG *In any case, I should go now really. It's late ... Well, I don't know a thing about cars, in any case. Ask Rob – he might.*
3 **In case** is used to refer to the possibility of something happening. EG *Take your umbrella just in case it rains ... I've got some extra money in case we see something we want to buy.*
4 The **case** for or against a particular plan or idea. EG *Most people argue the case against using nuclear power.*
5 A **case** is also a person with a particular illness or problem, who is being treated by a doctor or social worker. EG *Who's dealing with her case? Dr Adams.*

choice 3

1 The one you want. EG *Which one did you choose, what was your choice?*
2 The things from among which you choose. EG *Inns, guesthouses and farmhouses provide a wide choice of accommodation.* (35)

choose 3

To decide which one you want. EG *Did Catherine choose the same route as you?* (131)

claim 8

1 If you **claim** something is true you are saying that it is true even if other people say that it is not true. EG *I have a friend who's a waitress who claims that she gets about $20 an hour.* (42) *I thought he was wrong but he claimed it was true.*
2 If you **claim** something, you are saying that it is yours and should be given to you. EG *Tell the shop you want to claim refund of VAT before making your purchase.* (126)
3 A **claim** is a statement that something is true. EG *I could not accept his claim.*
4 A **claim** is the right to have something. EG *I want to make a claim for a refund.*

class 6

1 Social grouping. EG *... a middle-class society ... He has an upper class background.*
2 A group of students who are taught together. EG *... students in your class.*
3 An indication of quality. EG *He travelled first class ... It's a top class restaurant ... As a tennis player, he's in a class of his own.*
4 To **class** someone means to categorise them. EG *At the age of 19, you're still classed as a teenager.*

clear, clearly 4

1 Easy to understand, free from confusion, and with all the details well explained and in a sensible order. EG *Excuse me, but I'm not clear about ... erm ... He explained it all very clearly.*
2 Obvious and evident. EG *It wasn't clear whether the meeting had begun or not ... Women are clearly underpaid in some jobs they do.*

3 Easy to see or hear. EG *Write your address in clear handwriting ... He speaks very clearly.*
4 Easy to see through. EG *The sea was so clear that you could see everything on the bottom.*
5 To **clear** a surface or a place means to remove things from it. EG *He cleared some newspapers off a chair.*

community 1

1 All the people who live in a particular area or place. EG *What is best for the community? ... It's quite a close community.* (27)
2 A particular group of people who are all alike in some way. EG *... the business community.*

complete, completely 4

1 Totally. EG *... we've got it completely wrong ...* (49)
2 Finished. EG *... began in 1974, completed last year ... Can you complete the story?*
3 To fill in a form. EG *Take your completed form to the point marked 'Service'* (117) *... Just complete the attached form ...* (82)
4 Having everything. EG *... a house complete with swimming pool.*

concern 14

1 Worry. EG *Growing public concern over the economy. Lack of teachers is a matter of serious concern.*
2 To be affected by something, or involved in it. EG *Crime prevention concerns everyone.* (178)
3 To be about. EG *Do you know any stories concerned with fortune-telling?* (188)

condition 2

1 The particular state that someone or something is in. EG *You can't go home in that condition ... Second hand car for sale – in a very good condition.*
2 The **conditions** in which you live or work are all the factors such as heating, hygiene, safety, etc. which affect the quality of your life or job. EG *... living conditions ... ... bad housing conditions ...*
3 The **condition** of a group of people is their situation in life. EG *... the condition of black people in the United States.*
4 A **condition** is something which must happen, be true, or be done first before it is possible for something else to happen. EG *What is the condition that you have to satisfy?*
5 Someone's state of health. EG *He was in good physical condition.*

consider 2

1 If you **consider** a person or thing to be something, you have the opinion that this is what they are. EG *They consider themselves to be very lucky ...*
2 If you **consider** something, you think about it carefully. EG *He had no time to consider the matter.*

contact 7

1 If you **contact** someone, you telephone or write to them in order to ask or tell them something. EG *If you have any problems contact us and we'll try to help.* (91)
2 To be **in contact with** someone means to communicate or spend time with them. EG *I'm in contact with a number of students in other classes.*

control 8

1 **Control** of a country or organisation is the power to make the important decisions about the way it is run. EG *The Communist Party has control of the country.*
2 **Control** of something is **2.1** the ability to make it do what you want it to do. EG *You should have control of your car at all times.* **2.2** the ability to prevent yourself behaving in an excited or emotional way. EG *Don't get angry, keep control of yourself.*
3 If you are **in control** of something you are able to make it do what you want. EG *Man was not yet in control of his environment.*
4 If something is **under control** it is being dealt with successfully. EG *Everything is under control.*
5 To **control** a country or organisation (refer also to 1 above). EG *His family had controlled The Times for more than a century.*
6 To **control** something (refer also to 2.1 above).
7 **Controls** are **7.1** the methods that a government or other organisation uses to prevent prices, wages, etc from increasing. EG *If we remove controls, prices will rise rapidly.* **7.2** the parts of a machine that enable you to make it do what you want. EG *The ship was sinking but the captain stayed at the controls.*

cover 9

1 If you **cover** something you place or spread something over it. EG *Cadbury's take them and they cover them with chocolate . . .* (120) *. . . chocolate covered nuts.*
2 To travel, go. EG *We covered two hundred miles.*
3 To **cover** a topic means to explain it or talk a lot about it. EG *We covered a lot of words last lesson.*
4 To have enough money, food etc for your needs. EG *Enough to cover the day's needs plus an extra £5 to cover emergencies.* (206).
5 To **cover up** can mean to hide, or not to tell. EG *He covered up his plan to escape.*
6 You can be **covered by** insurance.

dead 6

1 No longer living. EG *The person who'd had the bag had been dead for a year.* (78)
2 Not lively; used in informal English. EG *The place is dead.*
3 Not working. EG *The batteries are dead.*
4 Exactly, completely. EG *It landed dead in the centre.*
5 Very; used in informal English. EG *He's dead nice.*
6 A **dead-end** is a road that stops, so you have to turn round and go back.

deal 1

1 A lot. EG *A great deal of rain fell in the night.*
2 An agreement in business. EG *That was the best business deal I ever did.*
3 To **deal in** means to sell. EG *He deals in cars.*
4 To **deal with** something means **4.1** to take action about it. EG *They can deal with any kind of emergency.* **4.2** to be the subject of something. EG *The film deals with a meeting between two men.*

dear 14

1 Used as a form of address. EG *How are you, dear?*
2 Used at the beginning of a letter. EG *Dear Sir,*
3 Used as an exclamation. EG *Oh dear! . . . Dear me!*
4 Very fond of. EG *Her mother is very dear to her.*
5 Costing a lot. EG *I can't afford it. It's very dear.*

degree 1

1 Amount, how much. EG *We can do it by degrees . . . She speaks with a high degree of accuracy.*
2 A unit in measuring. EG *The temperature was still 23 degrees centigrade . . . . . . an angle of 45 degrees.*
3 A course of study taken at a university or the qualification you get when you pass the course. EG *He had taken a degree in music at Cambridge.*

depend 6

1 If you **depend** on someone or something, **1.1** you need them. EG *Children usually depend on their parents until well into their teens.* **1.2** you trust them. EG *You can depend on me.*
2 If you say that something **depends** on something else, you mean that it might only happen under certain circumstances. EG *It really depends on the time you've got available . . .* (69) *It really depends how long you've got though, doesn't it?*

direct 9

1 Moving in a straight line. Of an aeroplane, without stopping. EG *Flying direct from Sydney.* (33)
2 Not involving any intermediate stage or action. EG *. . . London stores are able to send goods direct to an overseas address . . .* (126)
3 Plain, frank, honest. EG *She's very direct.*
4 To show someone where to go. EG *Can you direct me to the Post Office?*
5 To lead or organise a group of people or a project. EG *The film Dreamchild was directed by Gavin Millar.*

discover 3

1 To find out about something for the first time. EG *Discover the North Pennines.* (35) *He discovered the door had locked itself.* (104)
2 If you **discover** someone or something, you find them, often by accident. EG *A false wall was discovered in the . . .*
3 To find a place, substance or fact which nobody knew about before. EG *Columbus discovered the largest island in the Caribbean . . . Penicillin was discovered by Alexander Fleming.*

draw 4

1 To make a picture. EG *. . . draw maps for a new book . . . I can't draw.*
2 If a vehicle **draws away, draws out, draws off**, etc it moves away, out or off etc smoothly and steadily. EG *Before she could reach the bus stop, the bus had drawn off . . .*
3 If you **draw away, draw near** etc you move away, near etc. EG *As the people drew near . . .*
4 If an event or a period of time is **drawing near**, it is approaching. EG *Their wedding day was drawing nearer all the time.*
5 To pull something smoothly. EG *Can you draw your chair in a bit further, please?*
6 To pull across. EG *He drew the curtains.*
7 To take out money from a particular source. EG *. . . draw money from or out of a bank . . . He drew fifty pounds . . .*
8 To **draw** a conclusion means to arrive at that conclusion.
9 To attract. EG *The film was drawing huge crowds.*

drop, dropped 6

1 If you **drop** something, you let it fall. EG *I dropped a glass and broke it . . . He dropped the belt on his lap.* (179)

2 To leave out. EG *He played so badly that he was dropped from the team.*

3 You **drop** someone when they get out of your car. EG *Every day he says to me when I've dropped him: 'Don't know when I'll finish. I'll get back on my own.'* (75)

4 To **drop** something can mean to stop doing it. EG *I'm not very good at English. I think I'll drop it.*

due 12

1 If something is **due** at a particular time, it is expected to happen or be ready at that time. EG *We were due in London at 2 a.m. . . . When is our homework due in?*

2 Used of something that is owed to someone. EG *That money was due to me and I have not had it . . . Thanks are due to all the students who took part.*

3 Because of. EG *His death was due to natural causes, not poison.*

4 **Due** north, south etc means exactly in the direction of north, south etc.

5 **Due** attention, consideration etc is the proper amount of it under the circumstances. EG *He gave my comments due consideration.*

easily 2

1 You use **easily** 1.1 to emphasise that something is very likely to happen. EG *She might easily decide to cancel the whole thing.* 1.2 to emphasise that there can be no doubt that something is the case. EG *This car is easily the most popular model.* 1.3 to say that something happens more quickly than is usual or normal. EG *I make friends very easily.* (27)

enable 12

1 To make it possible for someone to do something or for something to happen. EG *Safety systems would have enabled the pilot to land safely.*

energy 2

1 Ability and strength. EG *You must eat to give you energy.*

2 Determination and enthusiasm. EG *Michael praised Tony's diligence, energy and ambition.*

3 **Energy** is also the power from electricity, coal, wind, etc that makes machines work. EG *Wood is an efficient source of energy.*

eventually 10

1 After some time or some distance. EG *The B6279 eventually runs into the B6278.* (132)

2 At the end of a situation or process, after many delays. EG *We eventually finished work just before midnight.*

expect 3

1 If you **expect** something to happen, you think that it will happen, because of what you know about the situation. EG *You have to expect rain.*

2 If you **expect** a person, you are waiting for them to arrive, because you have invited them or arranged to see them. EG *She would expect him at eight.*

3 If you **expect** someone to do something, you require them to do it as a duty or obligation, for example as part of their work. EG *He is expected to put his work before his family.*

4 If you **expect** to do something, you plan to do it or hope to achieve it. EG *I don't expect to be in England very long . . .*

5 If you say that a woman is **expecting** a baby, she is pregnant.

experience 8

1 Knowledge and skill in a particular job, gained by doing that job for a certain time. EG *My experience as a teacher is valuable.*

2 All the events, knowledge and happenings that make up someone's life. EG *In my experience it doesn't happen very often.*

3 Something that happens to you or something that you do, especially something important that affects you. EG *A friend of mine had a similar experience on a Greenline bus.* (110)

express 7

1 If you **express** an idea or feeling, **1.1** you put it into words. EG *We hope that students will express their ideas to us.* **1.2** you show it by the look on your face or by your behaviour. EG *Her eyes expressed her excitement.*

fact 14

1 Something that really happened. EG *How much of the book is fact and how much is fiction?*

2 A **fact** is a piece of information or knowledge. EG *The report is full of facts and figures.*

3 **The fact that** . . . is a way of referring to a particular situation or state of affairs. EG *. . . the fact that there was going to be this neat twist.* (193)

4 **In fact** . . .; **in actual fact** . . .; **as a matter of fact** . . . mean really or truly. EG *This is in fact what happened.*

fall 2

1 If someone or something **falls**, they suddenly move downwards, especially by accident. EG *Be careful, don't fall in the water . . .*

2 If a building **falls**, it collapses onto the ground. EG *. . . fallen buildings after the bombing.*

3 To go down. EG *The US $ fell sharply . . . Falling numbers of students in school. . . . The temperature fell at night.*

fear 7

1 **Fear** or **a fear** is the feeling you have when you think that something unpleasant is going to happen or something is going to go wrong. EG *Early fears about safety have now been largely dispelled.* (91)

2 If you **fear** someone or something you are frightened because you think they may be harmful in some way. EG *He is very brave. He fears nothing.*

3 If you **fear** something unpleasant you are worried that it has happened or is going to happen. EG *When I heard about the accident I feared that you might be badly injured.*

4 If you take a course of action **for fear of** something, you take that course of action because you do not wish that thing to happen. EG *They did not mention it for fear of offending him.*

5 If you say there is **no fear** of something happening you mean that it is not going to happen so there is no need to worry. EG *There's no fear of rain today.*

feel 11

1 If you **feel** a particular emotion or physical state, you experience it. EG *You'd feel exhausted when you got there ... I still feel at home when I go back there.* (9)
2 To believe, to be of the opinion that. EG *I've taken you onto B roads because I feel it's far more scenic.* (131)
3 If you **feel like** something, you want it or you want to do it. EG *I feel like something to eat ... We felt like going home ... I'll feel like putting on clothes of a different colour.* (128)

feeling 11

1 An emotion that you experience. EG *Just a sort of sinking feeling ...* (152) *Some people cannot put their feelings into words.*
2 Physical sensations. EG *A feeling of hunger ... I've got a funny feeling in my arm.*
3 An attitude, opinion, thought or idea. EG *I have a nasty feeling that something's going wrong ... I have mixed feelings about it.*

fight 13

1 To try to stop something happening. EG *Fight crime – protect your home!* (176)
2 To make something happen. EG *Fight for your rights!*
3 To take part in a war. EG *They fought in the First World War.*

figure 6

1 A person. EG *I saw a tall figure running towards me.*
2 An amount or price. EG *Could you give me some sort of a figure for your expenses?* (80)
3 An important person. EG *He's a controversial figure.*
4 A picture or diagram. EG *... see Fig.1.* (68)

find 3

1 To discover someone or something that you have been looking for. EG *... to find a partner ... ... be sure of finding comfortable accommodation ...*
2 To work out an answer to a problem. EG *Did you find it easy to get here today?* (140)
3 To have an opinion about someone or something. EG *Oh! I find it very difficult to tell anybody anything about ...* (20)

follow 5

1 To go along behind someone or something. EG *He followed her.*
2 To happen after something else. EG *Then followed a much longer pause before the waitress returned.*
3 To be true as a result of something else. EG *If x = 2, it follows that 3x = 6.*
4 To come next in a piece of writing. EG *If you are in London with no place to stay, ring one of the following: ...* (162)
5 To watch something that is moving. EG *Eric and the others could follow the man's finger as it moved across the map.*
6 If you **follow** advice, instructions etc, you do as you are advised. EG *Follow the directions on the London Underground.*
7 To understand. EG *The story was very difficult to follow ... Do you follow me?*
8 To take an interest in. EG *Do you follow any particular sport?*

foreign 1

1 Belonging to, coming from or made in a country which is not your own. EG *... foreign imports ...*
2 Not naturally part of and coming from outside an organism or substance. EG *He found some foreign object in the bottle of milk.*
3 Not characteristic of something or not usually experienced as belonging to something. EG *Such beliefs seem foreign to our way of thinking.*

form 6

1 A **form** of something is a type or kind of it. EG *Bus and coach travel are probably the cheapest forms of transport ...* (69) *Bed and breakfast is a form of holiday accommodation.* (39)
2 A paper where you write facts or answers to questions. EG *An application form ...* (2) *She had to fill in this form.* (80)
3 To develop an opinion or habit. EG *He formed the habit of taking long walks.*

general 4

1 **General** is used to summarise a situation or an idea. EG *The general standard of education there is very high ... I think in general they don't get equal pay.* (47)
2 **General** is used to describe a statement that does not give details. EG *In very general terms ... They went in the general direction of the school.*

ground 8

1 The **ground** is **1.1** the surface of the earth. EG *... on the ground. ... ...* **1.2** the soil and rock on and beneath the earth's surface. EG *The ground all round was very wet.*
2 A reason for something. EG *You have no real grounds for complaint.*

grow 5

1 To increase in size. EG *How tall our girl is growing!*
2 If you **grow** a plant, you put a seed or a young plant in the ground and look after it.
3 To change gradually. EG *The sun grew so hot that they were forced to stop working.*
4 **grow up.** To gradually change from being a child to being an adult. EG *It was not a very pleasant place to grow up in.*

hang 4

1 To attach something in a high place or position so that it does not touch the ground. EG *He should hang up his clothes.* (186)
2 Something that **hangs** somewhere is heavy or loose so that it swings slightly or can move freely. EG *There's something definitely hanging down.* (49)
3 To kill someone by tying a rope around their neck and making them fall. EG *He tried to hang himself.*
4 To **get the hang of** something means to understand or realise how a particular thing is done.
5 To **hang about** or **hang around** means to stay in the same place doing nothing.
6 To **hang on** means to wait.
7 To **hang up** the phone means to end a telephone call, by putting back the receiver. EG *'Thank you. Goodbye.' He hung up.*

heavy 4

1 Weighing a lot or weighing more than is usual; difficult to move. EG ... *carrying heavy weights about* ... (47)
2 Great in amount, degree, or intensity. EG ... *heavy rain* ... *The traffic is heavy now* ... *A man with heavy shoulders* ... *Heavy meals* ...
3 Very large and powerful, used for example of machines. EG *Heavy industry* ...
4 Involving a lot of work. EG *I've had rather a heavy week.*
5 Using a lot of something. EG *Our old car was very heavy on petrol.*

hold 14

1 To have something in your hand or arm. EG *He held it carefully in his hand.*
2 To contain. EG *This box will only hold about twenty bottles.*
3 To keep in the same place. EG *He held it there with his foot.*
4 To **take hold** means 4.1 to take something firmly in one's hand. EG *Here, take hold of this.* 4.2 to become established. EG *When the disease takes hold* ... (191)

hope 2

1 To want or wish. EG *I hope to see more of the world in the next ten years* ... *Can you come? I hope so.*
2 A wish or desire. EG *She expressed a hope to see more of the world.*

huge 8

Very large or surprisingly large in size or degree. EG *He looked like a huge human rat.*

idea 3

1 Something in the mind, a thought. EG *Tell each other the ideas you have.* (189)
2 A plan or suggestion. EG *Here are some ideas on how to enjoy yourself for absolutely nothing.*
3 A belief. EG *Some people have funny ideas about how to bring up children.*
4 Knowledge of something. EG *I can't remember where you stayed. Got absolutely no idea.* (29)

imagine 7

1 If you **imagine** something, your mind forms a picture or idea of it. EG *Imagine you were writing to a computer dating agency.* (20)
2 You say 'I imagine ...' or 'I would imagine ...' when you are not sure about something or when you are being polite. EG *I would imagine* ... (7)

immediately 10

1 If something happens **immediately**, it happens without delay or hesitation. EG *You turn left in Eggleston and then immediately right.* (132)
2 You use **immediately** 2.1 to refer to something that can be seen, understood, used, etc without any delay. EG *It was immediately obvious.* 2.2 to refer to someone or something that is closely involved in a situation. EG *We were not immediately concerned with the problem.* 2.3 to refer to something that is next to or very close to a particular thing or place. EG *Immediately to the right of the school is the shop.*

interest 3

1 A desire to pay attention to something and learn or hear more about it. EG *People who have taken an active interest in the project* ... *No one took any interest in me as a child.*
2 A sum of money that is paid as a percentage of a larger sum of money. EG *You receive interest on money that you invest and pay interest on money that you borrow.*
3 The advantages, well-being, success and happiness of a person or group of people. EG *They were acting in their own interests* ... ... *in the public interest.*
4 If you are **interested** in something, you are keen to know more about it or to do it. EG *I'm fairly interested in sport.*
5 If you find something **interesting**, it attracts your attention. EG *That's a very interesting question* ... ... *some very interesting people.*

involve, involved 8

1 If something **involves** a particular type of activity or behaviour, that activity or behaviour is part of it. EG *Social activities which involve meeting and talking with people* ... *Write about what you have done in the past and say, very briefly, what it involves.*
2 If you are **involved** in something you take part in it. EG *Have you ever been involved in an accident like one of these?* (106)

lead 8

1 To be in the front of a line of moving people or things. EG *Jenny was leading, Chris was behind her and I was at the back.*
2 To take someone to a place by going with them. EG *He led the way there.*
3 To go to a particular place. EG *Roads leading to the forts can be crowded* ... ... *stairs leading up to a house* ...
4 A **lead** is a length of wire covered in plastic that is used to carry electricity. EG *Make sure that you've got the leads plugged in to the correct sockets.*
5 The position of being ahead in a competition or contest at a particular time. EG *New Zealand went into an early lead* ... *Manchester are in the lead by 3 goals to 1.*
6 To be the most successful or the most advanced. EG *Japan and America now lead the world in computing science research.*
7 To be in control or in charge of a group of people. EG *The Labour Party is led by Neil Kinnock.*
8 The most important thing or person. EG *She's the lead singer in their rock group* ... ... *the lead story in a newspaper.*
9 **lead to** means to result in. EG *It will lead to trouble.*
10 To pass or spend your life in a particular sort of way. EG *I lead a hectic social life.*
11 **Lead** is a soft, grey, heavy metal that can be poisonous.

least 4

1 **At least** means 1.1 a minimum of. EG ... *seven at least* ... (18) *That's at least 8+ hours work each day.* (47) 1.2 a good point despite something bad. EG ... *had left his name and address so, at least, he could make a claim* ... (112)
2 **At least** can be used to modify what you have already said. EG *This is an island – at least I think it is!*
3 **The least** means that an amount of something is as small as it can be. EG *My least favourite* ... (58) ... *which person spends the most and the least money* ... (80)

leave 1

1 To go away or to depart from places, people and institutions. EG *My last train leaves Euston at 11.30 ... It's a very pleasant school and I'd be sorry to leave it. (2)*
2 To allow or cause to remain in a particular condition or place. EG *We decided to leave the office as it was ... Can you leave the door open?*
3 Remaining. EG *I hope there's enough left ... I'm the only one left ... Which sentences are left over? (13)*

line 7

1 **Line** is used in the following ways. **1.1** A **line** on a surface is a long thin mark which is drawn, painted, printed, etc. EG *We did a line across the middle of the cake. (100)* **1.2 Lines** are found on paper, for writing on; on a road, to show where you can park your car; on sports fields and pitches; on someone's face when they grow old. EG *A plumber had parked on a double yellow line. (150)*
2 A **line** of people or things is a number of them standing side by side or one after the other forming a continuous row.
3 **Line** is used to refer to groups of words, numbers etc in a piece of work such as a book, speech, song or play. EG *Can you guess the last line of the story?*
4 **Line** is used to refer to a long, narrow piece of string, wire, pipe or metal on which you hang wet clothes to dry; with which you catch fish; along which electricity or telephone messages are sent; along which trains run. EG *Get the Victoria Line.*

little 1

1 Small. EG *A little village.*
2 Young. EG *Two little girls, Marion and Mabel.*
3 A small amount of. EG *I speak a little bit of Italian, a little Spanish, and a tiny bit of Greek.*
4 Not much or not enough. EG *John and I had very little money left ... I studied Latin and French, but they made little impression. (12)*

live 1

1 To stay in a place which is your home. EG *Where do you live?*
2 To behave in a particular way. EG *My sister and I lived very different lives ... We lived very simply.*
3 To be alive. EG *We need water to live ... People cannot live without air.*

machine 8

1 A piece of equipment that does a particular type of work. EG *A washing machine.*
2 A well-controlled system or organisation. EG *A propaganda machine.*
3 If you **machine** something, you make it or change its shape using a machine; a technical term.

make 9

1 **Make** is one of the most common verbs in English. It is often used in expressions where it does not have a very distinct meaning of its own, but where most of the meaning is in the noun that follows it. EG *Make a purchase ... (126) Even if you do not intend to make a claim. (108)*
2 If you **make** something, you produce it. EG *Some days I am a receptionist, other days I make the tea. (52) I usually make a cheese flan. (86)*
3 To cause someone to be angry, happy, sad, etc. EG *This made him very happy. (179)*
4 A **make** is a type of product. EG *What make of car do you have? A Ford.*

mark 9

1 A **mark** is a small part of a surface which is a different colour because something has been dropped on it. EG *A dirty mark ... ... grease marks.*
2 A **mark** is a written or printed symbol. EG *An exclamation mark ... ... a question mark.*
3 If you **mark** something, you put a written symbol on it. EG *Teachers were marking children's writing.*
4 A point on a scale. EG *Unemployment is now over the 3 million mark.*
5 To label. EG *Can you mark where your house is on the map?*
6 German currency. EG *The German Mark was worth about 25p.*

matter 9

1 An event, situation or subject which you have to deal with or think about, especially something that involves problems. EG *That's a different matter ... It's a personal matter.*
2 If something **matters**, it is important, it is something that you care about or that worries you. EG *Your happiness – that's the only thing that matters.*
3 **Matter** is written material, especially books and newspapers. EG *Reading matter ... ... printed matter ...*
4 You say 'What's **the matter**?' to someone when you want to know what the problem is. EG *What's the matter with your arm? I broke it playing football.*
5 You say 'It doesn't **matter**' to tell someone who is apologising to you that you are not angry or upset.

meet 2

1 To make a new friend; to get to know someone for the first time. EG *I would need to meet somebody who also had a sense of humour. (20)*
2 To come together, usually for a particular purpose. EG *Let's meet at 11 o'clock tomorrow.*
3 Roads, rivers etc **meet** when they come together. EG *... the B6274 will meet the A688 ... (131)*

nor 6

1 **Nor** is used after 'neither' in order to introduce the second alternative in a negative statement. EG *Neither Margaret nor John was there ... He could neither read nor write.*
2 **Nor** is used after a negative statement in order to add something else. EG *That wasn't the whole story, nor anything like the whole story.*
3 **Nor** is used after a negative statement to express agreement with that statement. EG *'I haven't got a car.' '... nor have I.' (69)*

notice 8

If you **notice** someone or something, you become aware of them. EG *I think maybe the pilot had noticed, but certainly no one else on board had noticed ... (173) He couldn't help noticing a note to his secretary ... (55) Noticing a woman reading the menu ... (93)*

obviously 10

1 Used to show that you expect your hearer to know or understand something. EG *Obviously we'll have to think carefully about it.*
2 Used when something is clear or evident. EG *One of the beds had obviously been slept in.*

odd 5

1 Strange or unusual. EG *Isn't that a bit odd? ... We thought she was rather odd.*
2 **The odds** are a measurement of how probable it is that something will or will not happen. EG *The odds were against me, so I gave up the plan ... ... The odds are that it will rain tomorrow.*
3 Various. EG *Odd jobs ... Odd bits of shopping.*

offer 9

1 To ask someone if they would like to have something. EG *He offered her his chair ... It was always the smaller cars that offered you a lift.* (97)
2 To say you are willing to do something. EG *'We could do it for you,' offered Dolly.*
3 An **offer** is something that someone says they will give you or do for you. EG *Thanks for your offer of help.*
4 You can **offer** someone information, advice, help, an explanation, congratulations, thanks, friendship etc. EG *May I offer my congratulations.*
5 To provide. EG *Some stores offer relief from VAT.* (126)
6 Referring to a quality that makes things attractive, useful etc. EG *The latest that computer technology has to offer ... The best of everything that London has to offer.*
7 If something is **on offer**, its price is specially reduced.
8 To say you will pay a certain sum of money. EG *Make me an offer ... The original price was £10, but I'm open to offers.*

operation 12

1 An activity that involves many actions. EG *The speed with which he performed this difficult operation was incredible.* (126)
2 A planned series of military actions. EG *The Cambodian adventure had been the most successful operation of the war.*
3 A business or company. EG *The whole of the Vauxhall operation in Britain.*
4 A form of medical treatment in which a doctor cuts open part of the patient's body in order to repair it or to cure a disease. EG *Some 200 heart operations a year are performed there.*

part 5

1 One of a number of things that makes up a whole. EG *... a part of London.*
2 To **take part in** something means to do something or share an activity. EG *Even taking part in sport?*

partly 5

To some extent, but not completely. EG *The door was partly open ... That's partly because they live in unattractive conditions.* (25)

period 12

1 A length of time, usually a fixed length. EG *The payment period is within ten days of completion of the job.*
2 A particular time in history. EG *British paintings of all periods.* (157)

pick 14

1 To choose. EG *You can pick whichever one you want.*
2 **pick up** means 2.1 To lift up. EG *A million housewives every day pick up a can of beans and say ...* (120) 2.2 To give someone a lift in a car. EG *A motorist who had a brand new BMW car picked up a hitch-hiker.* 2.3 To find or collect. EG *You're quite likely to pick up a few bargains ... Pick up a copy at your nearest newsagent.*

plain 12

1 A large, flat area of land with very few trees on it.
2 Entirely in one colour and without a pattern, or without printing, writing, etc; used of surfaces and of cloth, paper, etc. EG *I'll tell them to put it in a plain envelope.*
3 Designed or prepared in a very simple way; used of buildings, clothes, food etc. EG *She was wearing a plain black dress ... Good plain food.*
4 Easy to recognise or be aware of; used of facts, and of difficulties, advantages, etc. EG *I'd say it's pretty plain that they got the baby to cry somehow.* (164)
5 Not beautiful. EG *A plain, plump person.*

point 12

1 Something that has just been said. EG *He makes a good point about people keeping dogs who know nothing about their real needs.*
2 A detail that occurs as part of a fixed procedure or process. EG *The main point on the agenda was left till the end of the meeting.*
3 Used to refer to a particular part of someone's character or abilities. EG *That's his best point, I think.*
4 The reason for saying or doing something, often used in negative expressions or questions, to show that something is useless or not worthwhile. EG *But that's not the point! What jobs need skilled hands?* (167)
5 A particular place or position, especially a precise one. EG *The two roads would merge at that point.* (131)
6 The sharp end of a pin, needle, or knife.
7 A particular time or moment. EG *At some future point, he may have to think again.*
8 **Up to a point** means partly but not completely. EG *Up to a point I agree with Catherine.*
9 A score in a game. EG *We won by five points to three.*
10 If you **point** to or at something, you show it to people. EG *She pointed to the bathroom door.*
11 To face a particular direction. EG *One of its four toes pointed backwards.*
12 To hold something, especially a weapon, so that it points towards someone. EG *My kids are forbidden even to point toy pistols at people.*
13 **point out** means to give an important piece of information. EG *Japan, he pointed out, has a huge population.*

policy 8

1 A **policy** is a general set of ideas or plans agreed by a government or party. EG *Washington has changed its policy with regard to the Soviet Union.*
2 An agreement with an insurance company. EG *You have to renew the policy every year.*

position 12

1 An attitude or point of view. EG *That is my position and I'm not going to change my mind.*
2 A condition or situation. EG *The party making an official statement is in a better position than the one who does not.* (108)
3 The place where something or someone is. EG *It stands in a good position overlooking Belfast.*
4 A job. EG *John anticipates some difficulty in finding a suitable position.* (52)

post 9

1 The **post** is the public service offered by the Post Office for collecting and delivering letters. EG *Send it by first class post ... Write by return of post.*
2 A strong pole made of wood or metal. EG *... a lamp-post ... The ball hit the goalpost ... The finishing post at the races.*
3 A job or position at work. EG *John was applying for a new post, the post of head of department in a school.*
4 **post-** is used to form words that describe something taking place after a certain date, event, or stage of development. EG *... post-war housing ...... post-graduate students ...*

powerful 7

1 A person, organisation or government is **powerful** if they are able to control other people and events. EG *... powerful and effective trade unions ...*
2 A person or animal that is **powerful** is very strong.
3 A machine or engine is **powerful** if it can exert a lot of force. EG *The powerful engine growled and grunted impatiently.* (97)
4 Other things that can be described as **powerful** are smells, lights, voices, blows or kicks.

produce 11

1 To cause or create. EG *With the hovercraft, the cushion is produced by a ring of airjets ... (73) ... once the door is opened, the microwaves stop being produced.* (91)
2 To manufacture. EG *Factories producing electrical goods ... It produces a third of the nation's oil.*
3 To show or supply. EG *From his pocket he produced a small black notebook.* (152).
4 To manage or organise. EG *They produce their own plays at school.*

professional 4

1 Relating to the work that a person does. EG *He started his professional life as a singer.*
2 Having an occupation that requires special training and education. EG *The flat is ideal for the professional single person.*
3 Having a job in which you receive money for doing an activity that many people do as a hobby, for example sport, music, or acting. EG *A professional footballer.* (43)
4 Showing great skill and high standards. EG *Piers Paul Read's a very professional writer.*

provide 3

1 To give or lend. EG *All meals will be provided by the hotel.*
2 Used to introduce a condition. EG *You can get a Cheap Day Return ticket at a reduced rate, provided that you do not start your journey before 09.30 hours.*

pull 11

1 Of a car, **1.1** to **pull in** or **pull over**. EG *I would say he would probably pull in to the side if he were by himself ... (136) If there was a policeman beside me telling me to pull over I would certainly pull over.* (136) **1.2 Pull up** means stop. EG *He pulls up at a traffic light.* (78)
2 To move something by getting in front of it and drawing it towards you. EG *Can you help me pull these things over here?*

push 5

1 To press something or someone, for example with your hand. EG *She pushed the button that locked the door.*
2 The act of pressing something or someone. EG *I gave her a push.*
3 To move something along. EG *Castle pushed his bicycle up King's Road.*
4 To try to cause someone to make progress by constantly persuading and encouraging them. EG *They didn't push you in that direction.*
5 **push on** means to travel onwards. EG *We must push on before nightfall.*

raise 11

1 If you **raise** something, you move it so that it is in a higher position. EG *Raise your hand if you want to ask a question.*
2 To increase in some way. EG *When he spoke next he raised his voice so loud that I jumped.* (147)
3 To grow. EG *Farmers raise crops.*

rate 6

1 The speed at which something happens. EG *... the rapid rate of change in the modern world ...*
2 The number of instances of something that occur during a period of time. EG *What is your success rate? ... A rising divorce rate among the middle classes.*
3 The level or amount. EG *... bargain rates ... Children at half the adult rate ... Interest rates rising to 12%.*
4 **Rates** in Britain are a local tax paid by house-owners (rate-payers), to pay for water, roads and other local services in their area.
5 To **rate** someone or something means to think a lot of them. EG *He was a highly rated goalkeeper.*
6 **At any rate** can mean 'anyway'. EG *I don't know exactly what he did, but at any rate he was very successful.*

reach 3

1 To come to a place or person. EG *It was dark by the time I reached their house.*
2 To speak to or send a message to someone. EG *I tried to reach you at home several times, but no-one answered the phone.*
3 To touch or take hold of something by stretching out your arm. EG *I can't reach that shelf unless I stand on a chair.*

relationship 5

1 The connection between two people or two groups of people. EG *The relationship between friends.*
2 The connection between two things, events, or ideas. EG *My exams bore no relationship to my being a doctor.* (64)
3 The type of family connection between two people. EG *'What is your relationship to the patient?' 'I'm his daughter.'*

remain 1

1 To stay in a particular condition and not to change. EG *Mrs Oliver remained silent ... Her husband remained standing. ... important that we should remain Irish ...* (9)

2 To stay in a particular place and not move away. EG *I was allowed to remain at home.*

3 To still exist, especially when other parts or other similar things no longer exist. EG *He was cut off from what remained of his family.*

4 To still exist and to be unanswered or unsolved, in spite of what people have said or done; used especially of problems and facts. EG *These problems remain ... The fact remains that they mean to destroy us.*

remember 14

1 If you **remember** people or events, your mind still has an impression of them. EG *Some of 'em can't even remember their own names ...* (193) *Do you remember Ireland at all?*

2 If you **remember** to do something, you do it when you intended to. EG *Remember to lock the door when you go out ... I remembered to put all my things away.*

repeat 1

1 To say or write something again. EG *'Is she quite dead?' – 'Quite dead', he repeated.*

2 To do or make something again. EG *I try not to repeat silly mistakes.*

3 A **repeat** is something which happens again. EG *... a repeat of the programme ...... a repeat performance of the play ...*

rest 6

1 What remains. EG *Let's turn over and read the rest.*

2 A period of time during which you do not do anything active. EG *I need a rest.*

3 To relax, and stop working or doing anything active. EG *'Try to rest', the doctor said.*

4 If a duty or responsibility **rests** with a person, that person must do the duty. EG *The decision rested with the headmaster.*

5 To lean on. EG *No more than a couple of fingers resting lightly on the wheel to keep her steady.* (97)

rich 14

1 Having a lot of money or possessions. EG *It must be nice to be rich.* **1.1** ' **The rich**' means people who are rich. EG *I only go after them as can afford it. The winners and the rich.* (189)

2 **Riches** are valuable possessions. EG *The young man set out in search of adventure and riches.*

3 The word **rich** is used to describe: **3.1** food, containing a lot of fats, eggs, cream etc. **3.2** soil that is very good for growing crops. **3.3** clothes that are beautiful and valuable. **3.4** voices and musical sounds that are strong in a pleasing way.

round 13

1 Of shape, position or direction. EG *... the belt from round the driver's waist ...* (174)

2 Near to, or moving from place to place within a certain area. EG *The policeman came round to my open window ...* (147) *Can you picture me goin' round kids' parties ...?* (174)

3 Approximately. EG *We should get there round four o'clock ... They live round about here.*

4 To **get round** something means to solve a problem. EG *If you don't know whether to put Miss or Mrs, you can get round it by writing Ms.*

5 A **round** can be: in sport – a round of golf; in politics – a round of talks.

scene 4

1 A part of a play, film, novel etc. EG *All we saw was about three scenes ... ... great love scenes ...*

2 A picture of a particular place or kind of activity. EG *It seems to be a street scene.* (49)

3 The place where something in particular has happened. EG *The scene of the accident.* (108)

4 A particular activity or part of life.

5 A fight or argument. EG *There was a scene, and Father called Christopher a lot of rude names.*

secret, secretly 4

1 Something that is known about by only a small number of people, and not told or shown to anyone else. EG *We had to promise to keep the secret.*

2 Happening or acting privately, with the intention of preventing other people from finding out. EG *They met secretly to discuss the plans.*

3 Something that is the best or only way of achieving a particular result. EG *He asked the popular one for her secret.* (55)

4 Something that has never been explained or understood. EG *The secret of life is to become very, very good at something that's very hard to do.* (121)

security 13

1 The precautions (safety measures) that are taken to protect a country from spying, to protect people from being attacked, to prevent prisoners from escaping etc. EG *Airport Security Check ... Top security prisons.*

2 A feeling of **security** means a feeling of safety. EG *People need job security.*

sense 5

1 If you have a **sense** of something such as justice, you believe in it. EG *a sense of right and wrong ... She's gained a sense of independence ... ... a sense of humour.* (20)

2 Meaning. EG *In the strict sense of the word ...*

3 The five **senses** of touch, hearing, smell, taste, sight.

serious 12

1 Causing worry or fear. EG *I suppose you know you're in serious trouble ...* (161) *... serious illness ... ... seriously ill ...* (145)

2 Important. EG *I think this is a serious point.*

3 Dealing with important matters. EG *A serious newspaper.*

4 Not joking or pretending. EG *At first I thought he was continuing the joke, but he was serious.*

5 Thoughtful, quiet, not joking. EG *A rather serious girl ... Don't look so serious!*

service, services 6

1 An organisation or system that provides a public need, especially related to transport or communications, health, education etc. EG *Bus services within the county.* (82)

2 The Army, Navy or Air Force.

3 Help or aid given as part of a job. EG *Thank you for your services.*

4 Being served in a shop or restaurant or hotel. EG *They give excellent service.*

5 The state of being used. EG *New vehicles brought into service ... This computer has been in service for years.*

sharp 11

1 A **sharp** object has a very thin edge that is good for cutting things. EG *A sharp knife.*
2 Clear. EG *... the photo was so sharp ...*
3 Sudden, quick. EG *Car prices have risen sharply.*
4 Spoken abruptly, often with anger, without warning. EG *'Who are you', he asked sharply.*
5 Exact time. EG *The train leaves at 8 o'clock sharp!*

sight 12

1 The ability to see. EG *For man, sight is the most important sense.*
2 An occasion of seeing. EG *We tried to get a sight of the president as his car shot past.*
3 Places, especially in a city, that are interesting to see and are often visited by tourists. EG *... the sights of London ...*
4 The distance or area within which it is possible to see someone or something. EG *He roared off up the road out of sight.* (161)

simple 7

1 If something is **simple** it is easy to understand; if a problem is **simple** it is easy to understand or solve. EG *The problem is a simple one.*
2 Something which is **simple** is straightforward without any unnecessary parts or complications. EG *Very simple language ...* (95) *A recipe for a simple dish.* (87)

simply 8

1 Used to give emphasis. EG *I simply can't believe it.*
2 Used to show that there is only one thing, reason etc. EG *I simply didn't look.* (106)
3 If you say or write something **simply** you do it in a way that is easy to understand. EG *Let me put it quite simply ...*
4 If you live **simply** you have an uncomplicated and cheap way of life.

somehow 14

1 You use **somehow** to show that you do not know how something was done. EG *It has somehow come out that way.*
2 To show that you do not know why. EG *Somehow I couldn't get to sleep.*

sorry 1

1 Used to apologise. EG *I'm sorry I'm so late ... I'm sorry about this but there's nothing I can do right now.*
2 Unhappy. EG *It's a pleasant school and I'd be sorry to leave it.* (2)
3 Used to disagree with someone. EG *I don't agree with you, I'm sorry.*

source 12

1 A person, place, or thing from which you get something that is useful or needed. EG *One of the world's main sources of uranium.*
2 A person or thing that provides information, especially about events that are reported in the news. EG *Sources close to the President report that ...*
3 The point or circumstance from which something comes or where something has its origin. EG *They're trying to trace the source of the trouble ... They come in useful as a source of disruption, I suppose, babies.* (164)

special 6

1 Different from normal, more important than usual. EG *Do you have any special skill, like typing?*
2 Particular: something that belongs to/is relevant to/is intended for one particular person, group, place, situation. EG *Travelcard is a special ticket.* (82)
3 Greater than usual. EG *Pay special attention to spelling ... He made a special effort to be helpful ... My special interest is music.*
4 Specialised. EG *Special schools for handicapped children.*

spread 2

1 To open, arrange or extend something, often over a place or surface, with the result that all of it can be seen or used easily. EG *He took the envelope and spread the contents on the table ...*
2 To put a thin layer of something over a surface. EG *... spreading jam on bread.*
3 To move outwards in all directions; to travel further. EG *... stop the fire getting out of control and spreading ... ... rats can spread disease.*
4 The activity or process of spreading. EG *... a result of the spread of fire ...... the spread of higher education.*
5 **spread out.** To move away from each other. EG *They followed him and spread out nervously in the forest.*

stage 7

1 A **stage** is a particular point in a continuous process. EG *To get creamy scrambled eggs be careful at this stage.* (87)
2 If you do something **stage by stage** you complete one part after another. EG *You must work through it very carefully stage by stage.*
3 A **stage** is a platform in a theatre on which the performances take place. EG *I walked on to the stage and started to sing.*
4 **The stage** is the profession or career of acting, or the activities connected with the theatre. EG *My Aunt Mabel was on the stage.*

step 10

1 A pace. EG *She took a step back ... I had to retrace my steps.* (140)
2 To **step on** means to put your foot on. EG *She stepped on his toe.*
3 A **step** is a stair outside a building. EG *She was sitting on the top step.*
4 A **step** is also a stage in achieving something. EG *This is a step on the road to victory.*

strong 13

1 **Strong** people can carry heavy things, work very hard, or are powerful. EG *Though the way be long, let your heart be strong ...* (201) *... some strong thread.* (172)
2 You use **strong** to describe something which affects you very much. EG *... strong feelings about ... She felt and argued strongly in support of equal pay for women.*

struggle 1

1 To try very hard to get or to do something that is difficult for you and that other people often are trying to stop you from achieving. EG *A nationalist movement that has had to struggle for independence ... I struggle through reading Italian.*

2 Very great efforts that you make to get or to do something that is difficult for you and that other people often are trying to stop you from achieving. EG *The conference called for a renewed struggle against racism.*

3 To twist, kick, and move violently in order to get yourself free when you are being held by another person or by a trap or ropes. EG *The guard was standing hitting him whenever he struggled.*

4 To manage with very great difficulty to move through a place, or to stand up, sit down, etc, for example because you are tired or ill. EG *He struggled forward for about half a mile.*

5 An activity which is very difficult for you to do and which you have to try very hard to achieve. EG *Reading, on the whole, was a struggle.*

support 13

1 If you **support** a political party, or a sports team, you want them to do well. EG *He supported Manchester United.*

2 To help people by paying for their food, clothes etc or by giving them practical advice, kindness, etc.

3 To take the weight of. EG *Will this shelf support all those books?*

supposed 8

1 If something is **supposed** to be done or not **supposed** to be done, you mean it should or should not be done because of a law, custom or rule. EG *You are supposed to report it to the police as soon as possible.*

2 If you say something is **supposed** to happen you mean it is expected or intended to happen. EG *Where are you supposed to be going?*

3 When you say something is **supposed** to be true you are reporting a statement or belief that is not your own. EG *It's supposed to be very difficult, but I don't know.*

surely 11

1 Used when making a statement to express surprise, or to contradict the other person. EG *Surely he must have known? ... You haven't finished all that yet, surely!*

2 In American English, **surely** means 'yes, certainly'. EG *Will you excuse me for a second? Surely!*

surprise, surprised 4

1 A sudden or unexpected event, or something that happens in a way that you do not expect. EG *The British government might be in for a surprise when the report is published.*

2 Something unexpected, especially something pleasant, such as a gift. EG *What a lovely surprise! ... I have a surprise for you.*

3 Feeling slightly shocked because of something unexpected, for example an unexpected event or piece of information. EG *'I'm not surprised,' said the plumber. 'Neither did I when I was a ...' Were they surprised when you went to University?* (64)

take 13

1 To move something from a place to another place. EG *Just complete the attached form and take it to any of the places listed here ...* (82) *What's the use of taking an umbrella when it's not raining ... They broke the window and they came in and took the video.* (178)

2 If something **takes** a certain amount of time, you need that amount of time in order to do it. EG *It takes me about twenty minutes I suppose to come in ...* (80) *He took plenty of time slowing down.* (147)

3 If you **take** a road, you choose to travel along it. EG *Take the second road on the left.*

4 The most frequent use of **take** is in expressions where it does not have a very distinct meaning of its own, but where most of the meaning is in the noun which follows it. EG *It is negative to take the attitude that 'It cannot happen to me ...'* (178) *Please take note of these points.* (178)

test 7

1 A **test** is **1.1** an event that makes clear how well something works or what it is like; EG *Stringent tests for electrical safety and microwave leakage.* (91) **1.2** a series of questions you must answer in order to show how much you know. EG *An English test.*

thick 7

1 Something that is **thick 1.1** has a particular distance between its two opposite surfaces. EG *The piece of wood was about six centimetres thick.* **1.2** has a greater distance than you would expect between its two opposite surfaces. EG *A thick stone wall.*

2 Someone who is **thick** is stupid. EG *He's a bit thick.*

3 **Thick** liquids are fairly stiff and solid. EG *I made the sauce too thick.*

top 3

1 The highest point. EG *Very lucky to get to the top of it ...* (24) *We actually managed to reach the top.* (29)

2 More important or better than other people or things. EG *... Top twenty records ... The very top of the profession.* (189)

3 A woman's shirt or blouse. EG *That's a nice top!*

towards 10

1 The form **toward** is also used. In the direction of. EG *The policeman came strolling slowly toward us.* (147)

2 Of attitude. EG *He felt friendly towards them.*

3 Just before. EG *Towards the end of 1987.*

trade 9

1 The activity of buying, selling or exchanging goods or services between people, firms or countries. EG *France is dependent on foreign trade ... Trade with Eastern Europe.*

2 A business. EG *The tourist trade.*

3 A kind of work. EG *I'm in a skilled trade.* (121)

4 A **trade union** is an organisation formed by the workers to improve their working conditions and wages. EG *He will meet the trade union leaders tomorrow.*

treat 9

1 If you **treat** someone in a particular way, you behave that way towards them. EG *You will be treated as a royal guest.* (39)
2 If you **treat** something in a particular way, you deal with it that way. EG *Electricity is dangerous so treat it with respect ... Treat it as a joke.*
3 To **treat** an illness, an injury, or sick people. EG *Only two doctors and eight nurses treat 300 patients.*
4 To give someone something they will enjoy. EG *A finger of fudge is just enough to give your kids a treat!* (120)

trouble 4

1 Difficulties or problems. EG *My bank manager had a lot of trouble with his hot water system ...* (45) *What's the trouble, mate?* (103)
2 To make someone feel worried, doubtful or uneasy. EG *What's troubling you?*
3 A problem. EG *Our flight was delayed because of engine trouble.*
4 A situation in which someone is angry with you because of something you have done. EG *I don't want to get you into trouble.*
5 Unpleasant or strongly felt disagreement which may result in bad quarrels or even fighting. EG *He's the sort of person who always makes trouble ... ... trouble in Poland ...*
6 Someone or something that causes you a problem in some way. EG *If it wouldn't be a trouble to you, could I ask you to give me a lift? ... Please don't go to a lot of trouble on my behalf.*
7 To do something that requires a special effort or that is difficult. EG *I'm sorry to trouble you, but I wondered if we could have a word some time ... I do apologise for troubling you, especially on a Sunday.*

union 4

1 An organisation which has the aim of improving working conditions. EG *If it was union work, a union would insist on a wage of at least £108 a week.*
2 A group of countries or states which have been joined into one for political reasons. EG *The Soviet Union.*
3 The act of joining two or more things so that they become one; also the state of being joined in this way. EG *... the union of the two countries.*

various 8

1 **Various** means that there are several different things of the type mentioned. EG *Various kinds of sweets.*
2 **Various** can mean 'varied'. EG *His excuses are many and various.*

view 12

1 A belief or opinion. EG *To give vent to their views on politics, the price of butter, religion, anything.* (157)
2 You say '**In my view ...**' when you want to emphasise that you are stating a personal opinion. EG *In my view, it's a long way to a United States of Europe.*
3 To think of something in the particular way that is mentioned. EG *Once you see China, it's impossible ever again to view America as you always had.*
4 Something which is seen from a particular place, especially something which is thought to be beautiful. EG *From the top there is a fine view of the sea.*

voice 11

1 When someone speaks, you hear their **voice**. EG *He spoke in a deep voice ... He raised his voice so loud ...* (147)
2 People's opinions. EG *The powerful voice of the people ... The voice of reason.*

way 6

1 **Way** refers to the manner in which a person or thing behaves or acts, or the certain style someone or something has, or feeling or attitude of a person. EG *Just look at the way he eats! It's horrible!*
2 **Way** refers to the means or method by which something is done, or how it happens. EG *The best way of getting to Paris is by train and boat.* (64)
3 Used with reference to a direction, distance, route, road, path or journey somewhere. EG *'Which way do I go?' 'Turn right at the shops, and go all the way down that road.'*

while 6

1 During the time that. EG *Maybe she sneaked out while he wasn't looking ...* (78) *It was fun while it lasted.*
2 A short time. EG *... for a little while ...*
3 Although. EG *While I like his paintings, I would not want to spend all that money.*

wish 8

1 A **wish** is a longing or desire for something. EG *She told me of her wish to leave.*
2 To want, desire. EG *I wish I were going with you.* (114)

wonder 12

1 To want to know something. EG *I wonder how they made it cry.* (164)
2 Used to make what you are going to say sound more polite. EG *I wonder if you'd mind closing the window?*
3 To think or silently ask yourself about something, especially because you feel doubtful, uncertain, or worried about it. EG *I am beginning to wonder why we ever invited them.*
4 A surprising thing that you would not have expected. EG *It was a wonder that she managed to come at all; she's so busy nowadays.*
5 Greatly admired or widely praised because of having surprisingly good results or more skill than anyone else. EG *The wonder boy of American racing.*

Words followed by a star (*) occurred in Level 1 of the Course, but further new uses are covered here. Words followed by 'L' are explained in the Lexicon on pages 111–125. Figures refer to sections where examples of the word can be found, either in the Student's Book or in the transcripts. 'T' after a reference means your teacher will give you the word to help you with this section.

ability 126T
able* 121, 126
about* 4, 13
above* 142
abroad 126T, 130
absolutely 14, 27
absorbed 91
academic 14
accept 153, 156
accident 103
accommodation 35, 39
account L 115
across* 100
action 108
active 28, 29
activity 28T
actually* 132
add 164, 170
addition 161
additional 161T
adult 82
advance 157, 162
advantage 91, 93
advertising 120
advice 162, 170
affair 178
afford 34
after* 186, 189, 197
afterwards 18
against L 112, 142
agency 20
agreement 84
ahead L 142
air* 68
aircraft 68, 69
airport 82
allow L 143, 150, 156
almost* 157
alone* 206
along* 67
alright 13
although 68, 69, 84
altogether 161, 167
among L 93
amount 47
analysis, analyses 120
ancient 28
angry 78
animal 25, 26
announce 193
annoyed 103
annoying 103, 130
anybody 42, 57
anyway* 57
anywhere 49
apart L 12
apology 112
apparent 18
appeal 95
appearance L 112T, 87T
appear L 87, 112
apply 52, 57
approach 144, 147
area 176
argument 21, 27
arms* 63
around 165, 179, 184
arts 157, 158
artists 157, 159
ask* 136, 137

assistant 43, 55
associated 78
association 80
atmosphere 35
attack 206
attach 82
attempt 178, 184
attention L 64
attitude 178
audience 157
authority 178
away* 57, 67
awful 57, 103, 130
back* L 27
background L 17
bad* 186
ball 188
bar 161
bargain 116, 126
base 73
based 82
basic L 89, 47
basically L 122
be* 8, 37, 66
beach 28, 35
beautiful 28, 35
beauty 35T
because* 69, 80
become* 131
bed* 39
beer 93T
before* 120, 126
behave 164, 165
behind* L 133, 141, 142
beings 202
belief 161T
believe L 69, 161, 185
belong 171
below L 142
bend, bent 179
beneath 142
beside 136, 142
beyond L 136, 142
bill 117, 130
bird 25
bit L 24, 27
blame 106
blind 189
block 150
blood 63
board L 39
boat 29
bored 14, 26
boring 14T, 26T
body* 63
boss 75
bothered* 152, 156
bottle 93
bound 152
box 117, 124, 138
brain 63
branch 131
bread 101T
break, broke, broken, breaking L 161
breast 152
breath 188T
breathe 188
brick 152
brief 52

bright 128
brilliant 193
bring, brought L 9
brochure 205
building* 152, 156
burn, burned/burnt L 184
business* L 104, 114
but* 19, 27, 155
by* 91, 96
camp 133
capital L 1
captain 104
care 167
career 64
careful 147, 152, 156
careless 147T
case 123, 138
cash 117, 130
castle 131, 134
catalogue 117
catch 110
category 25
caught 110
cause* 76
central 41T
centre* 82
certain* 178
challenge 136
character 14T, 20T
characteristic 20
charge 68, 82
chest 63T
childhood 64
chin 49
choice L 35, 41
choose, chose, chosen L 35T
Christian 28
Christmas 38
circle 100
circumstances 150, 153
claim L 112, 115
class* L 68
clean 120, 130
clear L 48, 57
clearly L 48
close* 186
closely 186T
coast 29
cold* 95
collection 157
come, came, coming* 131, 142
comedy 157
comfort 35T
comfortable 35
community L 2, 9, 13
company 52
companion 93
compare 89, 134
completely L 49
computer 20
concern L 188, 197
condition L 25T, 108
confidence 152T
confident 152
connect 104T
connection 104
consequences 64
consider L 14
contact L 91
contents 171, 184

continue 131
control L 104, 115
conversation 97T
cook 86
cool 152, 156
copy 152
correct 186
corridor 172
could* 151
count 152
countless 152T
country* 33T
county 1, 2
course* 114
court 143, 161
cousin 78
cover L 120, 130
cream 87T
creature 25
crime 176, 178
criminal 176
cross 131
crowd 28
cry 189, 193
cup 85
curious 200
cut 18, 100, 138
damage 150
danger 58
dangerous 58
dead L 172
deal L 1, 25
dear L 188, 197
decided 55
decision 57
deep 73
definition 67
degree* L 12
dentist 42, 45, 54
department 52
depends L 69
design 116, 157, 159
details* 97
device 91
die* 172
diet 186
difficulty 52
direct L 126, 130
dirty 186
disappear 78, 167
discover L 35, 41
discovered 104
discuss 69
discussion 69T, 84
disease 25
distance 131T
divide 100
division 100T
do, did, done, doing* 32, 36, 162
dog 25, 26
dollars 46
doubt 176, 178
doubtful 176T
down* 170
draw L 52
dreadful 206
dream, dreamed/dreamt 64
driver 97
drop, dropped L 75
dry 29

127